A
Journey
Into
Solitude

From Priest-Professor
To Hermit-Heretic

by

Richard W. Kropf

A Journey Into Solitude
Copyright © 2016 by Richard W. Kropf

Kropf, Richard W. 1932-

275 pp. with index

ISBN-13: 978-1530050888
ISBN-10: 153005088X

As updated November 19, 2017

Stellamar Publications
P.O. Box 315
Johannesburg, MI 49751
USA
www.stellamar.net

Front Cover Photo: Stella Maris Hermitage in Winter (by author)
Rear Cover Author Photo Portrait (by Bud Palin , Gaylord, MI)

In memory of my parents,
my teachers, my mentors, and my friends,
and in gratitude to God
in whom "we live and move, and have our being."

Contents

Acknowledgments

I want to acknowledge my debt to Mary Karr's book on *The Art of Memoir* (Harper Collins, 2015) for helping give me the courage to finally publish my own life story, and to thank Robert Chamberlin, Maureen Derenzy, Mary Flinn, Charlene Ford, Ruthann Galbraith, Robert Horning, William Joseph, Anthony Morse, Lorene Parshall, Joseph Rettig, John Riordan, and Patrick Stonehouse for their encouragement and their advice, and especially for their aid in the nearly impossible task of being one's own proof-reader.

Richard W. Kropf
June 20, 2017

Introduction

Recently, I read about a young man who hiked all the way up the coastal range of mountains from the California border with Mexico to the Washington State border with British Columbia, taking a "selfie" picture of himself with the scenery in the background just about every mile of the some thousand and a half miles, and then posting most or all of it on the Internet.

In writing this, the story of my journey through life, I ask myself if I'm not guilty of much the same, even if I would have preferred to keep the focus of my mental camera on what I was seeing around me, and only occasionally on myself. But even with that hoped for shift in emphasis, one may wonder, during this age of incessant self-promotion, what would prompt someone to attempt to write the story of his whole life. Who would I think might be interested? Why spend hours, even days digging up memories of the past, some of which I might prefer to forget if I had the choice to do so?

These are questions I felt I had to answer before I brashly decided to try to finish what began as a spiritual exercise during the Lenten season of 1992, only to be laid aside for about a decade before resuming the project around the time that I turned seventy years of age. By then, I guess that my project had begun to take on, at least in my mind, something of the same purpose as Saint Augustine's "Confessions", or something like Cardinal Newman's *Apologia* for his life, or Thomas Merton's *Seven Storey Mountain*; all of them attempting to explain how they ended up the way they were, but in my case, in particular, with an emphasis on Merton's influence, both by his writing and in my case, his personal advice on my life.

I have used the term "spiritual exercise" in all seriousness. If the saying, attributed to Socrates, about "the unexamined life is not worth living" is true in broad philosophical terms, then it is perhaps even more so in terms of psychology and the life of the spirit. For if what distinguishes us from animal life – which is certainly conscious or knowing according to its own immediate needs – is that humans are unique in having *reflective* consciousness, that is (to use the phrase coined by the paleontologist Teilhard de Chardin), to be able to "know that we know." It is this ability to reflect on the past and weigh its consequences for the present and the likely future that is the key to human freedom. Without it, we all end up the victims of circumstance. It's not that circumstances such as birth, upbringing, family or even ethnic culture and what is going on in the world around us doesn't have a great influence on what we become, but without the ability to go beyond or rise above all these influences, we can hardly be said to be free. How much freedom there really was in the choices that I made in the course of my life is perhaps up to the reader to decide, especially if the reader is something of a psychologist.

Nevertheless, it seems to me, looking back on it all, that my life has followed a path that I recently discovered in the first chapter of the 14th century English spiritual classic known as *The Cloud of Unknowing*. There the anonymous author tells us that there are "four degrees and forms" of Christian living, and "they be these, Common, Special, Singular, and Perfect." He then went on to tell us that "Three of these may be begun and ended in this life; and the fourth may by grace be begun here, but it shall ever last without end in the bliss of heaven."

As I write this introduction, I find in this unknown author what seems to me to be the basic outline of this account of my life, beginning with the common experience of growing up, although in my case it was in an uncommon number of different locations, even if the last one lasted six whole years.

Next, there was the decision to enter the "special" state of life known as the priesthood, including the long preparation, leading to nine years as a parish priest and its four what seemed to me to be increasingly difficult assignments. This was followed by a year of searching, which in turn culminated in the decision to enter theological grad school in Canada and seek two doctoral degrees. This led me to about nine more years of teaching, with one school year omitted to begin working on my second book.

Chapter 7, however, recounts what I see as perhaps the most

crucial time of my life, beginning with my mother's death in August 1978 followed by my father's death in April 1979. In the autumn of the following year I took a long postponed trip to Alaska, after which I returned to spend several months of a renewed trial with an eventual rejection by the Camoldolese Hermit-monks in Ohio. This was followed by nearly five months of study and travel in the Holy Land, with short excursions in Egypt and Greece. All this was to be, it seems, in preparation leading me back to my home in the north-woods of Michigan to live as much as possible — into that strange or "Singular" state of life, as the author of *The Cloud* seems to have envisioned for his readers — "in solitude".

Having thus come this far, I will recount (in Chapter 8) the initial process of building and settling into both my hermitage-cabin and making provisions or plans for the type of life that the Church expects of a vowed "hermit" or "anchorite" and the particular joys as well as trials that inevitably come with it. Among these I will also tell of one for which I seem to have been particularly unprepared and at a loss, leaving me, at least at the time, in anything but the bliss of undisturbed contemplative life. Looking back on it today, it was a kind an emotional trial by fire or testing of all my well-laid plans.

In the final chapter I have focused more on intellectual and faith matters — the kind that are apt to occur especially when that so-called "hermit" also feels called to continue to write and speak out as a theologian. It is this latter conflict, still unresolved, that has led me to write and rewrite Chapter 9 several times and to warn the reader that it still remains unfinished and that if I live long enough, might yet be rewritten still again. (For this reason, the copyright or publishing information page will contain information as to when any particular version of this book was published as "updated as of...."). Thus this last chapter, as well as the "Afterthoughts", might even, in fact, be read first by those who are particularly curious about this aspect of my life as a theologian, or, on the other hand, be skipped entirely by those who have read most, or at least some, of my other books.

Introduction

The reason for all this rewriting is not just because I'm still alive and my opinions are still liable to change, but also because of my hesitancy as to letting people, especially those not in touch with current theological thought, know just what I am really thinking. Thus the subtitle for this book (*From Priest-Professor to Hermit-Heretic*) as well as the question posed as a title for that last chapter, "Hermit or Heretic?" I chose those titles as a kind of warning that my own beliefs as a theologian do not always square up exactly with those expressed in the official catechisms. In fact, as I see it, especially as a theologian, *beliefs* are not the essence of *faith* itself, but are attempts (in our head) to express why we have faith in our will or "heart". Not only that, these beliefs gradually change or even to some extent *must* change as our view of the world around us changes, much as Pope John Paul II warned theologians in an address to the Pontifical Academy of Science that evolution is more than just a hypothesis and must be taken seriously.

However, for those who wish to understand the full background or the genesis of my thinking — which I suppose is the reason I began writing this book to begin with, that is, even to try to understand it myself — I would recommend reading the whole story, from beginning to end. Yet the fact that it to some degree remains unfinished is perhaps an indication that even now, over thirty-five years since I began this solitary life, I am still in the throes of negotiating my way through this personal confrontation with the still largely unknown God who can only be experienced when we have reached the point of letting go of all our human conceptualizations and surrender ourselves to this state or "cloud of unknowing".

Among these attempts to reach the unknown there have been times in my life when I believe that I had already experienced, no matter how painfully, on that occasion, was the state that had led up to it, a taste of that heavenly "bliss". And if heaven is anything like that, then I suppose I should be in a hurry to die and get there. But unfortunately, even despite the fact I'm now well into my eighth decade and suffer some increasingly troublesome joints, over all I seem to remain, for a man of my age, unusually healthy. So I suppose I'll just have to wait a bit longer before I can say I know anything for sure.

Conscious of the paradoxical warning once given by Mohandas Gandhi, the father of modern India, that "He who would be friends with God must either remain alone.... or make the whole world his friend", I have decided that, after all these years of seclusion, it is perhaps high time that I maybe begin to share more of my life experience with those who know me, or have maybe read some of my many short essays or even a book or two of mine. So having begun this account of my life in 1992, I now feel prepared to hand it over to others, no matter how unfinished and typo-ridden it is — or as imperfect I still remain — to make it available to those who care or have the patience to read it in the hope that my "Journey into Solitude" will in some way eventually lead all of us into a greater communion together in God.

+++

Now, a bit over a year after having, it seems, rather prematurely first released this personal account of my life for publication, (fearing, it seems that on the brink of turning eighty-five years of age that I might not have a chance to do so if I put it off any longer) I ask myself if even now, after having several times made further corrections, clarifications, and additions, might I still end up adding even more? My answer to that question is that it all depends on a number of things.

The first question is, of course, how much longer I will continue to live? But even aside from that, I have since discovered that during this past year I that in writing this long story that I had even forgotten one whole, and very crucial, year – the one that followed my father's death in April 1979. How could that have happened? It seems now, looking back to that period of time, that although I had deliberately decided not to make any big decisions following what was for me, due to my closeness to my father, a very traumatic event. It also seems that I also had more or less put my life on hold, shutting down not only my thoughts but my feelings as well, so much so that I had almost completely forgotten what transpired during that year. It was only after trying to put together a "chronology" to serve as an "Appendix" of sorts – still unfinished – that I discovered I had somehow missed a whole year!

Reflecting now on that strange gap, it makes me wonder about what else I may have inadvertently left out, what other memories (good or bad) have been erased, or what hurts I may have inflicted upon others, or what apologies I may have failed to make or what debts I may owe that still remain unpaid. If this is the case, I especially invite those who have known me in past years, and for whom this book has been especially written, to refresh my memory so that I may fill in those gaps.

Richard W. Kropf
Stella Maris Hermitage
Montmorency County, Michigan
November 19, 2017

Chapter 1
Beginnings

In June of 1929, the month my father finished college and married my mother, the nation's economy was roaring and the unemployment rate was only 3.2%. Then came the stock market crash on September 4th followed by "Black Tuesday" on October 29th. From then on the economy spun into a nose-dive. By 1932, the year I was born, the unemployment rate was to reach 23% only to reach 24% by 1933 when Franklin Delano Roosevelt, who had won the presidency by a landslide the previous November, took office shortly after I became one year of age on January 9th. So you might say that while my earliest years were spent in the depths of the Great Depression, they were also to be affected, at least some, by FDR's promise of a "New Deal".

Despite my father's Republican skepticism of all things Democratic, and although he had finished near the top of his class at Michigan Technological University (then the small but renowned Michigan School of Mining and Technology) and had even been elected class president, none of this landed him much of a job in his chosen field, metallurgical engineering. He was fortunate even to have his job in the yard of the Globe Steel Tube Company, a small Milwaukee industry where he help prepare scrap metal to be fed into the furnaces for melting. Not an auspicious beginning for a man of his talent. But it was a job that insured at least some income while he went to night school to earn his master's degree in metallurgy.

My father was from Madison, Wisconsin's capital city but still a small college town when he was born there in 1907. His mother, Mabel Bartlett, was the only daughter of George H. Bartlett, the son of a blacksmith and farm tool manufacturer from Bristol, Vermont. The Bartletts had moved on over from Bartlett, New Hampshire, nestled beneath the slopes of Mount Washington, early in the nineteenth century. They were undoubtedly of English extraction, but my great-grandfather's mother bore the name Vidum, said to be

Chapter 1

of French Huguenot origin. Great-grandfather Bartlett, after moving his family to Madison, ended up spending the latter half of his adult life travelling around the world setting up dealerships for the then-new International Harvester Corporation, and, it seems, about half of that time in Czarist Russia, escaping from Moscow back to the United States mostly via Vladivostok on the still unfinished trans-Siberia railroad after the way back through western Europe was blocked by the outbreak of the First World War. If I seem to have doted a bit too much on this particular ancestor whom I never met, it's because I have read the fascinating letters he wrote to his wife describing his adventures, and the autobiography he had started when relatively young but never finished, apparently having planned to do so in his retirement years. His plans were aborted by a fatal case of pneumonia within a short time after returning home. Surely, there is a lesson for all of us in that!

As far as my paternal grandfather goes, things were a bit less exciting, although not without their effect. Madison-born Rudolph Richard Kropf was the son of a local tavern owner himself the grandson of a widowed immigrant farmer who came from Eisleben in Saxony to settle near Black Earth, Wisconsin, in the early 1850s. The names are telling, as Eisleben was Martin Luther's hometown and the eventual place of his death, and Black Earth, whether intentional or not, is also the English translation of the name of Luther's principal theological advisor, Philip Schwartzerd, better known by his Graecized pen name, "Melancthon". One branch of the Wisconsin Kropfs stayed very Lutheran with even a minister or two in its ranks. My grandfather's branch was less so. In fact, Rudy was, in effect, excommunicated, because as a rising young businessman (banking and insurance) he had become a Mason. So my father was, as were both his older and younger sisters, raised in the Congregationalist Church, despite his mother's death from diabetes when he was twelve, not too long before insulin was made available. The loss of his mother had a profound effect, I believe, on my father's psyche, probably as great as that of another tragedy that occurred many years later and about which I was to learn only many years after that. At least that was the story I was told.

Beginnings

A recent DNA test that I decided to take seems to indicate very different roots to my father's Germanic background unless they were so thoroughly Saxon that it is they are indistinguishable from the Anglo-Saxon element of his mother's New England background. In any case; the test identified my DNA as being 47% "British" without a drop of German blood. Either that or perhaps I should pay for another test.

On my Irish mother's side there also seems to be a bit of mystery. She was born in the small town of Dollar Bay in Michigan's Upper Peninsula, the fabled "Copper Country" whose boom or bust economy had inspired Horace Greeley's famed advice "Go West young man, go West!" and whose infamous winters drove even more to the copper buttes of Montana and Arizona in the years to come. She was the youngest daughter of Francis William Foley, born in County Leitrim, Ireland, in 1857 and Mary Slattery, the American-born daughter of immigrant Irish grocers in the smelter community of Ripley along the lake shore near Hancock, Michigan. Gramp's father, a tailor, had brought his brood to the new world to Worchester, Massachusetts, and then more or less left them on their own when he returned to Ireland as a salesman for Singer Sewing Machines. Whether this amounted to outright desertion I'll probably never know. My mother once indicated that her grandfather was not a popular subject with the clan. Since both the Foley as well as the Slattery clans were originally from County Leitrim, all this fits in accurately with my DNA being 43% from the "northern midlands of Ireland" just as the test results specified.

But if 47% the Saxon/German element seems a somewhat mysterious combination, the test's claim that I have 6% "Iberian" DNA seemed even more so, until I remembered my grandfather's talk about "the black Irish". It is a term sometimes used to refer to the survivors of the Spanish armada that had been defeated by the British in 1588 and its remaining ships driven out further into the Atlantic only to be wrecked by a storm that left many castaways stranded on the coasts of Ireland and Scotland. So apparently some of those sailors decided to stay put. But this still leaves me with 4%

Chapter 1

unidentified DNA. Perhaps that is where the Hugenots enter in.

In any case, whatever his more remote origins were, my Irish grandfather was the major source of lore for a century to come. A feisty fellow whose major sources of recreation were the bottle and fighting roosters raised out in the back yard (and later at a nearby farm he bought as a refuge from grandmother), he had reputedly survived falling off the gangplank when the ship docked from Ireland, quit school at age ten to work in the woolen mills, and at nineteen (according to family lore) was picked out personally by old man Roebling of Brooklyn Bridge fame to train as a foreman for Roebling's new operation in the Copper Country, to take advantage of the vast quantities of pure native copper that were discovered there (probably the largest deposits of that type in the world) in 1843. Gramps eventually became manager of the whole local operation for Roebling. He seems to have put off marriage in true Irish style for some years and was, by my reckoning, about twelve years older than my grandmother, and survived her a dozen years more, finally dying in 1952, his several beers a day along with his daily boiled egg, and innumerable cigars not slowing him down a bit. My mother had three older sisters, and two older brothers, and one younger brother, all of whom played a significant role in my life. I was taken back to the old family home every summer but one or two (those during World War II) that I can remember until I finished high school. My mother never adjusted to the summer's heat anyplace south of Michigan's "U.P." as it is generally called. I remember long rainy Junes when woolen jackets were the only thing that would keep you warm, but this followed by gorgeous Julys and Augusts with long sunny days, the scent of pines, and cool twilights. But these long summers were all too short as far as I was concerned. Grandma used to announce around the 4th of July that summer had finally arrived, followed with a premonition, usually around August 15th, that there was already "a tinge of fall in the air." My dad usually made it up for about two weeks near the end of August, but sometimes even for a weekend courtesy of the Army Air Force Reserve that allowed my uncle, an airline pilot married to one of my mother's sisters, to get away on "training flights" from Chicago where we all lived at the time. But the most thrilling thing each year was that June trip on "The Copper Country Limited" out of Chicago via the Milwaukee Road and its northern extension the "D. S. S. & A" — the Duluth, South Shore, and Atlantic (which local wags claimed really stood for "Damned Slow Service and Abuse.") It was never that as far as I was concerned. It was the highroad to paradise from the steaming cities of Milwaukee, Chicago, Cleveland, and a host of others.

I really don't remember much of Milwaukee. We were there only three years. I had been baptized in the hospital by the chaplain at the insistence of my grandmother who still didn't trust her Protestant son-in-law's good faith. She wasn't aware that he was taking another more complete set of instructions from a local priest to make up for what he didn't get before marriage when he became good friends with the Dollar Bay pastor, Fr. Navarre, paddling around with the priest in his canoe before his marriage. Eventually my father received "conditional" baptism (just in case his Congregationalist one hadn't taken) and was not long after confirmed by Archbishop Stritch. He took Saint Joseph as his patron, very seriously so as I was to learn.

We lived at two different locations in Milwaukee. One was in an apartment building near the outskirts of the city, near railroad tracks I seem to recall. The other place was in a neat little bungalow in a residential section. Probably most of my memories are reconstructed ones, partly from old photographs, and partly from my parents' descriptions. But there are two or three that I know are the results of being engraved first hand in my brain. One, probably the result of repeated occasions, was with my nose pressed against the cold winter glass of the living room window waiting for my dad to arrive home from work. The others were, as far as I can tell, singular occasions, yet all the more memorable for that. Once, I remember walking around that apartment looking for my mother only to have her suddenly jump out at me from a closet with a big "Boo!" The other, I was in our car alone with my mother as she drove toward the apartment, while she, a big fan of Sophie Tucker's, was singing over and over again "You're going to miss

Chapter 1

your big fat mamma one of these days."

I suspect I was visibly upset. She, I think, liked to tease me or perhaps she was teasing herself, gaining some weight after being a petite "five foot two, eyes of blue" for half her life up to that point. I don't know, but it didn't seem to bother her. As the years passed I learned that she was a rather insecure and even frustrated woman. She was, I believe, the only one of the four sisters to complete college. She had a bachelor's degree from the University of Michigan, majoring in English and with a minor in Art, and yet, once she completed school in 1928, my grandmother had not allowed her to even accept a job teaching for the girls high school connected to Saint Mary's College in Notre Dame, Indiana. When my father, still a college student, met her, she was living a very active social life, but was very much, like the rest of her sisters, on a short leash. She also, it seems, suffered disturbing dreams about her mother throughout most of her life. Later on, after I had studied some psychology, I probably could have helped her deal with all this. But tired of hearing her complain about these dreams for so many years, I failed to do so.

I remember a great deal more about Chicago. My father had finally landed a job as a consulting metallurgist for the huge south-side Republic Steel Corporation. We lived in an apartment on University Avenue, just off 55th Street. The Field House or gym for the University of Chicago was just across the street and the pseudo-English Gothic atmosphere of the campus began just beyond the stadium just down the block — where I was to learn, much later in life, that Enrico Fermi was then about to conduct his first experiments on splitting the atom! A block or two farther west on University Avenue was the university's "union" or social hall, where on Saturdays movies (this being years before TV came upon the scene) were shown for the neighborhood kids. I became especially attracted to "The Lone Ranger" with his white horse named "Silver", but not much enthused about his Indian companion "Tonto", who seemed to me, even back then, as just a kind of prop so that in the radio versions we could hear what my hero was thinking, especially because otherwise he, like me, was alone.

But just around the corner, on 55th Street, was another world entirely. Kosher delicatessens and meat-markets, fives and dimes, dry cleaning establishments, and my favorite place, the Dutch Mill ice cream parlor were all connected by a red brick thoroughfare and busy trolley tracks. About a mile down the street was the "El", the elevated railway to the excitement of the Chicago's downtown, "The Loop". Beyond the El tracks were Grant Park and the shore of Lake Michigan. In the other direction, to the west, lay Midway Airport where my dashing uncle Harold flew his American Airlines late night "Owl" flights to New York via Buffalo in shiny DC-3s, first as a pistol-packing co-pilot (the little .32 automatic he carried was supposed to protect the mail bag) and later, as a full-fledged Captain. My greatest ambition for some years was to have a pair of AA pilot's "wings", the badge of their rank and profession — even the little set of Army Air Force wings (due to his connection with the Air Force Reserve) he gave me really wouldn't do!

Before long I was sent to the nearby Saint Thomas the Apostle parochial school. I started a bit late in my estimation. It seems that Chicago (or Illinois, because the same thing happened to my cousin out in LaGrange whose birthday was two days from mine) had this rule that you couldn't start kindergarten until the first full school year after your sixth birthday. So I began kindergarten at over six and a half. As a result, I think I was a bit bored by it. But those early school years were a curious experience. The Sinsinawa (Wisconsin) Congregation of Dominican Sisters was into "progressive education". We were enrolled for music classes in second grade, but after my audition with the sister who taught piano, my mother was advised that I'd probably do better in the harmonica group. We were also exposed to some lessons in the French language early on, but I'm afraid I wasn't much impressed with the idea at the time.

But I presume that I learned whatever else I was supposed to learn, passed to third grade without a hitch, having made my first Communion at age eight, remembering on that morning, since it took place at a later Mass, having attempted to say a whole rosary

Chapter 1

by myself. Dad, always an early riser, had always taken me to the earliest Sunday morning Mass. He was also much taken with the pastor who appeared in kind of a wall-balcony pulpit and gave never more than five minute sermons that, as dad said, left you waiting for the next sentence only to find out that he was all done (too bad I haven't followed that model in later years).

Midway through third grade, however, my parent's decided that we had had enough of the city and we moved out to nearer my uncle and aunt and cousin in LaGrange, renting a nice suburban two story frame house. Then came a shock. I was transferred to Saint Francis Parish school where I was amazed to find that my fellow third graders, under the exacting old-fashioned standards of the Franciscan sisters who taught there, were writing two and three syllable words long-hand, where back at Saint Thomas I can remember only printing one syllable ones. I don't think I ever quite recovered from that blow, or at least my abilities in hand-writing never caught up. Years later, in junior high, I gave up on longhand, and trained in mechanical drawing and lettering, adopted my father's more than half-printed style. I also found that a backhand slant helped me decipher my scribbling. The other big shock was having had to play the part of a leprechaun in a school play. I was given no choice and my costume, much to my chagrin (and everyone else's amusement at my expense) was a pair of green-dyed long johns (trap door rear included). After these two traumatic experiences at the hands of the good Franciscans, I never felt seriously attracted to the Franciscan order. It was now 1940 and Wendell Willkie was running for president against Roosevelt.

I remember also that my dad was on the road a lot on business trips. Part of the reason we had moved to LaGrange, I guess, was so that my mother and her sister could share their regular weeks of "widowhood", while Uncle Harold was off on the New York City run and dad was on his monthly trips to Minneapolis, Davenport, Springfield, or wherever. This brought me into more direct and constant contact with my young cousin, still a small child of four, and even worse, a bratty girl in my estimation. She was a precocious child with an almost photographic memory. But my main problem with her was that she was a girl. Two years previously one day my mother greeted my return from school with the news that I had a new cousin — another girl. I remember it as the first time that I ever swore out loud in my mother's hearing. I think she was amused. But at that point the younger one was no threat. But my LaGrange cousin, also an only child, now was under my feet much of the time, and now even our treasured visits to the Copper Country were often in tandem. It would be years later before I could accept her as the closest thing to having a kid sister, and by then it was too late to really share a past treasured together.

I underscore, perhaps even exaggerate, this reflection because it has taken me so many years to realize the deprivation that being an only child imposes. About that time, or shortly after, my parents did what now seems to me to be an incredible thing. They asked me if I'd like a baby sister, an adopted one like a friend of mine (who was also adopted himself) had. But I, of course, already being accustomed to being an only child, blurted out an immediate no. Why would I want to have to share all the attention that I was getting with someone else? But looking back on all that now, it seems that if I thought my 4-year old cousin was a selfish brat, what must I have been? It is too bad my parents let me get my way for even nine or ten years. It would prove a handicap in years to come.

However, the domestic scene was about to change radically. Dad came home one day to announce that he was going with a new company, Copperweld Steel Corporation of Warren, Ohio. We soon were to move there, living in a rented house on the outskirts of town where I wandered the fields and surprised coveys of Bob-White quail. My mother bought me a bow and taught me to shoot it (that, along with ice skating, had been her favorite sport in college). Dad presented me with my first bicycle, a narrow-tired English style Schwinn. I was not only the new boy in the neighborhood; I was also the one with the queer bike. I also began my first stint in a public school. I don't remember much else, except feeling alone a lot. That and an eerie display of pinkish and greenish Northern Lights one winter night which struck me as being like an omen of some sort.

Chapter 1

Soon after we moved again, this time to Shaker Heights, on the south-east edge of Cleveland. My father was to work for the Cleveland office of the same corporation, which specialized in making a copper-covered steel wire that was proving very handy for specialized industrial applications. There we lived in the upstairs of a duplex apartment and I attended the local public grade school. I also joined the Cub Scouts and was soon a little less lonely. I also began to notice girls (favorably) a little more — especially a red-headed Russian Jewish girl (there was also another red-head back in 2nd grade, but she was way ahead in 5th or 6th).

Two other memories are noteworthy from this period. One was an accident we had on the way to church one bright Sunday morning. We had to go quite a distance then, over to the edge of the John Carroll University campus. As we pulled out from a stop sign across a main thoroughfare, we hit the side of a car rushing through the intersection at better than twice the allowable speed. Although technically it was our fault, the sun was in my father's eyes and we just didn't see the car approaching at such a terrific rate. I can still remember it, as if it was a TV replay in slow motion, like it was just yesterday, with the other car doing a complete spin around to a stop and seeing all the chrome slats of our front grill (and there were many on the 1942 Mercury) showering down as they shimmered in the bright sunlight. It was a very close call. If we had entered that intersection a half a second earlier we could have been all dead.

And then there is another memory, a very private one, of suddenly experiencing a case of the scruples that lasted for a week or two. I'm not sure, nor whether it happened before or after the nearly fatal accident, but I suspect that it was after. It was a kind of irrational fear of whether or not my sins were truly forgiven (what sins I may have had then are beyond me — I suppose it was over honesty of some sort). But I know that by this time my religious education had begun to suffer. No longer having Catholic schools handy, my parents did not find catechism classes much available either. The mild case of scruples cleared up soon enough, but the situation that in part accounted for them, the lack of a deepened understanding of the basics of faith, was beginning to tell. But soon there were even greater distractions and excuses. There was the trauma of Pearl Harbor.

It was another one of those things that, I guess, one never forgets. December 7, 1941 was a Sunday morning that dad and I had spent in the basement after Mass and breakfast, setting up my electric train. I remember our land-lord, a Mr. Johnson, coming into the room and asking if we'd heard — "The Japanese are bombing Pearl Harbor: it's still going on!"

From that point onward it seemed like the pattern so recently established in our lives became almost permanent. We remained in the Cleveland area a short while, but soon dad said we were headed for Washington, D.C. He had the choice of either going into the Navy as an engineer at the Navy Department in Washington or else serving as a "Dollar a Year" man on the War Production Board — an arrangement by which his company would continue to pay his normal salary but volunteer his services to the government. So in mid-fall of 1942, all our furnishings were put in storage and we drove down to Washington in our car loaded with enough clothes to get us through however long it would take until my dad's services would no longer be needed.

I remember first staying there in a dingy hotel where I cut out paper airplanes to keep amused until my dad had located a nice furnished home in Virginia that was available for at least a couple of months. It was in a beautiful wooded residential area just off Military Pike (my father and I relocated the place just a week before his death nearly 40 years later and it still looked much the same!). I went to the local public school, a very small building up the pike, and roamed the scenic woods down to the Potomac shore with the local kids. It was exciting to find the depressions of old civil war trenches and earthworks back in those woods; it was like stepping back into another world. Then the lease was up and we had to move again.

So this time we located over in Westgate, Maryland, just north of the capital. There were woods there, but they weren't as extensive or as exciting. But trips to downtown brought all the

Chapter 1

excitement of a nation in the sweep of a great war effort. Uniforms were everywhere; American, Canadian, British, French and a host of others. Many government buildings had sandbagged machine gun emplacements on the corners of the roofs. Heavier antiaircraft guns could be seen on the edges of golf-courses and other open areas. One day some federal investigators came to ask questions about the people from whom we had rented the house. We knew next to nothing about them and all that we could learn in return was that the questions were part of a routine investigation being conducted as part of something called "The Manhattan Project". It was only after the war ended after the atomic bombs had been dropped on Hiroshima and Nagasaki that we learned that the "Manhattan Project" was the code name of the effort to build those bombs.

In Maryland it was suggested that I take a bus to a parochial school some miles away, but after a week or two there, with its near impossible overcrowding, I begged to go to the small public school just down the street. By now I felt quite comfortable in them, more so than in Catholic schools. I was also beginning to learn how to make friends in a hurry, and at the same time not to count on such acquaintanceships lasting for long. The house we had rented was on a corner and had a large garden which we planted. After the people who owned the house in Virginia came and reclaimed the cat, now with kittens, that had come with that house, my parents thought I should have a dog, and bought me a buff & white cocker spaniel I named "Zipper". But the dog really didn't pay much attention to me – probably because I didn't pay all that much attention to it either.

More attention was paid by a dark-haired girl my age who lived next door and who shadowed me so close on one occasion that as I swung a golf club in the front yard, the back-swing hit her across her forehead, leaving a nasty gash. It was hardly intentional, but it did put girls back in their place (this one anyway). My other would-be friend was a drawling southern boy whose father was a career Army officer. Charlie and I had some big arguments over who won (or should have won) the Civil War, but we never came to blows. I seem to have reserved those for girls.

In ten months or so, the steel allocations at the War Production Board were worked out, so my dad was free to leave. My mother and I had already made our annual summer trip to the Copper Country, and so our return to Washington (by train all the way in those days) was soon followed by packing and our return, this time by car, up north. We moved to a house in Jackson, Michigan, where most of my mother's displaced relatives (the U.P. copper industry never having recovered from the depression) had relocated, while Copperweld Steel tried to decide whether it wanted a Detroit area office. Apparently it looked as if they would, as we went over one day to a small Detroit suburb named Birmingham where my aunt had lived at one time and now some friends of my mother were living. It seemed like a long way from downtown Detroit (15 miles to be exact). But we continued on in Jackson and grandpa lived with us for awhile so as to give my aunt and uncle (my godparents, who were childless but who lived just down the block) a spell to themselves.

I played with the neighborhood kids out in the fields and especially just across the street where we had a complex of dirt bunkers and ditches where we played soldiers. One older boy in particular, who I guess was pressing fifteen in age, played the role of our commanding officer. He told us, as he had us wielding shovels and rakes, that we were building "The Burma Road" under hostile fire. It was a great game. In hardly over three years later I was nearly rocked out of my wits to learn that he was killed on Okinawa, shot between the eyes by a Japanese sniper. Tommy had passed all too quickly from kids games to the real thing. He had joined the Marines as soon as he turned eighteen. I was twelve and joined the Boy Scouts, and nearly got drowned (metaphorically speaking), I remember, in a washout of a Scout "camporee" in the local park.

During those war years I also experienced human grief for the first time. I was still too young in 1939, I guess, to remember grandma Foley's death, except to remember that they sent me and my younger cousin Frank to stay at his aunt's house. But midway

Chapter 1

through the war, in 1943, we were visiting in LaGrange when my aunt received a telegram from the war department. Her flyer husband, Harold, who had become an Air Transport Command pilot, was dead. I remember her shrieking in grief. My little cousin was too young to understand. I was rather impassive, as I recall, but wondering already about the irony of a man who had flown literally millions of miles in civil and military aviation suddenly dying of a heart attack on the ground at age 37. I guess that's always given me pause to think. My own grief, however, was much less serious. My dog was run over and I remember, after an afternoon of crying, insisting that I never wanted a dog again.

Shortly after that, word came that Copperweld had finally made up its mind. They wanted a branch office in Connecticut instead of Detroit, so we packed up again. This time we took a rather novel route east, gas rationing still cutting deeply into the freedom to drive and 45 mph war-time speed limits making a trip that long take what seemed an eternity. We ended up taking one of the last D & C (Detroit & Cleveland) side-wheel car-ferry steamers eastward the length of Lake Erie from Detroit to Buffalo, retracing in reverse part of the lake route that all of my ancestors (including my great-grandfather George Bartlett on his first big trip as a teenager out of Vermont) had taken in the Midwest.

Arriving in Connecticut, my folks placed me in a summer camp (Lantern Hill Camp for Boys) just out of Old Mystic, while they spent six weeks looking for a home in the Hartford area. The camp seemed an exciting place, but I was terribly parent-sick (how can you be homesick when you have none?), but it was a growing experience, both psychologically and physically: I think I gained over 20 pounds and at least two inches or so that one summer! Some years back I cruised up a side road out of Old Mystic and located the camp, now just a day camp for small children. How strange it seemed. The big lake had shrunk to a small New England pond, and craggy Lantern Hill seemed now only a rocky outcrop. Be it as it is or was, that summer I changed too, I was no longer a child.

But neither was I quite an adolescent. That fall I began "junior high school" as it was then called in the East. No longer confined to a single classroom, we moved around from room to room for different subjects, and my "homeroom teacher", if I recall rightly, was a man, the first male teacher I had ever encountered, who also taught what was for me another new experience at school, a "shop class" where we learned drafting, carpentry, and type-setting.

We also lived out in the country, or rather in what was still a rather unsettled section of West Hartford's suburbia. The house was on a road that ranged north to south on top of a ridge of land that looked westward towards the first of the low Berkshire Mountains. There was a golf course across the road, and at the bottom of the hill below our back yard, what locals called the "Mill Pond". The boys who lived two doors away had a corral and small stable with ponies and later, a magnificent white Arabian mare. I began to learn to ride, and one day almost got myself killed trying to get off a run-away rented riding stable horse when out riding with the youngest of the two neighbor boys. When we reversed course, my horse took off at a full gallop and was about to cross a four-lane highway despite my doing my best to slow it down or bring it to a halt. Somehow I managed to swing myself off the saddle and land on my feet even while the horse kept on at top speed.

Later that winter, my father bought me a pair of steel-edged skis with cable bindings and boots to match. I also began to take local jobs, like mowing a neighbor's yard and for a short time, while they were away on vacation, caring for another neighbor's prize bantam chickens. Except for the gas rationing, I seem to have hardly been much aware of the war, though I remember helping the scouts to collect scrap paper and empty crushed tin cans as part of the war effort and taking part in a school project where in art class we competed drawing posters to sell "War Bonds". We also made a trip to Boston to visit my oldest cousin and her husband, a US Navy pilot, who was able to get us on a tour of the Boston Navy Yard. I remember boarding the USS Arkansas, a World War I vintage battleship with an enclosed observation tower straddling the bridge on a tall tripod structure. I also remember going down to the train

Chapter 1

station in Hartford with my mother to see President Roosevelt on the campaign trail for his final election, and my mother exclaiming, when he appeared on the observation coach platform, maybe 60 to 80 or so yards away from where we were standing, that "he's all made up"— his ashen cheeks rouged to try to make him look fit. Within a couple of months he was dead.

I also remember that same year as being one of some stress both for me in school as well as for my mother who was unhappy in what she considered something of a New England exile. Nor was I exactly happy either. Although I seemed to have plenty of acquaintances, I felt I had no real friends. But I can't remember feeling that I was missing anything when we traveled north to Vermont several times during that period to visit my father's two sisters, the older, Wilhelmina — whom everyone called "Billie", whom my dad helped support on a small farm which she shared with another woman near Montpelier, and his kid sister Georgia, who lived in an apartment in Burlington with her two daughters who were one and two years younger than I. In fact, I rather enjoyed these excursions to the rugged Green Mountain country and the expansive shore of Lake Champlain. Something about Vermont drew me, like it did my two aunts, even though they had grown up in Wisconsin. I guess it was something of an ancestral homing instinct.

Maybe another reason I found Connecticut uncomfortable was that it was at that time that I began to feel that somehow, being a Catholic, I was different. Maybe it was partly because my folks decided it was time I be confirmed and dutifully hauled me to catechism class once a week. But I also remember feeling a bit uncomfortable when in homeroom each morning we recited the Lord's Prayer in what I took to be the "Protestant version", since in those rather unenlightened pre-Second Vatican Council days Roman Catholics were not used to the old "For Thine is the power and the glory..." etc. ending — which I only later learned that Protestants had lifted from the Eastern Rite Church. I even seem to have thought it might be a sin to say that part. My sense of isolation was not helped either by the realization that the only other self-identified Catholic in my class was a girl whom a lot of kids laughed at behind her back, as she reeked of what the Lifebuoy Soap ads on the radio ominously called "B.O."

As for the Confirmation itself, two things still stand out in my mind, the first being that I couldn't decide on a new Confirmation name, so I decided to take my middle name over again. But when the bishop addressed me as "Gulielmus" I thought he'd made a mistake — no one having warned me that "William" sounded that strange in Latin!

The other lasting impression from that ceremony was having sprung on us, without advance warning, that we were now expected to take the pledge against drinking any alcoholic beverages until we turned twenty-one years of age. This was something of a shock to me, as just that year my folks had on very special occasions allowed me a small glass of beer. But since everyone else around me stood up to take the pledge, I also stood up and took it — and apparently I took it quite seriously, as I never touched the stuff again until I turned 21. But looking back at the whole thing now, I still feel that although resuming catechism lessons was a good idea (as probably was the pledge — considering some of the fellows I ran into in high school a few years later), Confirmation itself could have well waited several more years.

About this time I also had several experiences that shook whatever confidence I had in myself. One was my failure as a Boy Scout to become an effective Cub Scout "Den Leader" when in the course of trying to teach these nine-through-eleven year old boys some knot tying, my den (or maybe I should say "pack") ganged up on me and tied me to a basement pillar. I think that I remember that the "Den Mother" was upstairs in her kitchen and had to come down into the basement to rescue me. Such was the end of my first efforts at youth leadership. And whether the story of that incident had made the rounds first, I no longer remember, but I do remember being bullied and humiliated in front of my Boy Scout associates by two or three of my peers without much of a physical struggle at all. Perhaps it was my memory of my having felt guilty over having struck a playmate some years before and sending him home crying, or of more recently having struck a small boy who had been pelting me with small stones when I had been hired by his parents to mow their lawn and had warned him to quit or else. Or maybe it was because I had suffered a concussion when I "headed" a place-kicked ball in a school soccer match and got knocked flat on my back and saw stars. In any case, it seems that by my early teens I had developed an aversion to physical combat of any sort.

Although V-J Day came not too long after and although I vaguely remember my folks and I driving to downtown Hartford to watch people celebrate, my most vivid recollection of the war's ending was accompanying my father on a business trip to the Springfield Armory in Massachusetts just a few weeks after V-E Day. After he made his call, we crossed the Connecticut River to Westover Field to watch a flight of 8th Air Force B-17 "Flying Fortress" bombers coming in from England. One by one they were touching down, many of them with obviously patched fuselages, tails and wings. It wasn't until then that this sight (along with the news of my old friend Tommy getting killed on Okinawa) drove it home to me that a lot Americans had been dying while I complained of snail-pace driving, food ration coupons and the limited amount of gas.

That fall my father confirmed that a job he had applied for some months before was now his to take and we prepared to move again, this time to Cincinnati, Ohio, where he was to open a new office for International Nickel Company. So despite my having been somehow nominated to run for vice-president of the student council and my having to stand up in front of the whole junior high assembly and give a campaign speech (I can remember saying something like "Don't vote for me as we'll probably be moving again soon") my mother and I finally got our wish to move back "west". Although it was probably too bad in a way, as I recall someone telling me that I had won the vote because a lot of the girls thought I was handsome or cute. It had been my first public speech and I, on the contrary, again, felt very much like a fool. Thus over-all, as much as I loved the countryside and the history of New England, I was rather glad to be headed back to the Midwest.

Chapter 2
The Cincinnati Years

If the Vermont farmer who thought I might run into Indians "out west" in Cincinnati sounded a bit out of it, he was hardly more so than the town itself, which still proudly called itself "The Queen City of the West". Built on seven hills (like Rome) ranged around the flats along the Ohio River, the town seemed to me (after the country-side of semi-rural western Connecticut) to be a jumble of old buildings that ranged from the seedy and broken down in the valleys to the old, but elegant mansions that commanded the heights. But there weren't many, or even any, wild Indians I could see. They had been long ago replaced by mostly German immigrants, mostly staunch Catholics with names like Vogele, Breitenbach, and Oberschmidt — just to name a few of my soon to be friends. But to my surprise, one of my high school classmates was part Sioux and one of my best buddies, partly descended from a northern Michigan family of French ancestry, certainly looked like he was part Odawa (Chippewa) — as so many of these families in fact are.

For some reason undisclosed to me my parents decided to place me, for my eighth grade, in a rather small and exclusive Catholic school known as "The Summit School for Boys" which had a "Headmaster" rather than a Principal and featured a lot of sports along with academics that included use of a college level English grammar and composition text. This choice was made even though our new home was only a block away from the local parochial grade school at Christ the King parish, named "Cardinal Pacelli Grade School" because it had been blessed in person by the future Pope Pius XII on a visit to Cincinnati not long before he became pope. I guess my folks were counting on me getting involved with the top layer of local society for my high school years. If so, they must have been rather disappointed when, after finishing eighth grade, I insisted on attending the closest diocesan-run high school, staffed by the Brothers of Mary, rather than the more prestigious

Chapter 2

Jesuit-run Saint Xavier High School. The deciding factors were, I guess, the long ride to that shabby old downtown and ancient civil-war era school building, plus the fact that the first fellow I met who lived just a few blocks away had decided on the same school as well. The choice, at least for me, turned out to be a mistake.

Not that I didn't enjoy my two years at Purcell High. I went out for the swim team and was immediately selected when the coach asked us to dive in the pool and swim as far as we could under water and I went what today would be for me still an amazing length. I soon specialized in the 100-yard freestyle dash. During the second year's season I did well in an all state meet but soon I had to quit on doctor's orders after a prolonged series of sinus infections. The coach, a local diocesan priest, thought it was a shame, for as he told me, if I had ever "really learned to swim" (he meant with any real coordination) I could have been the "fastest guy in Ohio in that particular event."

The college preparation that I had hoped to get at Purcell, particularly in math (as I aspired to become an engineer like my father), was disappointing. So I decided on my own to transfer to Xavier High beginning my junior year. With my background of many schools (eight different schools in my first eight years) transferring schools and making a new set of acquaintances was no big deal for me. Not that Purcell High had not given me some other challenges. For one, our religion teacher had required us to outline and sum up the contents of every page of our text book, so I decided, because my handwriting was so sloppy, to teach myself to type. The other big challenge was a rather madcap brother — my Latin teacher — who cornered me in the hall one day and asked if I'd ever thought of becoming a priest. I hadn't and quite resented being put on the spot that way.

But perhaps there was another reason that I reacted so negatively to that suggestion. If I had already suffered through a bout (even as a fourth grader), with what religious manuals called "scrupulosity", the problem came back at me with a vengeance during my adolescent years. No doubt an emerging sexuality had a lot to do with it. At least sex, or thoughts about sex, certainly exacerbated whatever cause was already there. At one point I actually developed something of a nervous tick, apparently based on the belief I could literally shake "dirty thoughts" out of my head. And to some extent, that maneuver even seemed to work. But all the other things that seemed to bother me this way, like worries as to whether or not our gas water heater in the basement might asphyxiate us all unless constantly checked (the thing did have a way of unexpectedly losing its pilot flame) or that failing to inform my friends that "a perfect act of contrition" could save one from going to hell even if one had neglected to go to confession, could itself put me in jeopardy of eternal damnation. All these couldn't seem to be so easily shaken out of my head.

I think too that I also half-instinctively recognized that the brother who had cornered me about becoming a priest also suffered from the same psychological affliction as I, something that was confirmed when, on another occasion, he stopped me in the hallway and tried to impart to me, in what seemed to be a contest to boil it down to twenty-five words or less, the basic "facts of life". Despite that, I didn't make any clear connection in my mind between his strange way of approaching people and religious life in general. The rest of the brothers in the school seemed to be real regular guys except for the "Prince Albert" type black frock coats some of them still wore as part of their religious order's teachers "habits". But, back then, the idea of becoming a teacher did not attract me, and I that the idea of somehow being responsible for the salvation or damnation of others would have been a thought that would have, and in fact did, scare the bejeebers out of me, and would continue to bother me for years to come, even after I decided to become a priest.

The one remedy that did seem to work at the time, however, was the help given to me by a young assistant priest in a neighboring parish (I was sure in my own mind that the rather gruff acting pastor of my own parish would probably thrown me out of the confessional on my ear) and the command that this priest gave me. He said I must not — and he repeated *not* — confess any sin in confession unless I "could swear on a whole stack of Bibles" that I knew for sure I was committing a mortal sin at the time. Now that proved a problem for me, and a stroke of genius on his part; for if I was never sure if I was really committing a sin or not, then how could I in conscience keep going over them in confession if he had commanded (almost under pain of sin) to stop dragging them up? He also turned out to be something of a hero figure in my mind, for not only had he solved my problem (well kind of) for me, but he had a way of sashaying his way down the church aisle wearing a dramatic black cloak over his cassock, something like a less colorful version of Bishop Sheen whose "Life is Worth Living" was soon to become a hit show on the new miracle medium of TV.

If this young priest's much needed kind but no-nonsense approach seemed to help me in the midst of my misery, something else more positive seems to have come out of the crisis in addition to an appreciation of the role of a parish priest. The affliction of "scrupulosity" although it shows all the signs of an obsessive-compulsive disorder, not unlike hypochondria, is also compounded by faulty religious training or a distorted image of God. Perhaps this is what prompted me, one summer morning, to take off on my bicycle to the public library, all on my own, to investigate, in a set of *The Catholic Encyclopedia*, the article on "Predestination". My mother seemed quite alarmed or perplexed as to why I, a mere high-school sophomore, would want to delve into such a mysterious subject. Nor am I still quite sure what motivated me to read that long article I could only barely understand. But I suspect it was the hope that I could be sure of getting to heaven no matter how bad I might be — or maybe the freedom promised by the futility of trying to escape hell if that's where the Almighty had, from all eternity, decided I'd end up no matter what. But I remember that I found the whole idea of predestination highly unconvincing no matter how persuasive the logic (that is, of God's foreknowledge) or the attempt to mitigate that logic by the reassurance that God only predestines the saints to heaven — providing they cooperate, of course — but never sinners to hell, since that is all their own doing. Yet if nothing else, I consider that bit of research, if not a particularly rewarding one, the beginning of my theological career.

But back to the subject of my switching high schools, another contributing fact or was the incident of getting shot, not in any way connected with the school, but accidentally by the buddy whose choice of schools had originally influenced me. My mother's older brother back up in Michigan's U.P. had, quite early on, taught me how to shoot. By age 13, after the summer at Lantern Hill Camp, my parents allowed me to own a single shot 22 caliber rifle. Later on, during my high school years, my uncle let me shoot, on one occasion, his deer rifle and on another — the first time I ever held a real handgun — a 7.65mm Luger one of my cousins had "liberated" while moving in with the US Army occupation forces in Germany at the end of World War II. As a result, I eagerly accepted the gift of some old 22 caliber revolver parts another uncle had come across as a result of his association with a fellow who had an electro-plating shop. All the essential parts, the frame with its barrel, the cylinder, trigger, and hammer, were there, covered by a thick new coat of nickel plating. All it really lacked was the internal springs to make it work.

One spring day, my friend was up in my room with me and was equally fascinated by the prospect of making the pistol shoot. I had foolishly shown him how a 22 cal. cartridge fit into the cylinder and (after removing the cartridge) let him play with the thing a bit. I was sitting in a chair and looked up when I heard him flipping the loose unsprung hammer back and forth. Right then I remember seeing an orange flash, hearing the report, and feeling an impact and then numbness just above my upper lip. I reached up and felt some blood trickling from my lip but also felt the bullet, lodged inside my lip against my gum. Apparently the old barrel had been full of rust that had not been removed before the plating job and the bullet barely had enough velocity to do any more damage than it did. I still remember the stunned look of terror in my friend's eyes, but being strangely very calm myself, more worried about what I'd tell my folks — my mother having left the house to grocery shop. I don't recall my friend staying around long enough to face her, nor do I ever recall him coming to our house again.

Chapter 2

The local doctor patched me up and said he'd have to report the incident to the police. I said that was OK by me but that otherwise I hoped he would keep the whole episode a secret. I was highly embarrassed by the stupidity of the whole incident. I even persuaded my folks to cooperate with my wish. Some months later I did have to go to the dentist for an X-ray, and he determined that the root of one of my upper front teeth was dying, and elected to do a root canal operation — the first I'd ever heard of, to save me the embarrassment of having to wear a denture at age 16.

One would think, of course, that after this I'd have nothing to do with guns, but quite the opposite. Years later, as a kind of psychological safety valve while a parish priest, I joined a local small-bore rifle team, reconditioned a few old guns, reloaded my own ammunition for shot-guns and center-fire rifles, and studied enough about ballistics to even find a use for those mysterious quadratic equations I'd been forced to learn in high school. I was even a proud member of the NRA!

Again, looking back on this incident and my long-undiminished fascination with guns, I'm hard-put to explain it. One would think that after such an incident one would swear off any interest in guns forever. But rather, that, and the fact that a local gunsmith I knew hobbled around with the help of a cane because of almost blowing his foot off in an ill-fated attempt to remove a stuck cartridge from a shotgun barrel, all this seems to have only given me a healthy respect for the danger such weapons posed, but in no way dimmed my fascination.

Perhaps, especially after building two muzzle-loading black powder rifles myself, it is the appeal of fitting a carefully fashioned piece of wood to an ingeniously designed mechanism that is capable of reaching out to strike a target many yards, even hundreds of yards, away. I seldom thought of these targets as being "living beings". They were instead "varmints"— hapless animals (crows, woodchucks, foxes) that the world (or at least the local farmers) didn't think much of, or in the case of pheasants, grouse, ducks, squirrels, deer, and in one case, a bear (taken on a fishing trip in Canada) as food to be eaten and in some cases, trophies to be shown off. It was only after the Kennedy and Martin Luther King assassinations that it began to dawn on me that there might be something more than a bit psychologically unbalanced in America's (especially American males') fascination with firearms. And it was shortly after those events that I gave up my membership in the NRA.

The whole incident plus the friendship that faltered as a result was one more factor leading to another change of schools. Or maybe it was my growing interest in theological matters even though I was switching to the Jesuit run high school to prepare to major in engineering. Yet the principal there insisted that I take third year Latin, which (Jesuit drilling of first and second years students being what it was back then) I nearly flunked. I kept getting lost in Cicero's long involved sentences. But at least the Jesuits spared me from having to take Greek. And math and science I did very well in, even though I could never figure out at the time, what might be any possible use for those quadratic equations. I also went on to take fourth year Latin and got A's in the subject. The young Jesuit Latin teacher, who later became a life-long friend, said he could never figure it out after I had almost flunked the year before. I chalked it up to being good at guessing the many uses of the ablative case in Virgil's epic poem *The Aeneid*, which had mercifully short sentences compared to the year before. But looking back now, maybe I should credit a new motivation that was already taking place in my mind and heart.

But first, perhaps it might be helpful to back up a bit and ponder my social life back then, or to be more specific, the subject of girls. As soon as we had moved to Cinci, my mother and a near-by neighbor lady who had two girls about my age plotted together to make sure that particular part of my education would not be overlooked. While still in eighth grade I was assigned the task of escorting those two sisters to dancing school so the three of us would all be ready to join, as soon as we were in high school, an organization called "Junior Dates". I was not very thrilled, to say the least. But to keep the peace I did my duty and continued to do so for the next several years. "Junior Dates" was something

Chapter 2

dreamed up by the good Catholic mothers of Cincinnati to make sure their kids, segregated by the separate boys and girls high schools, didn't fall into the trap presented by non-Catholic neighborhood kids. It was also supposed to, by means of a lottery system that picked your dates for you, prevent you from that major occasion of sin called "going steady" — although I soon enough noticed that certain older kids in the outfit seemed to be always assigned the same date. Obviously there was a bit of corruption in the system or some deliberate social engineering was taking place. But the system didn't prevent me from taking a shine to at least one girl, who was the kid sister of one of my newer Saint Xavier High friends. Yet on the other hand, due to that same system, I can remember taking that girl out to only one formal dance. Perhaps I was also a bit distracted by another Catholic girl I'd taken a shine to recently during my summers in Michigan's U.P.

One of those summers I was also witness to an ominous event. One day I was with my best friend up there, a fellow a year or so older than I with whom I had gone camping and whom I helped restore a rare old car (a low-slung 1938 Graham-Page) when his father received delivery of a new cabin cruiser. We'd gone down to the Michigan Tech dock and boat launching facility to watch the tractor trailer slide it into the water, then boarded the boat to start the inboard engine, which refused to start. My friend's father opened up the engine compartment to fiddle with the carburetor and repeatedly worked the starter, then suddenly collapsed. I went out on the deck to yell to the truck driver to summon an ambulance, thinking my friend's dad had been overcome by gasoline fumes or the like, but by the time the ambulance arrived and we managed to paddle the large boat back to the dock, his dad had lost all consciousness and his face had turned a blotchy purplish red. They got him off the boat and rushed him to the hospital, but we soon learned he was pronounced D.O.A.— dead on arrival. In fact, I believe I witnessed a death by a "coronary" first hand — the same way that years later I was to lose my own father. My friends and I, both boys and girls, did our best to share his grief.

But there were also plenty of other distractions from girls. One was that I'd gotten quite taken with horseback riding, partly under my dad's tutelage, he having been a rather accomplished rider himself. I learned to handle check-reins and to get one particular horse to "rack", — an unusual gait (most usually seen in "trotting" race horses) affording a swift ride that felt as smooth as a gentle rocking chair. But then the privilege of driving the family car came along and it was either money for gas or money for horses and the car won.

Then there was also the lure of one of my old Purcell High friends who lived out in the country and had a fish pond stocked with blue-gills. I also used to help him do things like rake and collect hay with an old surplus army Jeep, but these experiences of open skies and vistas — you could see downtown Cincinnati over five miles distant from their hilltop — soon had me half-consciously vowing I'd never willingly live in a city again. He and I, and some of our friends from either school also used to get together for more social things at my home. And there were fishing trips out of town, one a scout troop canoe trip on Michigan's famed AuSable river, and another one that my dad and I, and my country-dwelling friend and his dad, all took together way up into Ontario north of Lake Huron. It was a major expedition for those days before expressways, and for most of my southern Ohio friends, the psychological equivalent of going to the tundra regions of Canada's far north.

But the big distraction (at least from girls) came to me during the summer after my junior year of high school. Just before school let out (in fact, I think it may have been while we were writing our final English exam) our teacher, a Jesuit "scholastic" (the time that most Jesuit seminarians used to spend teaching before they go on to study theology) interrupted the class to tell us about a book he was reading. It was called *The Seven Storey Mountain*, written — not all that well he added — by a young Trappist monk by the name of Thomas Merton. The book was a fascinating story of conversion followed by a very special vocation to the strictest form of the monastic life to be found in the whole Catholic Church.

Now, I should say that previous to this, I had already become engrossed in the tales of the North American Jesuit missionaries and martyrs and had even prevailed on my dad, on the way to more fishing in Ontario, to take me to the site of their missions to the Huron nation on Ontario's Midland Peninsula along the south shore of Georgian Bay. There we even watched and talked to an archeologist as he dug to uncover the remains of the mission palisade that had burned when the Iroquois raiders had sacked the place in 1649. I had also avidly read the adventures of Fr. Hubbard, the "Glacier Priest" with his fascinating stories of the Jesuit missions in Alaska, and even went to see him when he came to Cincinnati to present a travelogue film on the Alaska Highway as part of the Xavier Lecture series. Some itch to do something or be someone heroic was already, I guess, grabbing my imagination. I can even remember making an attempt at writing a little poetry on the subject of the Jesuit missionaries — something I was to learn later on was a dire sign. My father and I also promised ourselves that some day we'd drive that highway to Alaska together, that is, if we could figure out what to do with my mother in the meantime (she was not what you'd call your average "happy camper" when taken out on the road — unless it headed straight back to Michigan).

That summer, however, forced to stay in Cincinnati a bit longer than usual by I can't remember what circumstances, I went to the local Catholic book store and bought Merton's book. I was utterly fascinated and taken by the idea of possibly becoming a Trappist monk myself. But I did not own up to the idea to my folks right away. In fact, I was a bit hesitant to admit anything, although I'm afraid I may have betrayed my cards a bit when later that summer, up in the U.P., I suddenly became very edgy about the idea of going out on dates or dancing with girls. Even though I very much liked at least a few of them, I figured that if I was going to give myself to the Lord, I'd better get used to doing without.

Looking back, I think there was something of a rather dark side to this as well. Although during the time we were still living in Connecticut I had begun to feel increasingly close to my mother and sympathy for her unhappiness at being so far from her beloved

The Cincinnati Years

Michigan and her extended family. But after the first few years in Cincinnati I'd become more and more estranged from my mother, especially her wild swings of mood, her complaining about this and that or whatever seemed to irk her at the time. I remember storming out of the house one evening after she went on what seemed to me to be a tirade over the flavor of the ice-cream I'd picked out when she asked me to run down to the store to buy dessert earlier that afternoon. I also remember vowing to myself on that occasion that on no account was I going to ever let myself get bamboozled into marrying anyone with a temperament like hers — and then wondering if maybe, sooner or later, all women turned out to be that way. No one really bothered to explain to me what menopause was all about. I can only remember her complaining about "hot flashes".

I also remember, about that time, gradually developing a strange feeling of satisfaction —or might I say enjoying a certain kind of melancholy mood? — when I found myself for any reason or other prevented from attending social events where I knew girls would be present, even to the point of on a few occasions deliberately not showing up when I had been invited. How to explain this? It seems to me now that however distorted my perceptions were, or impolite my actions, I thought that God was inviting me, or could I say enticing me, to be different, to resist the lure of the crowd, but especially, to declare my independence from women.

Added to all that was my frankly skewed and greatly distorted ideas regarding female sexuality. While it was obvious to me that young women were very much interested in landing a catch, the idea that they might be strongly drawn to engaging in sex itself seemed to me to be for some reason unthinkable. To my mind there were three reasons that they might agree to it: first, the overwhelming desire to have a baby; second, to please their husband or to trap a boyfriend; and third, if worse comes to worst, to earn a living. How I ended up with such weird or unrealistic ideas escapes me, but in a discussion many years later with my cousin (the one whom I considered to be a brat back in our childhood) she mentioned the strange attitude regarding that subject that she believed was our mothers' shared Irish-American family background. Although I would hesitate to accuse Irish Catholicism as having been particularly susceptible to this attitude about sexuality, I recalled how I learned, in one of the seminary Church History courses that I took years before, how the Church in Ireland, while under the thumb of British rule for centuries, had no choice but send its candidates for the priesthood over to the continent for training, particularly to France, where the seminaries were infected with what was called "Jansenism" — sometimes described, even by our professors, as a kind of "Catholic Puritanism". But it's not as if Jansenism (named after a professor at the University of Louvain who was an expert on Saint Augustine's thinking) was confined only to the French and Belgian seminaries. It's just that the effects of that kind of thinking for some reason lasted longer in Ireland and among Irish family culture than elsewhere. Nor was this rather distorted view of sexuality entirely the fault of my Irish Catholic upbringing. I believe that it was my Protestant-raised father who impressed me with the saying that in child-birth, a woman enters into or passes through "the valley of death". Whether this was intended as reflection on any difficulties my mother may have had with my own birth — if so, she never said anything about it to me — or simply as a fatherly warning, I'm not sure. But either way, it impressed upon me that sex was not to be trifled with.

However, a much darker event overshadowed my path the first few weeks of my eighteenth year of life. My U.P. buddy, the one who had so traumatically lost his dad before our very eyes, was now a sophomore at Michigan Tech, and was also dating one of my cousins who lived on the opposite side of the street from the University. I couldn't say for sure, but I think I even began to think of him as a future cousin-in-law. But as a member of Michigan Tech 's ice hockey team he was returning on January 14, 1950 from a game played down at Michigan State University, when on a curve on US-27, about seven miles north of Gaylord, the team's bus sideswiped another bus headed in the opposite direction.

The Cincinnati Years

According to the newspaper accounts, a cloud of snow, kicked up by a plow-truck, had momentarily obscured the bus-driver's vision. Bob was sleeping with his head against the window, just two or three seats behind the driver and he and another student hockey player were instantly killed — as were several persons on the other bus. I was ill with a cold or the flu at the time and can remember lying in bed in my room that evening when I was told the news and thinking how short and capricious life can be, and again thinking that perhaps God wanted me in some way to do something special with my life.

After high school graduation a few months later, my mother and I spent part of the summer in Jackson, Michigan living in a cousin's home while she was at their summer place and while I worked as a janitor and gardener for the apartment complex supervised by my widowed aunt. By then I had bought Merton's second book, a book of meditations called *Seeds of Contemplation*. By then it almost seemed that my mind was made up to join something along these lines, but I said little about the subject, except to my oldest cousin who asked what was on my mind. I remember that when I said I was thinking seriously about becoming a lay-brother on a monastery farm, she blurted out that I had too much brains for that and should become a priest like their pastor in town. So after my mother and I returned to Cincinnati I came clean with my folks and told them what was on my mind.

I can't remember my mother saying anything — she had, I think, guessed it all along — but I do remember my father breaking down and weeping a bit, the first time I'd ever seen him like that. For some reason or other it never dawned on me the real reason for this. It probably was the fact that with my decision his family name (or at least his branch of the Kropfs) would die out. It was his older sister who would raise that point openly later on. Nor did it ever cross my mind what this would also mean for my mother, but I would have to admit that at the time, had it occurred to me, I probably would have taken secret satisfaction in upsetting her own plans. Looking back on this period of time during my life, it is hard to figure how I could have been so scrupulous about so many things – yet so callous about other's feelings.

However, still being in a state of indecision, I entered the local Jesuit-run Xavier University in a general liberal arts program. And with the Korean War just having broken out in late June, I also became a member of the Reserve Officers Training Corps or ROTC, although I'm not sure we had any choice in that matter. We drilled in our smart uniforms once a week and were given instructions on how to take apart and reassemble an M-1 carbine. But, with the prospect of eventually studying for the priesthood in mind, I also decided I'd better begin to study Greek, just in case. Meanwhile, my folks prevailed on me to go to the university counseling department to take a battery of vocational aptitude tests. They came out saying that I was well suited to "social type work" like the priesthood, but should steer clear of any detailed administrative duties. I also consulted with the university's appointed student "spiritual director" who asked me why I didn't think about joining the Jesuits, to which I think I said something about not feeling particularly called to teach and adding what I must think was something of an unintended insult when I said I felt the Jesuits were not required to pray enough!

Not put off by that, however, he reminded me that there was a war on and that if I really did feel called to the seminary or priesthood, that I must realistically consider that should I be drafted, I'd be put back at least three years toward accomplishing my goal and that a vocation was not something to be trifled with like that. I countered that I felt safe enough because of my generally high grades and membership in the ROTC. Then he reminded me that one failed exam could change all that and suggested I transfer to the local seminary post-haste.

Looking back at all this over a half-century later, it seems to me that most of us college students felt at that point that the "engagement" in Korea was not any big deal. We figured it would be all over within a few months time, especially after General MacArthur's spectacular counter-invasion at Inchon resulted in the liberation of Seoul in September of 1950. But this was to be followed by the disasterous route of U.S. Marines and U.S. Army infantry by waves of Chinese infantry at the Chosin Reservoir in December after MacArthur recklessly ignored Chinese warnings and foolishly decided he'd completely conquer North Korea and wipe out its Communist regime.

So by Christmas break, arrangements for me to transfer to the seminary had been made. But first, I traveled by train down to Gethsemane Abbey south of Louisville Kentucky to make a short retreat and to look over the place that had so fascinated me in Merton's books. And it continued to fascinate me: in fact, I was overawed. The medieval atmosphere, the farm animals and smells (mules even — no tractors there yet), the absolute silence except for the round of chants, all that left an impression that has never faded even to this day. But I also knew, deep down, that I could not make that final of a break with my folks, at least not yet. So when they drove down to pick me up I returned with them to Cincinnati convinced that I was making the right step, at least for now. And I guess my mother was convinced that they at least had saved me from throwing my whole life away in a medieval monastery buried in the back hills of Kentucky.

My pastor at Christ the King was a personal friend of Joseph Albers, the Bishop of Lansing Michigan. Bishop Albers was from an old and prominent Cincinnati family and since we once lived in Lansing diocese (in Jackson) they arranged my release from any claims by the diocese of my birth (Milwaukee). I was fitted for a black cassock and scheduled to report at Saint Gregory's Seminary in nearby Mount Washington for the beginning of the winter term with the idea that I would transfer to Sacred Heart Seminary in Detroit once my dad's impending transfer to the INCO office up there was arranged. I was assigned a room with a second year student from the Youngstown Diocese in the old dormitory at "The Greg" as the place was called. The whole operation went so smoothly and quickly that I forgot to show up with a pair of black shoes to match and had to quickly find black shoe dye so I wouldn't stand out like a sore thumb.

I very quickly took to the life, and when, as the Korean warfare worsened, the rumor spread that we might be kept in studies in the seminary over the summer to make sure we retained our 4-D (D for "divinity") selective service status, I positively looked forward to the prospect. It was, as I saw it, except for the exams, almost as good as living in a monastery. But when one morning in chapel I saw one of the Trappists (in his white tunic and black hooded scapular) from Gethsemane who had stopped by overnight on his way to New York State where a new branch monastery was soon to be formed, I was stirred up with thoughts of a real monastic life all over again.

Meanwhile most of my former high school and college buddies continued college and after their graduations, became second lieutenants in the Army, two of them, twin brothers particularly noted for their brains (which figured — their father being a brain surgeon) in the Army Intelligence Corps, and going on from there to careers in the CIA. Years later, one of the two, having never married, became a priest.

Looking back on it all now, I have often wondered what might have happened to me if I hadn't run off to the seminary. One thing for sure, having done so, if I had later left the seminary for a career in politics, I sure would have had some explaining to do!

Chapter 3
Preparations

If the short, barely five-month, period at Saint Gregory's was a taste of longed-for monastic seclusion, the year to follow was just the opposite. Sacred Heart Seminary in Detroit was so crowded with candidates for the priesthood that all those who lived in the Detroit area, from second year college on down to high school freshmen, had to commute to school. This included me, my folks now living in Royal Oak, a suburb just about a dozen miles northwest of downtown Detroit.

So commute I did, driving with my father down Woodward Avenue each morning, stopping to pick up a few other seminarians, letting my father off at GM's stately Fisher Building where INCO had its office (nothing like being close to your major customer) and backtracking a mile or so to the seminary where I took a full round of classes until mid-afternoon. Then back up Woodward with my student passengers around 3 PM, and around 5 PM over to the local Royal Oak Grand Trunk RR station to pick up my dad as he arrived on the commuter train. The only thing really notable about that year is that we lived in the Shrine of the Little Flower parish (still with the controversial Fr. Charles Coughlin in charge — although he had stayed off the radio after the Archbishop had ordered him to) and I had also persuaded my father to turn in our 1949 Ford for a 1951 model with automatic transmission to cope with the stop and go driving involved in the long commutes. Though I can't remember Fr. Coughlin saying anything too bombastic that year, I do remember that block (neighborhood) rosaries recited to ward off any take-over by the Communists were a big thing.

The following school year I got to go back to living a semi-monastic life in the seminary again. One of the old large dormitory rooms had been partitioned off into single study-bedrooms, so I even had my own little monastic "cell". There were visitor days once a month, and some free afternoons we could leave the grounds, and occasionally we even had a whole day off. The seminary grounds, which took up most all of the equivalent of several city blocks, were now surrounded by the city, with an almost entirely black neighborhood to the south, a predominantly Jewish neighborhood to the north, and a more or less mixed neighborhood on the east and west sides. Classes in English, history, and philosophy just about filled up the scholastic schedule, but I do remember doing a paper for a sociology class on the "Rurban Community" praising Henry Ford's concept of the automobile allowing industrial workers to enjoy the benefits of rural life. (Years later I learned that the unions saw this concept as part of plot where the auto makers could lay off their workers without benefits, content that they wouldn't starve as long as they had their own garden plots!)

My classmates were from varied backgrounds. One, from Detroit's large Maltese community, brought his grandmother's prayer book to show off the novelty of Catholic prayers that began with the invocation "O Allah", while another, a Ukrainian-American, had the novelty of his own father, a local Ukrainian-Catholic pastor, say Mass for us in the Byzantine Rite.

One of my closest friends, a tall black fellow, was a convert from Pittsburg whose grandfather was an African Methodist Episcopal bishop, and together, for some strange reason, the two of us signed up for a class in the Polish language. Most of our philosophy courses were taught in Latin, and we had to write our exams in Latin as well. I became very adept at starting a sentence with a Latin noun, skipping down a line or two in the bluebook to write out the verb, then filling in the space with the object and whatever adjectives, adverbs, and other modifiers were needed in between. It was the closest I'd ever been to living in an international community, typical of the exotic mix that was Detroit at that time.

Not all was prayer and study, however. There were outreach activities like helping to take parish census or when another classmate and I went to give catechism lessons to a little boy dying of cystic fibrosis. And there were occasional excursions to Blessed Sacrament Cathedral where the seminary choir sang for special events like the mass adult confirmation services held in the spring. After one of those events, most of my classmates ended up at the nearby home of a classmate who threw a little party for them. Not having been invited (they probably figured I'd refuse to break the rule) I was one of the few who checked back in at the seminary in time. The others got quite dressing down from the Dean of Discipline.

Four other things of note happened to me while I was at Sacred Heart Seminary. It was after my parents bought what was to become our new family residence in Birmingham, Michigan (once called "Piety Hill") that my parents, renewed their friendship with a crusty old bachelor from Michigan's U.P., who lived a few blocks away with his elderly mother. One day as we were leaving after a visit, he said to me (out of earshot of his mother, a pious old Scottish Presbyterian) that he found it difficult to believe that a fellow as intelligent as I could swallow all the stuff they would teach me in the seminary. I don't recall exactly what "stuff" he meant, but somehow I got the feeling that he just wasn't referring to Roman Catholic pieties or papal "infallibility", but to the whole Christian system of beliefs. This impression was confirmed later when one summer day I ran into him in a local store, and again, he sidled up to me and said he figured that sooner or later I'd come to the conclusion that much of what I would be expected to teach was only so much "myth" — for the comfort of simple believers, but that I'd hardly take it literally myself. I don't remember what I said in answer, but I do recall reacting negatively to any such suggestion of pretending, for the sake of others, that I believed.

I also know that I took these challenges seriously as an incentive to investigate more thoroughly the historical and theological foundations of Christian doctrine and Catholic dogmas and that I resolved that I'd never allow myself to remain in a situation where I found myself forced to dissemble or conceal what I really did, or didn't, believe. It has not always been an easy resolution to keep.

During my final year at Sacred Heart I was put in charge of all janitorial work in the senior college dorm, which my mother thought was awful — this despite my pointing out that it was I who got to assign the other fellows to do most of the work.

Then I had my first published article — a short history of the Mormon colony (and its fall) on historic Beaver Island, Michigan. My

Chapter 3

folks and I had visited the place the summer before and I delved into the state historical collection in the seminary library to get the low down on the island's colorful past.

Finally, there was the MMPI (Minnesota Multiple Personality Inventory) test. The seminary staff had decided the year before that all senior college students who were intending to continue studying for the priesthood must take the test. The year before, the some forty or so seniors had taken it and about six of them were rejected for further theological studies as a result. About four or five of those went on to study for other dioceses out of state. But there was some apprehension. One wag in our class, when he saw the questions, wanted to know if the test correctors "wore stoles" — implying that it was a lot like going to confession and revealing one's deepest thoughts to a priest.

I answered the questions thoughtfully and honestly — perhaps too much so. I suspect that the test corrector must have been a woman, as to some of the questions I answered in ways not unlike the estimates of women found in Nietzsche or the Book of Ecclesiasticus (lightheaded temptresses not to be trusted, and that sort of thing). A month or so later the seminary rector told me I had come close to flunking the test, but they were going to recommend me for theology because in all other aspects they considered me a model seminarian. (At least I got back from choir duties on time!) But looking back on that now, maybe they should have had more worries about all the fellows who passed, with nearly half of them eventually leaving the priesthood and most getting married posthaste.

That summer I took a job as a counselor at Camp Ozanam, a summer camp for indigent boys sponsored by the Saint Vincent de Paul Society up on the shores of Lake Huron. I was assigned a group of inner city boys, the same as all the rest. I also (having a Boy Scout Life-Saving Merit Badge) did beach duty, and one gray overcast morning jumped in to pull out a boy who was definitely going under — he said nothing, but one could tell just from the look on his face. But otherwise, I didn't do very well there. I couldn't seem to keep order or keep these kids from fighting one another. I'd take long hikes in the country alone when I had the afternoon off just to work off the tension, and when my folks came to visit one Sunday afternoon I went for a ride with them on the country back-roads, and when a car passed us and threw a stone that cracked the windshield, I too cracked and broke down into tears. I quit the job a few days later and went home, feeling a failure in youth work.

In August my folks and I took a three-week trip to the South Dakota Badlands, the Black Hills, Yellowstone, Glacier National Park, and to Banff, Jasper, and Yoho Canadian National Parks. There we viewed elk, bison, and bighorn sheep. I was nearly run over by a bear while sleeping outside our tent at Yellowstone's Fishing Bridge Campground, and caught rainbow from our trusty little 15 ft. canoe in Yellowstone and Jasper parks and cutthroat trout from an alpine lake in Glacier Park. We even, on two or three occasions, persuaded my mother to sleep in the tent instead of painfully picked motels and tourist cabins — this despite her fear of all the bears.

That fall (it was now 1954) I began my theological studies at the still very new Saint John's Provincial Seminary north of Plymouth on a high moraine looking far to the east toward Detroit on the glacial outwash plain below. I know all these geological details because the first speech I gave in our "Sacred Elocution" that is, preaching, class, was a synopsis of a little book I was reading on the *Geology of Southeast Michigan* — not your usual Sunday sermon fare. But our professor urged us to talk on anything we wanted to or were interested in; so I did!

All of our instructors there were members of the Society of Saint Sulpice — a group of priests founded in France several centuries ago for the express purpose of preparing candidates to the priesthood. All of our professors were American except one — a real live Frenchman by the name of Fr. Michel Baron, an exotic it there ever was one. He'd been an artillery officer in the French Army and during the Second World War had been stationed, of all places, in Timbuktu, where of course, he saw no action to speak of, though later on he'd been transferred to French Indo-China, but was lucky enough for his enlistment to run out sometime before the disaster at Dien Ben Phu. On entering the Sulpician order, he figured he'd be assigned, with his engineering background, to teach mathematics in a minor seminary (that is, for high school age candidates) but to his surprise was asked to go to the USA, earn a degree in theology at Catholic University of America, and teach here instead.

I think we all found him fascinating (and somewhat amusing with his tendency to get the emp*ha*sis on the wrong syll*ab*les), but I saw in him even more. In the pre-Vatican II Church, it seems to have been the French who were coming up with the most innovative ideas and theological approaches. The Germans may have had the heaviest-handed scholars (and could add on the most footnotes), but it was the French who seemed to have had the most refreshing ideas. Even though it was his task to teach us "Patrology" (study of the ancient Church Fathers) and Fundamental Theology, it was exactly in these fields, particularly the latter, that I sensed that a lot of rethinking needed to be done. The "Sulps", as we called them, also had the good sense to ignore the rule about teaching in Latin. A lot of our text books were still in that language, but the discussion, and (thank God!) the tests, were not.

Then there was Fr. Castelot, who despite his French surname, was thoroughly American. He taught all of the courses in Sacred Scripture, and to us first year students thought able to handle the extra study required, basic Biblical Hebrew. There was also Fr. Charlie Kerrin, the Vermonter who had the unenviable job of teaching us Canon (that is Church) Law and who, believe it or not, whose humor actually made the course interesting, and occasionally real fun.

The Rector of the seminary, a very Irish Californian named Fr. Lyman Fenn, taught us introductory moral theology, and was most notable for the whole week he spent talking about the problem of alcoholism and importing a reformed priest-alcoholic whose story had made the front cover of *LOOK* magazine. We all, of course, suspected "Lymie" (as we all called him — but of course not to his face) of having once drained more than a few bottles himself. But considering the antiseptic discussions of our moral theology text (also still in Latin) these digressions were a welcome relief. They also represented the only down-to-earth training in human psychology we ever received (besides Fr. Kerrin's commentaries on how people avoided Church regulations). We were subjected to a course on scholastic psychology back in our college years, but it seemed to us that any resemblance between what the medieval philosophers thought made us tick and what really goes on in people's heads seemed purely accidental.

One of the features of Sulpician-run seminaries is that there was no official "spiritual director". Rather, the students were expected to pick one of their own from among the faculty. I chose, of course, Fr. Baron. And quite early on I confided to him my monastic leanings and to my surprise, he told me of his. It seems that before joining the Sulpicians, he had spent a good part of a year or so as an applicant at the famous old Benedictine Abbey of Fleury on the Oise River near Orleans in central France. And he told me he still had leanings in that direction. (Years later, when I spent a summer studying in France, he took me down to visit the place.) So he was very understanding of my dilemma, but urged me to just take one thing at a time. Studies kept me very busy of course.

But there also was plenty to do out-of-doors. Saint John's was a "Provincial Seminary" (so-called because it was supported and maintained by the whole ecclesiastical province of Michigan, consisting of five dioceses at the time) was one of the very few seminaries in the country that had its own golf-course. Mundelein Seminary outside Chicago was supposedly the only other one. This largely was Cardinal Mooney's doing. Mooney was an avid golfer, and in fact, one summer day, before I began there, I went out to look the place over and ran into the Cardinal who was standing in the midst of unfinished chapel in his golfing togs, surveying the construction progress. The Cardinal was of a mind, much like the people who feel that "the family that prays together stays together", so too, the priest who golfs is most likely to stay in the priesthood.

I, for one, did not much care to play golf. Truth is that I was lousy at it, with my coordination with a club not much better than my physical coordination at anything else. However, since golfers were required to put in extra hours on grounds maintenance, I golfed purposely, partly to get in line for the tractor-driver's job. I inherited that job rather quickly after one of the upper classmen almost turned the tractor, a low-slung 1942 war-surplus model Ford 2N, over on himself pulling a large rock up a steep hill. One of my friends in Cincinnati had in fact turned the same kind of tractor over trying to get out of a mud hole, so I was well aware of the do's and don'ts, yet still eager for the job. One of my long term projects was removing large glacial drift boulders from the golf course. After helping fellows dig around them, we would then roll or otherwise manhandle the boulders onto a large metal skid plate. I would then drag them off behind the tractor to a shallow depression which had a small watercourse, constructing what we soon nicknamed "Boulder Dam". (Many years later I was to acquire a similar Ford tractor, and when that one gave up the ghost, still another even older one, built in 1942.)

A group of us seminarians also decided to build an outdoor shrine in the corner of the woods between the fairways which we constructed of old flagstones cemented together. I took charge of scoring and cutting a large slab of sandstone that was to serve as an altar top. During the winter I cross-country skied on the grounds quite a bit, and developed a little ski jump in the ravine near the railroad tracks. During a couple of the winter breaks I drove north with some of my fellow seminarians and gave them skiing lessons. A few of them got quite good at it. I also engaged in a bit of archery on the grounds in the woods, at least once I came back during the summer with my .22 rifle in my golf bag to take care of some of the gophers who kept digging up the greens. I may never have turned out to be a golfer, but with further instructions from "Scotty", our imported Scottish grounds-keeper, I might have turned out to be a decent groundskeeper myself.

That first summer after the first year of theology brought a much bigger adventure. Since the Diocese of Lansing, for which I was studying, included extensive rural areas, ministry to Mexican laborers was a major concern. So I signed up to attend summer school in Mexico City along with two older seminarians from Detroit. We arranged to take a Ford "drive-away" car for delivery in San Antonio, Texas, and the three of us set off cross-country equipped with passports, a few clothes, and not much else. Our destination was the Seminario Conciliar in a little old colonial town called Tlalpan just south of Mexico City, and we arrived there just a few days later after dropping off the car, seeing the Alamo (both the building and the John Wayne movie which was premiering in San Antonio when we arrived) taking the train through Laredo down to Monterey, then flying the rest of the way into Mexico City. It was my first flight on anything other than my uncle's Army Air Force trainer, and I can still remember the thrill of that big old DC-4 (or was it a DC-6? — it had four engines anyway) descending rapidly from over the mountaintops surrounding Mexico City into the deep twilight of that ancient Aztec capital.

We were received with some curiosity by our Mexican counterparts. I remember a tumultuous awakening the next morning, that day being the Feast of John the Baptist, Mexico's patron saint. With all the firecrackers going off, I at first thought we'd arrived just in time for a revolution, there being an army barracks just down the street. After a breakfast that included fried plantanos (a large variety of banana) and coffee, we proceeded by bus past the impressive campus of the National University to the little campus (if you could call the assemblage of low framed buildings) titled "Universidad Ibero-Americana". It was actually a boy's secondary school run by the Jesuits, but serving as a summer school location mostly for students from Georgetown U. My two colleagues having taken basic Spanish, were assigned to a more advanced class, while I and a fellow from Georgetown who wanted to major in international relations (with the idea of going to work for the US State Department) were assigned to study with a young college senior (or maybe I should say "senorita") who was blonde, blue-eyed, and very good looking, and sported one of those double last names that adorn Latin America's upper crust. I suspect we were her first "Yanqui" students, or maybe I should say "Gringo" as many Mexicans still call us. She was definitely the youngest teacher I'd ever had — possibly younger than I — since maybe kindergarten or first grade, and by far the prettiest.

Now we were always told in the seminary that the most important time of our training was in the summer when were off on our own. The idea was that under such conditions in the real world our vocations would be tested by the proximity of girls and women. I could see right away that this summer was going to be a real test. But apparently she'd been cued in on what was expected or not expected of her. After a week or so of lessons, my fellow student and I tried to talk her into being our guide around the national art museum. It was no go. I can see why from the way some of the other Georgetown students were acting. But she needn't have worried because this fellow I was studying with was quite otherwise. He was very thoughtful and one day when we went to climb the nearest volcano (Mount Xitle — extinct of course) I was most impressed when he told me that although he was raised Presbyterian, he was an agnostic, but still hoped he wouldn't be one for long. I learned a great deal of respect for seekers from that encounter. I hope he found what he was looking for.

Since my older colleagues had different class schedule, and I had also signed up to take a course in architecture from a Spaniard who pronounced most of his t's and s's with a Castilian lisp (he wasn't that hard for me to follow because he showed slides of everything he talked about), I had quite a bit of time to explore things on my own.

I started visiting the old Carmelite church at San Angel, another ancient colonial village that had become a district of Mexico City named Villa Obregon (a Spanish mispronunciation of O'Brien), after the famous general who had been assassinated just down the street. One day, while exploring the church, a little boy came up to me and asked if I wanted to see "los mummios" and led me down into the church crypt. There encased in glass-faced coffins, were the bodies of two very short people, a man and a woman, dressed in colonial era finery, no doubt early patrons of the church they helped finance with colonial gold. I wish I could say they were well-preserved. But I paid the kid a few coins anyway. What he had showed me probably helped me keep my mind on my Spanish lessons rather than the Spanish teacher. Towards the end of my stay I asked one of the Discalced Carmelite friars about joining their Third Order. He got quite excited as he seemed to think I was asking about the First Order — that is, the friars themselves. Maybe I was in a way. They were one of the monastic orders I had thought of seriously four years before. He gave me a copy of the Third Order Manual in Spanish, and a year or so later I applied again in Detroit.

Preparations

My friends and I took a few weekend excursions, besides seeing all the old ruins, both Toltec and Aztec, as well as colonial Spanish, around Mexico City. We went to the old silver mining town of Taxco. Another trip took us to Vera Cruz down by the Gulf of Yucatan, where we ate shrimp out of buckets in the steamy tropical heat and watched a small coastal freighter leave the docks on a trip that was to end in disaster in a storm on the gulf later that same week. Another weekend one of the Detroit fellows and I took a bus down to the old town of Amecameca at the foot of Mexico's most famous mountain, the volcano Popocateptl, and stayed in a 16th century Franciscan friary, courtesy of the local parish priest. At Sunday morning Mass he conducted a double wedding for two girls and two boys from a local village, so we witnessed the distinctive customs of a Mexican marriage with the exchange of coins and the "lasso"— the cord looped around each couple to signify the marriage bond. Our plan was to take the local bus up to the Paso de Cortez, the gap between Popocateptl and Ixtecwatl ("the Sleeping Lady") and to climb up from the pass which is at about 12,000 feet above sea level, to as high on the side of Popo as we could get. Imagine our surprise to find the two newly married couples on the same bus, in all their finery. Their little village was on the mountainside up on the way to the pass.

Once up in the pass, well above tree line, my friend and I labored up the side of the volcano along with some other hikers, until we reached the snow line at about 14,500 feet. I'd wanted to climb all the way up the mountain and had even started making plans with a local climbing club, until an American priest warned me of the danger of snow slides or avalanches on the mountain in the summer, which is the rainy season when all the new snow falls. Several climbers had been lost the year before. But even that little way took over two hours, as at that altitude we found ourselves stopping about every 50 to 100 yards to catch our breath. It was like walking on the surface of the moon, except we were rained on, snowed on, and probably had some hail to boot. On the bus on the way home late Sunday afternoon, we were introduced to the Mexican custom of passing around a bottle of Tequila with a bite of lemon and a pinch of salt. I don't remember accepting the offer.

Chapter 3

Another weekend, while my friends went down to Acapulco (which I passed up, having a cold and not wanted to go anyplace where I'd regret not being able to swim) I went northwest of Mexico city on my own to the towns of Celaya and San Miguel de Allende and reveled in the exposure to old style Mexican town life. One night, in San Miquel, there was a serenade with guitar and several voices drifting up from the street, I peered out into the darkness where there was no street lamps and could see nothing in the moonlight. And then there was the Sunday morning market, when all the Indians came into town for church and buying and selling, with chickens under their arms, piglets in gunny sacks, and whatever, an incredible mixture of smells, colors and sounds, offering fantastic photo ops. Sometimes I was too timid to use all of them — particularly on one occasion when I saw a man standing by a little boy as the kid squatted down brazenly ignoring a sign stenciled on an old monastery garden wall which warned "Prohibe relevarse aqui."

Although on the long bus ride back to Mexico City I met an American fellow with whom it was a relief to be able to speak English after my immersion into getting along in Spanish alone, I discovered another thing; that traveling alone, in a strange land, can be an especially enlightening experience. Where two or three pairs of eyes might call attention to more curiosities, in going it alone you probably experience a great more in depth.

The summer in Mexico ended with a long way around trip by bus to Morelia, Guadalajara, and Mazatlan on the Gulf of California, then by an ancient DC-3 (with the outline of the old American Airlines lettering barely covered over by "Aereonaves de Mexico") back over the mountains via Durango and Torreon to Monterey, then home all the way to Detroit on the train. It was a summer to remember for the rest of my life. My Spanish is still very halting, but I learned a great deal about how the rest of America lives.

That following school year, however, I began to suffer increasing doubts about my vocation. But it was not over my exposure to my Spanish teacher (with whom I did exchange a few notes later on) but triggered by something I saw on one of my side trips without realizing it — a new monastic experiment near Cuernavaca run by a

Preparations

Belgian Benedictine attempting to adapt the ancient monastic rule and customs to develop a less clerical form of monastic life more along the lines of Saint Benedict's (who never was a priest as far as we know) original intent.

In a diary or journal that I began to keep about that time, I wrote on November 2, 1955:

> For seven years now I have thought about priesthood in terms of the professional holy man, the monk, and all the incidentals that form his life. The priesthood seemed to me to be the summation of the contemplative life, and to tell the truth, the diocesan priesthood, to my way of thinking, was [like being] a fish out of water, the very summation and perfection existing without the ascesis. This has changed. The parish priest, the missionary, has an asceticism all his own — that of the apostles. He has a form of contemplation peculiar to his state — "the prayer of the poor" — his poor. The more resplendent this idea becomes for me, the more I doubt my worthiness. I find that my "charity" was merely a lack of difficulty with others: I had few difficulties with my neighbors because I was neighbor to so very few ... Only a very few have the gift or vocation to love from afar, zeal for those whom one has never seen, the vocation of the apostolic contemplative. I once was sure I had it — now I am not... [Yet] what I seem to seek for the time being boils down to this: a life of work and prayer for souls with personal responsibility for none of them.

And then on November 19, 1955 I added, beginning, or so it seems, in a rather sarcastic tone:

> My "ideal vocation" . . . to be a monk in an agricultural monastery, and to be a priest — if to be one would not involve me in an active apostolate. After such a dictation to God's will and providence it seems that one should only kneel and beg for mercy!
>
> Contrast all these dreams with the cold reality, with the needs of the two million souls who live beneath the dull glow in the east among the lights which on the plain below us mark the gigantic mess of Detroit. I've gone from door to door in that city, into smelly tenements in the poorest section of Detroit where people seem to be the [more] genuine in a way. I've been in the confusion of

Chapter 3

Children's Hospital. I've been in many a home here and there and into those which are considered the nicest, and true to a young [parish] assistant's prediction, found them to be the coldest. Apart from the material circumstances, I've found the same moral bankruptness [sic], the same neglect, indifference and messes of marriage problems in all. With all of this going on can I hesitate because of squeamish sensibilities [or] self-centered and valued composure... In the last four months I have met, even if in a guarded way as census-taker, enough moral misery to inspire prayer of the intensest [sic] nature; yet what have I done—only daydream or weigh this or that preference against each other and occasionally sigh "what am I to do?" My vocation of the moment is to rid myself of self-centeredness... not until my vision is widened beyond my own ego can I even begin to be a real priest or monk or [for] that matter even competently choose one state or the other... How can one achieve charity until he has entered into the field in which he is to win, yet how can one choose the field in which the combat is to be fought before charity has liberated him from delusion?

I should, as decided at the beginning of the year, become a parish priest first before becoming a priest-monk... How often I'm tempted to run off and just be a hermit!

Apparently, the problem did not let up, even through Christmas break and a few days with my folks at home. At the first opportunity after returning to the seminary, I went to see my spiritual advisor to let him know what I was thinking and afterwards wrote these notes:

January 1, 1956 [After a conference with my spiritual advisor.] Tonight I got my answer — parish work. I'm relieved like one who is told he is going to be thrown to the lions; no more wondering whether or not he is going to the mines or the arena. This notebook is the main reason—vanity, psychiatric egocentricity. Not so much volitional pride, conscious egocentricity but just inborn, inbred self-centeredness with corners that must be rounded off if I'm ever to become a saint. If I see parish life as one big cross, I'm seeing the priesthood correctly . . . I'm to accept this decision for at least a year, to forget about everything but the parish that awaits me; and not so much precisely the parish but rather Christ who is waiting

Preparations

there in a special way. He is with me here all right, but He's waiting among the people with a big cross. I must never forget that it is his cross and that He will carry it. I need only disappear into Him and forget all else. Five years ago I was given a book called "Trust in God" — will I ever learn?

Then, in successive months, I added the following:

February 2, 1956. Some thoughts that continue to reoccur. I would like, nothing else considered, to be a hermit or contemplative monk. But the reality is, what does God want me to be? All I know is that I want God and sincerely wish that others would do likewise. As far as apostolic work is concerned I run hot and cold.

The monastic life is the perfect discipleship of Christ. It is the vocation of not letting anything stand in the way of seeking God. The priesthood is not mere discipleship: it is to be another Christ. Yet one presupposes the other as the cross presupposes two beams. The upright, planted in the earth and pointing to heaven is discipleship. The cross-beam, reaching out to the world, is the priesthood: this will fall without the first.

March 27, 1956. Tonight I signed and handed in my petitions for tonsure and the four minor orders. I have been told what to do and have done it—the rest, until the next set of petitions, is in the hands of the rector, the bishop, and God.

Last Saturday I wrote another petition and sent it off. It asked for the privilege of being clothed and received into the Third Order of Carmel... I look on [this] latter as a bulwark for something I must confess I feel no enthusiasm over, that is, the life of a parish priest. I still long for the monastery, but I still know that I have been told that the strict orders are not however painful, is something that I need.

I think I must be realistic and think of monastic life in its full rigor, as lived by the Trappists or Carthusians, and think of it under no other aspect. If I have a vocation to either of these orders, or to a Benedictine house of similar strictness, [which] I very well may have, it is at the same time a vocation which I must convince myself on other's authority that is to be delayed until I have undergone the trial and balancing effect of parish work. It is likewise a vocation

- 49 -

that I can not competently choose until I have undergone that purgation . . . and that I have no business embracing that life or [even] considering it until I have first paid the price.

April 22, 1956. In a day or two I will be obliged to speak for me and my disposition, that parish life is a remedy which, to the Rector about my intention to go on to the priesthood. Since Tuesday last, when I suffered indecision and scruples about the oath stating the intentions of perpetual service to my diocese, I have had only one short period, some six hours or so, during which I felt confidence enough to be able to state to the Rector that to go on was my intention. The rest of the time, up until today (Sunday) has been on the foolhardiness of going on.

The occasion for the interview, I believe, was our upcoming "tonsure" or formal induction into the clergy, plus conferral of a couple of the four "minor orders" that used to be part of the steps toward the priesthood. A snippet of hair was to be cut from the crown of the head, reminiscent of the days when all clergy, much as the monks of old, had their head, or at least part of it, shaved bald. The minor orders involved were those of "exorcist", "porter", "lector" and "acolyte". Ever since the Second Vatican Council, only the last two mentioned orders remain, and they are rarely conferred on those people who actually perform those functions (reading and serving at the altar) in most parishes, but, except in monasteries, are generally conferred only on those headed toward the priesthood.

My problem wasn't with the orders as such, which involved no permanent obligations. It was with the intention to perpetually serve the Diocese of Lansing. By this time I think I had told the rector that I was wondering about possibly joining the Sulpicians myself. But if I did, my aim was to teach theology, something that was unlikely to happen (according to the rector) if I were to join them right away. Those who joined them while still seminarians were generally assigned to teach in their minor (college and high school) seminaries. He indicated that I'd be much more valuable to them as a theology professor if I had several years of experience as a parish priest under my belt. He also pointed out, I think, that since the Sulpicians were not a "religious order" as such, but a "society" or association of priests on more or less perpetual leave from their respective dioceses, that technically speaking, they were continuing to serve their own dioceses, however indirectly. So I guess I was satisfied. Though I remember Fr. Fenn saying he was a little uneasy with my rather biblical response as to why or how much I felt called to the priesthood. I had quoted Saint Paul where he said "Woe to me unless I preach the gospel!" The rector had to remind me that a vocation is always an "invitation" not a certain command.

That summer I went to work as a catechist at the camp run by the Archdiocese of Detroit for deaf and hard-of-hearing children at "Boysville", a residential school that was run by the Holy Cross Brothers near Macon in the rolling countryside near the "Irish Hills" in southeast Michigan. The first two weeks were working with boys and I did better than my stint at Camp Ozanam. I even managed to summon enough authority in my manner to break up a fight or two, although on one occasion not quickly enough to prevent one kid from being knocked out cold. The second two weeks all I had to do was teach girls and let a couple of nuns worry about settling the girls' spats and squabbles. I also had to act as a life guard, which was not difficult. The job there was mostly to make sure some of these kids didn't try diving into the shallow end of the pool.

Later (it must have been that summer) I remember, while driving home alone with my dad from a fishing trip, his asking me if I was certain about my determination to become a priest. I said unquestionably yes. But again, on my return to the seminary that fall, I made a note that indicates some doubt if not about the priesthood as such, still about where or what kind of life I sought as a priest.

September 14, 1956. Truly I need a lot of smugness knocked out of me. Sometimes it seems sheer foolishness for me to become a priest, but as long as the priesthood, God, and souls remain the logical goal of [my] life, I should be glad or at least fiercely determined to enter the parish priesthood to be battered into a true parish priest or into a character made capable of a more cloistered vocation.

Chapter 3

That third year of theology went very quickly. If I wrote any more notes to myself, they seem to have been lost, as the beginning of my next notebook, in 1963, notes that I hadn't kept a journal for nearly five years. But I remember becoming the assistant to the director of the seminary book store and that my spiritual adviser, Fr. Baron, had also finally persuaded me that I should use my last free summer to travel in Europe, an idea I had so-far resisted increasingly after seeing slide-show after slide-show given by other soon-to-be-ordained seminarians after taking "The Grand Tour" before they became inundated with parish work.

But I do remember one other final sorting out of my intentions. I'm not sure; perhaps it was during Christmas break, or even during the following year, but I do remember going up to Lansing to confer with Bishop Albers and laying my dilemma before him – that I now felt torn between contemplative life and seminary teaching, and that in any case he probably could not count on me serving the diocese directly except for a quite limited period of time. He reassured me that he'd only be too happy to provide me with the parish experience that the Sulpicians would consider valuable and that he would also try to see to it that I would be assigned to parishes that would give me plenty of teaching opportunities, at least on the high school level, and when I felt ready to make any switch, just to come to him about it.

It is too bad I didn't keep detailed notes on this conversation, or even better, have it on tape. Nevertheless, I ended that third year without any real qualms about "taking the step" as we called it, the literal stepping forward when our name was called to receive the first of the "major orders" — that of "subdeacon". That step signified our willingness to undertake life-long celibacy. If we changed our minds after taking that step, even if we never became a priest, we'd have to be dispensed not by just our bishop, but by the Vatican in Rome. It also meant that I'd have to carry a "breviary" with me on the trip to Europe, the small book — really a set of books — containing "The Divine Office", that is, the prayers and scriptural and other readings recited each day by monks, nuns, and those in major orders.

Soon after I took that step I also learned from Fr. Baron something I found a bit disturbing. As usual, our moral theology professor requested that we write our answers to the ethical dilemmas he posed *"fusiter"* (Latin for "profusely"), even though we now wrote our exams in English. That semester we had been studying the tract on *"De Justitia"* or to put it in plain English, the ethical issues involved in buying, selling, and other such contracts. I found it particularly challenging to get down all the distinctions, sorting out the ethical issues from the legal ones. I had, in fact, with the help of a small compendium of moral theology, something other than our fat Latin textbook, outlined all the basic rules on large 4"x 6" file cards and memorized them, so I had walked into the exam more confident than ever before. I analyzed the questions, then wrote furiously and, I thought, incisively and then discovered, much to my relief, that I had actually finished about 10 minutes ahead of our full allotment of time. So I walked up to him, probably with a big smile on my face, handed him my blue book and walked triumphantly out of the room, unlike other times, when I had felt totally snowed under by his exams and rarely felt I had adequately covered the matter when the time would run out.

That turned out to be a big mistake. Fr. Baron told me that prof had almost vetoed my being allowed to become a subdeacon, and that he (Fr. Baron) had had to specially intervene in my behalf. He also urged me to go see that professor to find out why he was so upset with me. But this was only a few days before our departure to Europe, and I felt that I already knew why the moral theology prof was upset and that I'd only be forcing him either to admit he was jealous of the neat way I'd settled some very complicated issues or else dream up some other excuse for his opposition to me. But no doubt I was also too proud, fearing to hear that I had actually done a lousy job of answering the questions, which I felt was impossible, in that he had, after all, given me a passing grade, even though (I suspected) he thought me entirely too self-confident for my own good.

But putting that incident aside, on June 2nd my friends Jerry and Gabriel, both of whom were one year behind me in the seminary, and I took an overnight train to New York, then the subway and then a bus to Hoboken, New Jersey, where we boarded the Holland-American Line ship with the improbable name of the "Johan Van

Chapter 3

Oldenbarnevelt", an old diesel-powered liner (reputedly the first such in the world) of about 25,000 tons displacement and set off for Europe. It was an elegant old ship, with mahogany lined lounges, a swimming pool, etc. Put into summer service on the Atlantic, its usual runs, the rest of the year, were to the South Pacific. The crew was all Dutch.

The passengers were a predictable mix of college students, teachers, and tourists. There was another small party of seminarians. And then there was a group of Catholic college girls being herded around by one of their teachers and a Benedictine priest who was their college chaplain. And there was a rather talkative priest from California who told us proudly that he was headed to Italy to join the Camaldolese Order of Hermits near Florence, who in turn planned to send him back to California to start a new foundation there. He struck me as being a bit too outgoing to be a successful hermit — but I was to learn a few more things about hermit-types in ensuing years. The only real "foreigners" on board, besides the all-Dutch crew, were a small part of a group of Basque youngsters who had been in the US on an extended tour as folk dancers. One of them, a girl named Maria Pilar, came over to us one day at pool side and asked us if we'd consider visiting her and her family in a small sea-side town west of San Sebastian. She told us that her brother was also studying to become a priest and that he and his friends would be delighted to show us all around the Basque Country of north-central Spain. So we added the little town of Zumaya to our itinerary. Meanwhile, one seminarian from the other party (that couldn't seem to come to an agreement on their itinerary) came to us and asked us if we'd take him along with us. Since we had lined up a little four-passenger car to use, we agreed, so with the addition of Bernie, who was to join us in Paris, we were now going to be a party of four.

It took ten days to reach Rotterdam, with the Ile de France, (presumably with Fr. Baron aboard) passing us on June 10th—so quickly that it seemed our old ship was sitting still. On the 12th we spotted the remote Scilly Islands off Lands End in Cornwall, putting in briefly at Southhampton and later that day at LeHarve, our first view of France. Next morning we were landed in Rotterdam and on the next day we took a train south to Brussels and visited two

Preparations

Michigan seminarians and my old Saint Xavier High School Latin teacher, all of whom were working on their degrees at the Catholic University of Louvain. There we also saw the tomb of Fr. Damien Deveuster, the famous missionary leper-priest of Molokai.

Then on to Paris, where we picked up our little Renault Dauphine (straight from the Ballincourt factory door) and immediately set off for Chartres with Fr. Baron meeting us there as our guide. Next day, we began our tour of the rest of the whole continent, with an agreement to bring back the car within two months time, to be repurchased with no more than the allotted 10,000 Km. We were determined to use up every mile of that allotment. First we drove past the Chateau-Thierry battlefield to Rheims and its huge cathedral, and from there through Luxembourg to Trier and its ancient Roman ruins. There we also watched its famous Corpus Christi Day procession from a silversmith's shop and I also ordered a silver chalice to be made for my ordination a year hence. The night of June 21 we stayed at the famous Benedictine Abbey at Maria Laach — the first of many such old monasteries we visited, most of them having nice guest houses. Then we toured Cologne and its huge cathedral, headed up the Rhine towards Heidelberg, then back into France at Strasbourg, then back across Germany's Black Forest to Tübingen. There we bought six marks worth of bread and cheese and ate lunch alongside a wheat field, before we went on to Augsburg to meet a Bavarian girl, Frauline Groh, whom Jerry knew, and who showed us all around town and gave us her mother's address who, in turn, would guide us around Munich. From there we went down to Garmisch-Partenkirchen in the mountains where Frau Groh's son was a parish priest and would guide us in turn. We then spent a day in Innsbruck where I envied another Michigan seminarian for his having been assigned to study there, especially after he told us they had each Thursday free to spend on the ski slopes.

Leaving Austria we went over the Brenner Pass down into Italy, past Trentino (where the famously long council of Trent was held) into Venice, where we spent two days strolling the piazzas, visiting the famous Saint Mark's whose porch roof sports the famous horses stolen by the crusaders from Constantinople, and dodged pigeons with the rest of all the tourists to try to get pictures of everything we could. On the way to Verona we stopped to visit Riesi, the home town of the then recently canonized Pope Pius X who was still a hero to me, the biographies not mentioning what he had done to Catholic scholarship. We visited Verona's ancient Saint Zeno's Basilica and then the next day proceeded to Ravenna to see some of the most ancient Christian art, particularly the 5th and 6th Century mosaics. The next day we drove down the Adriatic coast to Loretto and its famous shrine of "the Holy House" (supposedly transported by angels from Nazareth!) then over the hot dusty mountains to Rome arriving there in the midst of a heat wave on the 4th of July.

We stayed in Rome for eight days, seeing everything we could in the mornings, and spent at least some of the afternoons out at the North American College villa on the mountainside near Castel Gandolfo, the papal summer residence. The villa had a swimming pool which made the heat tolerable to some extent. So did my first pizza in a tiny restaurant in Frascati washed down with a musty brown local wine. Among the things we did was to get a chance to go down into the newly dug excavations under Saint Peter's to have a look at what is believed to have been Saint Peter's tomb. We took in a performance of the opera "William Tell" at the Baths of Caracalla that included, as an extra, a little ballet.

We saw all three levels of Saint Clement's church, including the Mithric shrine in the basement — a relic of what early Christianity was up against. After driving out on the twenty-century old paving blocks of the Appian Way, we were privileged to assist at Mass said by an American priest in the small chapel down in the catacomb of Saint Callistus next to the tombs of six of the earliest of Saint Peter's successors. The whole place crawls and oozes history. I came away from all of this with an appreciation of why Rome, that is, the official Church, takes so long to change!

On the 12th of July we finally left Rome and went up to Assisi of Saint Francis fame. There everything began to look more humble and down-to-earth again. We also visited Orvieto and Siena, ending up in Florence. Next day, while two of my pals went to see all the museum pieces, one of the others (I think it was Gabriel) and I, still tired of cities, drove up east of Florence into the mountains to find this mysterious Camaldolese hermitage the priest on the boat talked all about. After going up twisty mountain roads to what turned out to be the "continental divide" of Italy's backbone, we found a turnaround filled with excursion busses. Now one would hardly expect to find a little collection of cottages behind a low wall arranged around a little medieval church to be a major tourist attraction. But there they all were. I began to feel a bit better about my secret desire to be a hermit. Apparently a lot of people didn't think the life to be so strange after all. In fact, I think the monks had the California priest temporarily working as a guide — or traffic cop!

That night the four of us attended an out-of-doors concert at a villa on the edge of Florence. The featured piece was Dvorak's "New World Symphony". Something about hearing those echoes of American folk music in a far country still brings a thrill, and that particular evening, tears to my eyes.

Next it was on to Pisa (of leaning tower fame) up the coast to Genoa (Christopher Columbus' home town), then Milan, and then to Lake Como and Switzerland and its cool icy Alps. There we visited the famous Abbey of Einsiedeln, hiked up to a glacier at Interlochen, and rode a cable car up to a mountain-top outside Lucerne. Then we drove down through the French side of the Alps to little town of Ars, where Saint John Vianney, the patron of parish priests, exercised his pastorate and where we paid our due respects. Much more exciting, for me at least, was our drive back up into the mountains near Grenoble to the famed Grand Chartreuse, the birthplace of the Carthusians, a strict order of hermit-monks who were begun back in the 12th century by Saint Bruno, a theology professor from Rheims who decided to chuck it all to pursue God in the wilderness along with a few friends. But again, this place also turned out to be a major objective of tour buses. I've begun to wonder if hermits don't make a mistake when they locate themselves in such spectacular sites.

From there we went down the Rhone into Provence, visiting the kind quaint villages that drew painters like Cezanne and Van Gogh. We attended an outdoor performance of "Carmen" at a music festival at Aix-en-Provence, visited Avignon, where the popes lived in courtly splendor for about 70 years, and the ancient Roman cities of Arles and Nimes where we ran into the Benedictine college chaplain who told us he was going nuts trying to keep his young female charges from running off with French sailors and the like. I resolved at that point never to accept an offer to be a tour guide. Now at some point along the way we abandoned Gabriel to meet his brother so that both of them could experience France as French-speaking "Canadiens" together. And some where along the way (I think it was in Spain) we met up with another fellow, a dental student from Creighton University, whom we had met on the boat and who joined us for several weeks.

Such as we were, we then made our way down over the eastern Pyrenees into Catalonia, Spain's Riviera, Barcelona and then up to the ancient Benedictine monastery of Montserrat, near where Saint Ignatius of Loyola, the founder of the Jesuits, made his decisive retreat. From there we went through the ancient city of Zaragoza (the Moorish mispronunciation of "Caesar Augustus") past the original Guadalajara (from the Arabic for "Rocky River") down into the comparatively modern city of Madrid. Of course, we went to a bullfight, saw the El Prado museum, drove down to ancient Toledo with its catacombs, El Greco's home, and the historic fortress, the Alcazar. After that we drove northward, stopping in Avila, Segovia, Valladolid, and Burgos where I insisted on seeing another Carthusian monastery, Miraflores — where for the first time in many monasteries, there were no tourist busses around. Years later I wrote one of the monks there, a retired American psychologist who had been both a Paulist priest and a Benedictine monk, for advice about following in his footsteps. He answered kindly and simply urged me to pray more. We also visited the famous cave at Altamira, where the vivid Cro-Magnon wall paintings date from some 20,000 years past.

In the Basque country we were feted by our new friends. And Maria Pilar was right. There were so many seminarians from Zumaya one wondered what the poor girls of that town were going to do. We were taken to see the town of Loyola and Ignatius' substantial family home. They tried to explain some politics of Basque nationalism (and the Basques who had been executed) in Franco's Spain, and of the

Preparations

intricacies of their ancient tongue (banned in public by Franco) unrelated to any other European language — perhaps the only surviving relic (other than a few fossils and those cave paintings) of Europe's first *homo sapiens* inhabitants, the Cro-Magnon people. One day I spent some hours alone on a high costal bluff overlooking the Bay of Biscay. There I wondered why people or peoples cannot be left alone to be themselves.

From the Spanish Basque country we went back over the Pyrenees into France, hiking in the mountains near Lourdes, visiting Poitiers where Charles Martel turned back the Saracens in 732, and Tours, where the famous Saint Martin (Patron of France) converted the country folk — early Christianity was mostly a town folks' faith — then northwestward over to Brittany where some Breton or Celtic is said to still be spoken, and then up into Normandy, where one night I slept next to an old German gun emplacement overlooking the English Channel. By that point, to save some money, the four of us, who had one sleeping bag and a few blankets between us, were exchanging places on alternate nights, two to an inn, two camping out (one on the ground in the sleeping bag, the other on the back seat wrapped in the blanket with his feet out the door suspended from a sling.) We all stayed one night at the old Benedictine abbey of Solesmes — of early Gregorian chant revival fame. We visited Lisieux, where Saint Therese (the sainted "Little Flower" of Fr. Coughlin's shrine church in Royal Oak, Michigan) is buried, and the town square and cathedral at Rouen, where they burned Joan of Arc at the stake. We arrived back in Paris on August 14, visited the palace at Versailles, the Louvre, and turned the car back in on the 17th.

The next day we all met up again in London where for the next few days we visited all of the usual tourist sites (The Tower of London, Westminster Abbey, Buckingham Palace, etc.) The two brothers who had done France together were grateful to be back in an English-speaking environment, as the two of them had been unmercifully ridiculed by the French for their Quebeçois pronunciations and accent. We took a tour of the ancient towns of Winchester and Salisbury and visited the mysterious prehistoric megaliths of Stonehenge. We then crossed the choppy Irish Sea to

Chapter 3

Ireland on a ferry boat to Dun Loaghaire where a driver met us with a Bentley that was too small to crowd in five passengers. So we went into Dublin where he exchanged the Bentley for a Chrysler, and swore at the American car's mushy suspension for the next three days as we toured the usual tourist sites in counties Galway, Kerry, and Cork, and the old monastic ruins at Cashel. There was so much in Ireland that I wanted to see, including my grandfather's birthplace in County Leitrim in the northwest. The driver, who was from the same area, assured me there wasn't much there to see. I can't believe that. In fact, by then we'd all seen so much touristy places that a little stone cottage on a treeless moor with an empty ocean vista sounded to me like heaven on earth.

We then took another ferry to Hollyhead in Wales, passed the famous station at Llanfairfechan and ended up in Liverpool where we shipped out on a little old Greek-owned passenger ship called the Columbia (built in Belfast in 1919) bound for Quebec loaded with Jewish kids from Canada and the USA who'd spent most of the summer in Israeli kibbutzim and some Irish and Scottish immigrants still looking for a wealthier place to live. After their summer in Israel the kids weren't willing to talk to us *goyim*, so for from August 25 to September 4 we amused ourselves trying to decipher thick boughs and burrs, holding impromptu music sessions (one of the Irishman had a set of Uillean pipes, another fellow played the tin whistle, and Jerry and I had our harmonicas.) I also read Melville's *Moby Dick* and between two paragraphs one day, looked up to see a whale spout. Now you'd never have any experiences like that today crossing the Atlantic overnight at 36,000 ft. The last day of the sea journey we passed between the rugged high coast of Labrador and the low northern tip of Newfoundland where I gazed through the mist at L'Anse Meadows, where the Vikings had built an outpost at the door of the new world.

However, sad news awaited me upon my return. My youngest uncle, my mother's youngest brother, who was an alcoholic, had, on August 15th, returned from a trip looking for a new job, but finding no one home (most of the family was at Mass) took a shotgun out into his garage and shot himself. I, of course could not be notified very easily at that point as my folks could not have known where exactly I was. A few years later I learned that one of my classmates, while still a seminarian, had tried to help him, and later on, I was instrumental in helping one of his daughters overcome her addiction to alcohol. But some years later was unsuccessful in doing the same for his only son. I mention all this because, although I very much enjoy both beer and wine, I greatly fear that my half-Irish ancestry might eventually catch up with me in that same regard.

Meanwhile I had brought some presents home for my parents. I had bought my dad a handsome Omega watch in Switzerland, and my mother some antique silver jewelry and a blue lace mantilla in Spain. I'd also bought five yards of fine unbleached Irish linen in a store in Cork so she could make me a set of Mass vestments which I still to this day occasionally use.

Yet, after all that crammed into just three months, what can one say about the next nine months back in the seminary? Well, for one, shortly after I returned, I was ordained a deacon – the first real rank of the sacrament of Holy Orders. This meant also that I officially started preaching, my first assignment being to literally captive congregations down the road at the Detroit House of Correction – the men's division on the south side, and the women's across the road on the north. A lot of our spare time was spent on just trying to learn how to say Mass. I was in charge of the bookstore by now, so I also had to learn a bit more about keeping accounts.

Still, one event in particular did cause me second thoughts that winter of final preparation for the priesthood. During our European tour, I thought briefly of trying to visit my old Cincinnati girlfriend who now lived with her husband, a US Air Force pilot, at a base near Koblenz. Her brother, I think, had given me their address and may have even written her to tell them I'd be stopping by. But I gave up the idea in deference to traveling buddies — in fact, I may have not have even mentioned the idea to them. But then I got word, I think it was in November, that her husband (who had been, for a year or so, a novice at Gethsemane Abbey before going on to the Air Force Academy) had been killed in a collision with another plane while on a training mission, while she was already pregnant with their second

Chapter 3

child. So I felt not only guilty for not having visited them, but not only that. I was also strangely moved, and even tempted for a few days, to wonder if God was not asking me to leave the seminary and my plans for the priesthood and to take this ex-monk's place, even though it would have meant at that point getting a special dispensation from the diaconate as well as from the obligation of celibacy undertaken with the subdiaconate the spring before. Somehow or other, I still cared for her enough, and was especially moved by the drama of this young man — whom I had never met but who had enough courage to at least try the monastic life I still longed for. That, along with my attempts to write poetry, I was to learn later on, at least for me, is always a bad sign.

Years later, on a visit to Cincinnati, I stopped by to visit her, still a widow. I hadn't realized that her second child (a second daughter) had been born blind. Sometime after that I also wrote her, and admitted to her how much I had been moved by her husband's death and what had passed briefly through my mind. She wisely never responded to that admission, but I hoped she appreciated that at least I still cared.

That brief hesitation out of the way, the time flew quickly our as final year of studies before ordination to the priesthood. But as the big day drew closer, it seemed to me that some of my classmates were losing weight. It also seemed to me, though I never took a count, that the number of people sitting at what we called the "ulcer table" (special diet table) doubled in those months. But I gained weight instead — about 15 pounds more than I ever have been the rest of my life. Was I storing up fat for lean years to come? Hard to say, because I had no real idea of what lay in store for me.

Chapter 4
Parish Priest

Seven of us were ordained in 1958 to the priesthood in the service of the Diocese of Lansing, one in Louvain, and the other six of us on June 7th in the old Saint Mary's Cathedral church, half a block from the state capital building. At that time the Diocese of Lansing, formed from portions of the Detroit Archdiocese and the Diocese of Grand Rapids in 1937, consisted of some fifteen counties stretching across southern lower Michigan from the area around the industrial city of Flint on the east all the way to Lake Michigan to the west. Except for Flint, it was largely rural but punctuated by small to medium-size business and manufacturing centers like Jackson, Battle Creek, and Kalamazoo. It also had the lowest percentage of Catholic population in Michigan.

The day before the ordination, we met with Bishop Albers who talked with us and asked us all to take a pledge against using any alcoholic beverages for five years, or anything but beer for ten. Unlike my confirmation pledge-taking, this one was not sprung on us by surprise. I'd already made up my mind I'd opt for the beer. We all stayed at the local diocesan-sponsored orphanage next to Holy Cross Cemetery, and early that next morning I read my breviary and meditated out there, taking a good hard look at the "priests' plot" that had been set aside near the cemetery entrance. I wondered if and when I'd eventually end up there.

My memories of the ceremony itself are a blur. We were ordained, I think, in alphabetical order, which made me third on the list. Eighteen of my classmates were ordained that same day in Detroit, and several more in Saginaw and Marquette. Grand Rapids probably had several others, but none of them had attended school with us at Saint John's. Most of my Michigan relatives attended the ordination, as well as a small contingent of my Cincinnati friends. My folks held a reception for me the next day after I said my "First Mass" – the first such occasion in Birmingham's new Holy Name Parish church. For two weeks I basked in glory, and then reported to my first

Chapter 4

assignment, Holy Redeemer Parish in Burton Township located on the south side of the industrial city of Flint.

First Assignment: Holy Redeemer Parish, Flint

Holy Redeemer was a relatively new parish, but due to Flint's astronomical growth in the post-World War II auto boom, had grown to become reputedly the diocese's largest parish — although nobody had any exact figures for sure. There were, I believe, some 1,400 families on the parish registration books and we had good reason to think that there were probably another 400 or so unregistered families in attendance. It was a very mixed population, both in the parish and the neighborhood. The first pastor, who had died only a year or two previously, was of French-Canadian ancestry, and because he spoke French, had attracted a considerable number of his own kind. The new pastor was of Slovak ancestry, but originally hailed from my mother's area in the U.P., although his father, a copper mine worker, had taken his family to Arizona to find work during the depression years. Many Flint residents, in fact, were migrants from the U.P. — many of them of Finnish ancestry, though these were almost always Lutherans. We also had many people from the south. In fact, I had been at the place only a day or two when the sheriff's department blocked both ends of the street that ran along one side of the parish rectory while they conducted a raid on a suspected still in a garage farther down the street. Apparently the tradition of southern moonshine liquor had moved north with the immigrants. One lady who worked for the parish told me that she grew up in Dayton, Tennessee, when the famous "monkey trial" had taken place, on a subject (evolution) that began to attract my interest the year before. Among other notable parishioners was a tall athletic-looking native-American, a Chippewa from Minnesota, who had played football at Carlyle University with the famed Jim Thorpe and was now a local MD. And there was also a Mexican fellow who told me that he had been involved with the "Christeros"— the armed Catholic uprising against the anti-Church government in Mexico in the late 1920s.

The parish had both its own grade school and high school, and ran a fleet of about ten school busses to bring in the kids. What it didn't have, at the moment, was a proper church. The school's combination gymnasium and auditorium served as the main church, and the school cafeteria doubled as a second location for Sunday Masses. Thus, while there were five or six scheduled Mass times on Sunday mornings, about nine Sunday Masses were actually said, divided up, on a rotating basis between three parish priests and a religious order priest who rode the bus from Windsor, Ontario, most weekends to help us out. Sunday afternoon baptisms were held in batches, some with as many as ten to a dozen babies to be "christened" at once. Most Saturday afternoons and all Saturday evenings were taken up with hearing confessions, as this being before Vatican II and Saturday night Mass. Between these weekend workouts were late Saturday evenings spent watching "Gunsmoke" and "Have Gun Will Travel" with a relaxing beer in hand. By Sunday afternoon, I was utterly pooped.

The rest of the week, especially during the school year was largely spent in school. The bishop had kept his promise and I, and the other assistant priest, were kept busy teaching religion classes, particularly in the high school. There were also three local hospitals to be visited on a regular basis, and during the summer we were sent out to try to locate unregistered parishioners or other recalcitrants.

Yet despite all this activity, I also found time to read. During the year before ordination to the priesthood, I became more and more aware of the challenge that evolution posed, not so much to the biblical accounts of creation (which I saw as manifestly symbolic or mythical in expression as suited to people of ancient times) but to our understanding of human nature and our relationship to the rest of the universe. One of my Sacred Heart Seminary friends had dropped out of seminary studies for a few years to pursue a degree in biology before he again took up his studies for the priesthood. I had written to him about my concerns and he had told me about the work of a recently deceased French Jesuit paleontologist, Pierre Teilhard de Chardin. He said that Teilhard's major work, *Le Phénomène humain*, was soon going to be published in English and that I should get a copy as soon as it came out, my friend already having had a chance to read some of it in French. So I bought a copy as soon as it came out as

Chapter 4

The Phenomenon of Man in 1959. It was slow going at first. I had to re-familiarize myself with a lot of the terms I had come across in reading my dad's geology texts, terms like "Cenozoic", "Precambrian", etc., etc. But I was impressed and even more so when his spiritual testament, *The Divine Milieu*, the second of his works to be published in English, came out the year after that. Here was a thinker to be reckoned with! What particularly impressed me was not just his ability to rethink Christianity in evolutionary terms, but as I saw it, to finally address, in terms of an evolutionary world view, the knottiest of all theological problems, that of explaining all the evil in the world in a way that could be reconciled with a loving God. But unfortunately, I was confronted with much more immediate distractions just then, ones that got in the way of much reflection on such deep subjects.

For me it had all started the first day I stepped out of my new Chevy coupe to walk up to the front door of the rectory, and to introduce myself at the parish where I was to spend the next several years. A seminarian met me right on the front porch and told me right off that I had been chosen by the pastor to help him cope with a very special situation, a parishioner who was a mystic and who had the "stigmata" like Saint Francis of Assisi — the marks of the nails used in the crucifixion of Jesus, in her hands and feet. Not exactly the kind of thing we were taught about in Mystical Theology 101. The bishop, I was told, had asked that we pay very close attention to what was going on. Later on, the pastor explained to me that the marks appeared only on Friday afternoons when the ladies of "The Legion of Mary", a pious organization, were at her house praying the rosary. I was to be the organization's chaplain, and was to oversee their weekly meeting in the school building as well as make sure I was over at that house every Friday from noon until three. I was to make sure that the ladies copied down anything our mystic said during her three-hour trance and to report to him (the pastor) anything I thought unusual. Unusual? — almost as if the whole situation wasn't somewhat bizarre to begin with!

I dutifully obeyed, but I'm afraid without much enthusiasm. Something of a born skeptic when it comes to these sorts of phenomena, my suspicions were further aroused by the woman in question herself. Fairly young (in her mid-thirties), not bad-looking, and a rather stylish dresser, all that I suppose was OK. But what really bothered me was her lavish use of rather pungent perfume. It just didn't jibe with my preconceived ideas of holiness. She also had a way of arriving at the Legion of Mary meetings just a bit late, making a dramatic entrance, and one time, when one of the ladies said something that upset her, she jumped up and ran from the meeting in a huff. I went out into the school hall to retrieve her and found her teetering over the railing of the stair well — like she was about to jump!

I rushed over to restrain her and discovered that most all of her weight was on the safe side of the rail. To say I was puzzled by all this would be an understatement, but just when I was about to seek counsel outside the parish, the pastor credited her with acting as an effective go-between in his efforts to reach out to a former or lapsed priest, with our mystic taking in his common-law wife while he began rehabilitating himself to return to ministry. Now that was quite a coup, one that made me stop and think.

Nevertheless, I still had deep doubts about what was going on, as other stories began to filter in about this woman, stories that began to reflect seriously on the pastor's judgment. When I first came to that parish, the other assistant, a year older than I, told me that he personally refused to have anything to do with the whole matter, a position I was beginning to wish I had taken as well. That assistant had been sent on to another parish and a priest a year younger than I was assigned, but the pastor did not involve him in the matter, still trusting me to be his main agent. But at this point the still unimaginable happened: the pastor, at age 53, suddenly upped and died.

It was just two days before New Year Day, 1960. He had taken several boys who had recently graduated from the parish high school and had gone about 200 miles north to the hunting and fishing cabin he partially owned with six other priests. The place had been built on forty acres along the Black River in northwestern Montmorency County that had been inherited by one of the seven priests and

Chapter 4

together they had formed a non-profit corporation which they named "Stella Maris", Latin for "Star of the Sea" – even though the river's outlet on Lake Huron is about sixty miles downstream. Fr. Blasko used to also give me the key to the place to use myself, and bought me, for Christmas, first a decent shotgun, then, the following year, a deer-rifle to use up there. On this occasion Fr. Blasko and the two or three fellows had gone up there right after Christmas, but had gotten snowed in and had ruined the high gear on his Chevy's automatic transmission trying to get out and when they did get out, had to drive home in low gear range. Perhaps the exertion had gotten to him, or the excitement of the new church dedication (and the challenge of paying for it), but I think it was more the mental stress of the whole situation as it began to unravel. In any case, a night or two after he returned home, I was filling in for another pastor nearby when I got a call around 1:30 in the morning from the other assistant priest telling me that the pastor had just died of a massive heart attack.

I rushed back to Holy Redeemer to find that the funeral home people had already taken his body and other priests from the area were beginning to arrive. The head of the deanery, an old part-French part-Chippewa priest from my mother's neck of the woods told me that as senior assistant, I'd probably be appointed the parish administrator or acting pastor, and that he would help me all he could. I appreciated that, but I was overwhelmed. The next day the part-time housekeeper let the pastor's relatives move in and begin carting out his personal effects, although there actually was very little. The pastor, generous to a fault, was known as someone who'd give you the shirt off his back. We found only a few hundred dollars in his bank account. The parish, of course, was in a state of shock. Two pastors felled by coronaries in little more than three years!

As for me, I felt like a robot, still in almost a state of shock myself. But I did try to take charge of the situation. In the meantime I'd managed to find a book on pastoral psychology and read with a shock of recognition a chapter on "Hysterics", so when our "stigmatic" called asking what she could do, I told her the best thing she could do is stay home and stay out of the way. The funeral went off without a hitch, except for one member of the Knights of Columbus honor guard who managed to knock his cockade hat off his head when he presented arms before the casket with his sword. (The pastor would have loved that — too bad it was too late for him to see!) I hung in there and managed to manage the parish for five months before a new pastor was assigned, with, I recall, only one serious altercation, a clash between myself and the nun-principal of the high school over a disciplinary matter. She insisted on expelling an unruly student, with whom I'd also had problems with in class, after he'd spit in a girl's face on the school bus. I suggested he just be required to walk to school for the rest of the year. Sister won. Some years later that boy was killed in a head-on collision while out with some other college students. Well, at least I'd done my best to both discipline him yet give him a break. I was also to be told about that time that the bishop's orders that had been actually given to the pastor regarding our stigmatic was to steer clear of the whole situation, but that the pastor had been too kind to carry the orders out. So it seems that we were both people who were inclined to lean the other way when it came to situations where others demanded a less "understanding" approach. Perhaps we were both naïve or taken advantage of. But what more can one do?

But I also knew what I wanted to do by then. In fact, some months before I had written the bishop telling him that even after less than two years I was certain that my calling was not to be a parish priest and that I hoped he would be willing to let me join the Sulpicians. I forget if he even answered me, but I do remember that the year before the bishop had invited me to drive with him down to Cincinnati to attend his nephew's ordination, and that I declined after the older assistant warned me to watch out, as the bishop was looking for a new secretary and that this was probably his way of testing me — especially to see what kind of a chauffeur I'd make. And I also remember that after my folks had come up for the new church dedication they told me later that the bishop had said to them that I was giving him a hard time. Instead, he left me there at Holy Redeemer another three months while the new pastor got settled in. Then I was assigned to Saint Joseph Parish in Battle Creek, following the same priest whom I'd replaced in Flint.

Chapter 4

Second Assignment: Saint Joseph's in Battle Creek, the "Cereal City"
Battle Creek, Michigan, originally "Waupakiska" — Pottowamani for "Bloody Creek" — was for me, very unlike Flint, both as a town and as far as my ministry was concerned. Saint Joseph Parish was much smaller, at least by two-thirds, than where I had been. The pastor was a gentle soft-spoken German-American who seldom got excited, if ever, about anything. There was no Catholic high school at Saint Joseph's, only at the older parish, Saint Philip's, downtown. But after all the turmoil in Flint, I was happy for the change. I became quickly involved with the Christian Family Movement which my predecessor had gotten started there before he volunteered to become a missioner in Peru. It was nice to be able to deal with people in small groups for a change.

I also became rather close to a Native American couple. He was an Army veteran who held a police/fireman/game-warden job at Fort Custer, the crumbling old military reservation just west of the parish. He was a local Pottowamani and she was an Odawa from northern Michigan. They had two teen age boys — the oldest of whom was continually in trouble and the younger one as good as gold. They confided in me, and told me a lot about what it was like to be an "Indian" in white society and the prejudices and the discrimination they experienced. I very much valued their friendship and their sense of humor despite it all. Besides, he used to guide me to the best hunting spots on the fort.

But there was another side to Battle Creek that often puzzled me besides its old-fashioned hometown ways. Something about the place seemed to draw mental cases. Maybe it was the proximity of the large V.A. psychiatric hospital on the edge of Fort Custer, or the smaller Battle Creek Sanitarium. It seemed to me that a lot of the alumni of these places had settled down close-by. Two of these people used to call the pastor quite regularly on the phone, one a paranoiac whose husband always seemed to have spies or secret agents out to get her, and the other, a crusty old woman who used to call and swear like a trooper over a long list of complaints whenever she got drunk. Neither of them ever identified themselves or asked if the pastor was on the line — they both just assumed that if someone (other than the cook) picked up the phone that we were willing listeners. I soon learned from the pastor to just lay the receiver across the chair arm, particularly with the one who swore, as when she got finished she'd simply hang up. She really wasn't looking for us to say anything in return. Then there was the little fellow who upon release from the hospital took it upon himself to begin to direct traffic at the nearest intersection, and when put back in the hospital, hanged himself.

However, about this time my growing familiarity with psychological matters became much more severely and personally tested. Somehow or other, I got word that one of my cousins, a daughter of the uncle who had killed himself only three-and-a-half years before, was in bad shape. She had been on the US Olympic Ski Team, but was severely injured in a training accident, had been unable to compete in the Olympics, had gone out west, married, but quickly ended up divorced and in an alcoholic treatment program in Seattle. Meanwhile, her mother had remarried and seemed to want to have nothing to do with her. Thinking that somehow I could rescue her, I prevailed on her to fly back to Michigan to get help. I went out to the Battle Creek Airport one winter night to meet her and she seemed to have missed that plane. Next morning I got a call. She had been on the plane but apparently had been suffering a "blackout" and next thing she knew she had ended up in Detroit. When she finally arrived back in Battle Creek, I took her over to the then unused student nurses' residence at the local Catholic hospital where I'd arranged, with the sister in charge of the hospital, for my cousin to board.

Things seemed to go well at first. My cousin attended some AA meetings, spent a fair amount of time talking things out with me and began to look for a job. But then I got a call from a local doctor who had taken a look at her, said she was in bad shape, but even worse, I was going to cause myself and the Church great scandal if I didn't get that girl out of town. So what to do? I went home to my folks and pleaded with them to take her in, and they did. She got a job as an instructor at one of the ski hills just outside of Detroit. But after a couple of months of that, she didn't seem to be getting any better — in fact noticeably worse. I then persuaded her to let us admit her to a local Catholic-run psychiatric facility, where after a couple of weeks the head physician told me that he was at a loss as to how to help her. So then I consulted with a psychiatrist at the VA hospital in Battle Creek and he told me about a program outside Milwaukee where she could not only be involved in the usual type of AA treatment, but be fully psychoanalyzed. So I wrote her mother and said we had done all we could do or could be expected to do and would she at least take responsibility of paying for her daughter's treatment out of her own family's considerable financial resources. She finally took the hint. Eventually, my cousin, after finishing that intense course of treatment, moved to Indiana where she lived with another uncle and aunt, married, and had a daughter of her own. But then her husband relapsed into alcoholism and died. Years later, after remarrying again, she became a specially-trained counselor herself. If it is true that the best helpers in this regard are those who have been through the mill themselves, I suspect that she has helped far more people than I ever could.

Meanwhile, I was beginning to feel more stress myself. While stationed in Flint, I usually took my day off, once a week, to go home and visit my folks and stay overnight, returning in time to celebrate Mass in the parish the next morning, as it was just a bit over an hour's drive to return to work. Usually, before I got to my folk's, I would spend the day hiking, snowshoeing, hunting, or fishing according to the season in one of the many state recreation areas located in the beautiful Oakland county countryside north of Detroit. I seldom spent the time with any others, except at a small cabin owned by two other priests near the village of Holly. But most of the time I was content to spend the day alone. If I shot any chance I had at various "varmints", maybe it was my way of avoiding throttling those I was supposed to help.

When I was stationed in Battle Creek, however, such quick trips home were less possible, with about two and a half more hours needed to return to Battle Creek in the morning, especially if there was rush hour traffic to contend with. But it turned out that the VA hospital chaplain had a small place out on a lake just about three-quarters of an hour drive away that he was very happy to have me use. Also, there was a place about an hour and a half north owned by the brother of the priest who had taken over in Flint. It was a tiny old farm house close to the South Branch of the Muskegon River. And I discovered excellent trout fishing on a branch of the Pere Marquette River just a half-hour's drive farther north. So, many times I went up to that little cabin, even in the midst of the winter. I'd fire up the little woodstove, tramp around the swamps and woods on snowshoes, make supper as soon as it became dark, read a bit, then crawl into a sleeping bag and leave early the next morning to get back in time for morning Mass. The place had no running water, just a hand operated pump, and often during the winter I would have to melt snow to brew tea. In the spring and summer I'd drive up to the Pere Marquette, fish and sometimes just camp next to my car overnight. I continued to use that little place during my next two assignments — for a total of about six or so years. It was also where I shot my first large buck deer. And it, and the other place closer to Battle Creek, were the places where I also began to realize that maybe I really was called to live alone.

However, there were a lot more hurdles to be jumped before that would ever come to be. Sometime during my assignment in Battle Creek I had arranged to see the bishop again and to ask him, face to face, whether he'd now release me to join the Sulpicians. But again, even more than before, my timing was all wrong. He had just released two seminarians, one, I believe, from the same Battle Creek parish where I was serving, to join the same group, so his answer was that I'd better forget about the idea, at least for five more years! Not even my argument that I even hoped I might be able to help, with my knowledge of Spanish, with the plans the Sulpicians had to start a new seminary in the country of Colombia seemed to move him, as after all, he'd released my predecessor in Battle Creek to do mission work in Peru — although this one lone diocesan missionary hardly began to fill the call that Pope John had made for the dioceses in North American to consider sending up to one fifth of their personnel to Latin America.

I'd rather expected his automatic refusals by now, so I then came to the conclusion that perhaps I needed to go outside of the diocese for help. So I wrote to a Trappist priest at Gethsemane, Fr. John Vianney, about the possibility of making a retreat specifically under his direction. I knew that this priest, who was from Cincinnati, had been a seminary professor there before becoming a Trappist monk. What I wanted to know, specifically from him, is why he, after doing what I'd been trying to get in a position to do now for several years without any encouragement or even with rapidly diminishing hope, would give it all up to become a monk.

He began with the normal kind of retreat considerations and all that, but after a day or two I pressed my question, and he said he honestly felt that he could help people more in a life of prayer than in a classroom teaching future priests. But then he said he thought I'd better talk to their "Novice Master". I objected to this suggestion, saying I no longer felt any specific attraction to the Trappists, even though I was very impressed with their life. At first he thought that maybe I didn't realize that the novice master was Fr. Louis — the religious name for Thomas Merton, the famous author. I said that of course I knew, and didn't feel I should waste Merton's time. But he insisted, picked up the house phone and called Merton and asked him if he would come over to the retreat house to meet me and talk. I was told to wait around for about twenty minutes and he'd be there.

Merton was very gracious. I explained things as best I could in about another twenty minutes, and Merton then said that he was relatively sure that I was called to a contemplative life. The only question was how soon. He felt I probably had talents that deserved to be developed and suggested that I keep seeking permission to teach or in some way become involved in academic life. But, he said, if I kept "finding the door closed", it probably would be a sign that I should enter a contemplative order directly, and that if I felt intimidated by the size of Gethsemane or the formality of Trappist life, he suggested that I look at the new Camaldolese foundation in southeastern Ohio as something that might fit my needs. And that was it. It was almost as if he he'd written a script for the rest of my life. I was only to find out some years later that Merton himself, frustrated in his efforts to be allowed to take up life in a hermitage, was casting his own eyes in the direction of the Camaldolese.

On the way back to Michigan I detoured northeastward up to southeast Ohio and went to inspect the small Camaldolese foundation located high up on a hillside outside McConnelsville. There were only about three monks there at the time but they made room for me and put me in their guest quarters overnight. The next day, before I left, I asked if I could return for a longer stay and the prior indicated that he'd consider it but be sure to write first.

The next spring I was driving back to Battle Creek from the diocesan retreat house north of Lansing, and taking an alternate route, drove through the little town of Grand Ledge situated on the Grand River about ten miles west of Lansing and found myself wondering what it would be like to be a priest in such a small town. I no sooner arrived back in Battle Creek and the pastor announced that he'd been reassigned to Jackson and that I been reassigned also – surprise! – to Grand Ledge.

Third Assignment: Saint Michael's Parish in Grand Ledge
The first information I received about the parish in Grand Ledge was a sympathy call from a close priest friend whose older brother, also a priest, had been assigned the year before as an assistant to the pastor, an elderly immigrant from Hungary. My friend told me that his brother had almost lost his mind in the place. The fact was that the parish was way too small to keep two priests very busy, despite the fact that the Rev. Dr. Anton Csaky was a near invalid. He had had cancer and, a heavy smoker, suffered from asthma and emphysema. But he still said Mass every day and frequently drove over to the parish grade school (about six blocks distance) to spend time visiting the classrooms and talking to the kids. He also told me, when I arrived, that "We don't wear [Roman] collars here, except in the school or whenever we go over to the Church — in a few weeks everyone in town will know who you are anyway" and that "The grade school is my [i.e., his] area" and finally, that I should never interrupt his enjoyment of the early Saturday evening wrestling matches on TV. Keep these simple rules and we'd get along just fine. I was to be mostly responsible for dealing with the high school kids,

and conducting most of the weddings and funerals — not a heavy work load in a parish of just over 300 families.

I have to admit that the Rev. Dr. Anton Csaky took a bit of getting used to. Descended from a noble Hungarian family (the Counts of Csak) he had been ordained for the Diocese of Estergom in what had been part of Hungary, had been a chaplain in the Austro-Hungarian Army during the First World War, and had earned two doctorates, one in history, the other in philosophy, at the University of Vienna. But he had become displaced as an ethnic Hungarian from his home diocese, it being made part of Czechoslovakia after the war. So, he had ended up teaching in a seminary in Budapest and was thrown into jail for a few months when the Communists took over the Hungarian government for a short time in 1922. He fled to the United States shortly after, took a parish among the coal mines in Pennsylvania, later applying for a Hungarian parish in Detroit but ending up in Flint instead. When Bishop Albers had gone over to meet him and discovered they had been on opposite sides of the Western Front, Albers (who had also been a chaplain and who had only one lung left) coldly said "You boys gassed us!" and never said much to him after that. Csaky had been assigned to Grand Ledge some time after he had quit his ethnic parish in Flint after Albers had refused to allow him to raise money to relocate the place.

Things went rather well for me there at least for the first year or so. I began to know people much more closely than I had in any other parish, especially the high school students and their families. Fr. Csaky also indicated to me that he wished me to advise him on how we should go about implementing all the changes in the liturgy that were in the works as a result of the Second Vatican Council, which had begun in 1962 and was still in progress. I also made some rather good friends, particularly with a high school teacher and his friends with whom I often went out to hunt or fish.

Nevertheless, all my unsettledness about my vocation persisted. In April of 1963 I began to resume keeping a diary or journal in which I began to pour out my doubts, though the entries remained rather sporadic for a long time. It was becoming ever clearer to me that I still was not resigned or even suited to remaining a parish priest. I had already written to Dom Verner Moore, the American Carthusian (and psychologist) in Spain for advice (his answer — "pray more") and had also written Fr. Maurice, the Camaldolese prior in Ohio, about my hopes to return.

But I also worried some about my ministry. It seemed to me to involve an excessive amount of time dealing with the problems of women and girls. I was well aware, by then, that in a parish situation, females will come looking for advice much more often than will men. Nevertheless, males, being roughly half the human race, were creating at least half, perhaps even most, of the problems. In the difficult marriage situations, I relied largely on a male counselor, Ed King, at the Catholic Social Services in Lansing, who seemed to have a special skill in dealing both with couples together and also with men. In turn, he would send out some of his clients who needed special help with "conscience situations" — and again, these were more often women than men. Nor did I feel that I was praying enough and resolved I must pray more.

In the meantime, Bishop Albers had become more or less permanently incapacitated, so I decided to consult with our auxiliary bishop, Joseph Greene. I explained to him my vocation problems and he more or less said I should give up all hope of ever getting permission to join the Sulpicians (which was no surprise by now) but (and this was a surprise — even a shock to hear) that he was sure I'd have no difficulty in getting the Bishop's blessing to enter a contemplative order "for the good of my soul". Had they heard something about me or suspected me of something?

Shortly after, I went to see my "confessor" or spiritual advisor, the pastor of a nearby parish and laid it all out on the line. Nor was I ready for his answer, at least not quite yet. It was that if, after five years of parish work, I still did not feel comfortable with parish work and was still drawn to contemplative life, now was the time to do something about it and to get myself to the Camaldolese Hermits for a serious trial of their life. So that very night (May 10, 1963) I wrote a letter to the prior there asking his permission to travel down to McConnelsville as soon as possible. Yet just as suddenly all kinds of reasons flooded into my mind: my parents, my possessions, even my

Chapter 4

"apostolate" such as it was. I found myself hoping that their prior, Fr. Maurice, would answer that they had no room for the next three years or so.

His answer, which finally arrived on June 4, did not say they didn't have room, but nevertheless tried his utmost to discourage me from planning to go down there, citing first, my need for greater maturity (I was still only 31 years of age and he said that in their experience, few were really ready for such a life until the late 30s), my long-continued state of indecision and that my talents indicate that I should still continue to try to teach. I wrote back giving six reasons why I thought I must go down there, citing among them, that when one has a bishop strongly hinting at it, a spiritual director strongly urging it, and yet with no real personal experience of the life, how could he expect me to decide? I also offered to bring down my own tent to live in so that they'd not have the excuse of "no room in the inn." It was then agreed that I could come down for a week's stay in July.

But there was still another hurdle. I'd said nothing of all this to my parents. So the last day of June I went over to Birmingham to tell them my plans that drew a shocked and somewhat angry reaction from my mother. Nor did Fr. Maurice seem overly pleased when I showed up at Holy Family Hermitage a week later, with my own camp-stove and my own tent. But to tell the truth, I was still hoping that after a few days of sampling their life, with its 3:30 AM rising for the long recitation of the divine office (shorter than Gethsemane's sung offices, but here in a flat monotone), boring work (they had me debarking logs with a two-handled draw knife) I too would decide it really was not for me. But instead, I found myself on a spiritual "high" and wanting to enter the life for good.

Fr. Maurice, a Frenchman, was still not convinced. Now, instead of my being still too young for the life, he took the line that while I may well have had a vocation to the monastic life while I was younger, I had missed that opportunity, and the result was I was now unsuited, through lack of monastic training, to take up their form of life. I protested, in vain, that seven or more years in the seminary certainly gave me a good idea of what monastic life was all about. So by the end of the month I was back in my post at Grand Ledge, no closer to a solution in my own mind, but with my mother no doubt greatly relieved. I spent the rest of that summer fiddling with my daily schedule to try to live a more consistent prayer life, and fending off temptations to spend what little money I had on trinkets (a new watch? a new gun? maybe a new car?) to distract myself or compensate for my growing despair. I began to think of alternatives. Perhaps (after watching a Maryknoll Missioners movie about their work in Guatemala) the foreign missions? Or again, how about becoming a military chaplain (the situation in Viet Nam was really beginning to heat up)?

In October there was the missile crisis with Cuba. But the seriousness of the situation really didn't hit me until a high-school girl (whom I recall had never been baptized — her mother being a fallen away Catholic and her father an atheist) came to see me and was actually shaking in fright. Then, on Nov. 22nd, President Kennedy was assassinated, but I wrote nothing more down about the event until, late the night of Nov. 30th, I copied this quote from a letter of Teilhard de Chardin:

> . . . but what an absurd thing life is, looked at superficially: so absurd that you feel forced back on a stubborn, desperate faith in the reality and survival of the spirit. Otherwise — were there no such thing as the spirit, I mean — we should be idiots not to call off the whole human effort. (*Letters from a Traveler*, p. 202)

Then I added:

> What Teilhard wrote at the death of [his close friend] Prof. Black struck me soon after the President's death. Today it struck me again. It is the very antithesis of Sartre's existential atheism and yet, at the same time, a confirmation of its logic.

That fall I also decided to go back to school at near-by Michigan State University to study psychology, although our new bishop, Alexander Zaleski, warned me that he would only tolerate this if it did not cut into my parish duties. Instead, thinking of all the time I

Chapter 4

had wasted working with people, beginning in Flint, with no formal training in psychology whatsoever, I signed up first for a course in Abnormal Psychology, and then for a course in Clinical Psychology. The dean of the School of Social Sciences, because of my extensive course background in the seminary, accepted me as a possible master's degree candidate.

My professor, an elderly Belgian woman by the name of Marian Kinget, had a Ph.D. from Louvain but had done much of her clinical training under the guidance of the American Carl Rogers of *On Becoming a Person* fame. Dr. Kinget (a devout Catholic) was what you might call a "humanistic psychologist" as distinguished from most of what she called "rat and squirrel cage psychology" that dominated the department at Michigan State at the time. As a result, her classes were packed. I also took a guided reading course from her and she helped me devise a personality assessment test to use with my teenage charges in Grand Ledge, something which gave me a real help in knowing these kids better, as most of them were very anxious, after taking the test, to know how they scored. A released time program with the near-by public high school gave me the opportunity to discuss the results with each of them for about 40 minutes or so. But after that, I dropped out of the masters program when the next hurdle was my having to take a course in "Statistical Analysis". I picked up a textbook on the subject and freaked out. Had hand calculators been available then I might have changed my mind, but the bishop's warning about not neglecting my parish duties began to sink in.

At the same time all my new knowledge in psychology also began to sink in, even in regards to my own case. I began to self-analyze myself, not just in terms of my own perceptions, but also in more theoretical terms. One of my journal entries at the time reads as follows:

The study of neurosis in my text[book] has been most enlightening...I've always known myself to be definitely if mildly neurotic but could never piece the response why together. The picture is not complete yet but it's getting clearer all the time. So far

Parish Priest

I see my scrupulosity to have been an obsessive-compulsive
syndrome typical in neurotics who are inclined to repression,
rationalization of conflict, avoiding acute anxiety states, and by
character tend to be orderly, clean, conscientious, idealistic, kind
and considerate, but also inclined to be stubborn and stingy. It was
like reading my own biography!

Although in later years I have become anything but orderly, what
surprised me most was that according to the author (Robert W. White
of Harvard University) *aggressive* impulses are generally the central
issue in such neuroses, and the light that this threw on what the
author saw to be inherent in the "overdriven strivings" of the
protective organization, which in my case was expressed in a
movement "away from people" which becomes "indiscriminate",
"insatiable", and is apt to provoke "disproportionate frustration"
when blocked. According to White, when this abnormal tendency
runs into one of the more normal inclinations "towards people" or
even "against" them, these latter tendencies fight back with an
abnormal vengeance. Was this the key to the phenomenon I first
noted as a teen-ager — the peculiar poignancy or melancholy feeling
that a sense of loneliness or solitude produced most of all when I
seemed to be pulled towards others? It seemed to me that these were,
as I described it...

...the times that I think most clearly, feel more profoundly, pray
more ardently, in short, life gains a certain dramatic, even heroic
quality that is lost when I'm moving in crowds, busy with friends,
teaching classes, or even when alone but in a light-hearted passionless
mood.

But if some sort of hidden aggression was behind all this, what
was it? I had no clue.

More recently, a friend who had also studied psychology at MSU,
but nearly two decades after I had taken those two semesters, came
up with another or what I might call an alternative diagnosis of my
problems: it is that I show many traits of what is called "Asperger's
Syndrome" – the term currently used for the mildest degree of

autism. Among the traits so listed by my friend were: a tendency to monologue, to go on and on with irrelevant details, and to be unaware of other's boredom; lack of eye contact and a failure to read other's body language, etc.; and that most of all, that I seemed unaware of it. Yes, all these traits, and probably more (like "adherence to rituals", which I consider to be a sign of faithfulness) seem to fit – except for one, and that is I have been to some degree aware of it, even seeing them, at least some of the time, especially when it came to my memory (some of my other friends have called me "a walking encyclopedia") as something of an asset, especially back when I was a teacher. I also have been quite aware of my shyness regarding eye contact: too much of that generally makes me feel that I am invading another's private space. My friend conceded that these traits often accompany people with a higher IQ than average – which I suppose I should consider a compliment. But I was told that over all, it generally adds up to being a "social deficit".

So which is it? Am I psychologically speaking somewhat neurotic? Or am I somewhat, even if mildly, autistic? Or maybe even both? Or are such attempts at psychological analysis apt to end up as futile or even self-contradictory, given what seems to be the ever-shifting trends (one might even be tempted to say "fads") within the pop-psychology scene. (The subject of autism or autistic behavior was barely touched upon in my 1950s-era 644 page psychology textbook, mostly in conjunction with mental retardation or else schizophrenia – neither condition being, as far as I know, something that anyone has ever suspected in my case.)

However, back then my immediate concerns were less theoretical, because later that spring I found myself distressed again over what I saw as the excessive role that ministry to women played in my life, especially the fact that I allowed them to take up so much of my time. Thinking of the story of Saint Dominic's deathbed admission that one of his lifelong faults was enjoying talking to women more than men, and to young women more than old ones — I admitted to myself that I reveled in the fact that as a compensation for not being married I would (if I remained a parish priest) always have these young women to talk to instead of being bored by the talk of just one who constantly grows older. I concluded that the true Christian's attitude toward the fairer sex should be something like our attitude toward flowers: a healthy respect for their beauty and a sadness at its short-lived frailty. To be blind to the first or to the second — either would be foolish.

That June, after having talked a Franciscan priest-psychologist into reading through my notebook and still not getting any answers (except that I obviously had some problems) I decided, while on retreat, to take another tack prompted by something I had read in a book on the spirituality of parish ministry (*Fathering Forth*, by John H. McGoey, SFM). McGoey suggested that if our plans to achieve perfection are fundamentally selfish or egotistic, the efforts will be inevitably erratic and inconsistent. Why? — because egoism requires instant and tangible results. And if I had any doubts about the validity of McGoey's logic, I found the proof of his argument towards the end of the book. He said that if one has to keep looking for the will of God, it is a symptom of our trying to avoid it! So I resolved to quit looking for the will of God and instead concentrate on finding his will in "what and where and who I am now." I would try to cultivate what McGoey called "holy indifference" — at least regarding my own fate.

Well, at least for two months, I really tried. Then I found myself either getting depressed in my work or whiling away my time with hobbies. In November of 1964, Bishop Albers became fully retired and Bishop Zaleski became our new "ordinary" that is, given full jurisdiction. My hopes picked up. Bishop Zaleski was a scholar himself, with a "licentiate" (a kind of church awarded master's degree) in Sacred Scripture. Maybe at least he'd have more sympathy for my own scholarly inclinations. My spiritual adviser agreed that I should go see him — which I did, in January, with high hopes which were quickly dashed. Study at home if you like, but — much as he had told me when I began taking psychology courses at MSU — make sure it doesn't interfere with your parish tasks, and if it in anyway does, drop it. At that point I felt like I had sprung a trap on myself.

Beginning in March of 1965 I was alone in the parish in Grand Ledge for nearly three months while the pastor spent an extended time in the hospital. It was both a relief and a further trial. A relief because I had found myself increasingly in open conflict with him in the months before that — as I was to be even more in conflict with him in months to come. One of the issues that was to emerge involved my being caught in the middle of a dispute between him and a newly ordained deacon (a son of some of the parishioners) and whose first sermon in his home parish was, if I recall, on the Good Samaritan vs. all the self-satisfied middle class whites, with the role of the poor beat-upon traveler being taken by our nation's blacks. It raised quite a stir in little old Grand Ledge whose boast at one time used to be that the town was devoid of Catholics, Jews or Blacks — substitute a less acceptable word for that last one. By my time there the town had one Jewish family (who ran a dry goods store) and certainly quite a few Catholics. But there was not a single black face in town. In fact, the local Presbyterian minister had lost his job when he advocated some kind of cultural exchange between his Grand Ledge church and a black congregation in Lansing or Detroit. I also found my own Christian Family Movement group starting to fall apart over the issue of open neighborhoods – especially after I had gone down to demonstrate in Lansing over support for an open-housing clause in the new state constitution. Meanwhile, the pastor refused to allow the deacon to preach in his home parish again. And the deacon (whom I considered a friend) told me frankly that I tended to be too submissive or accommodating. Yet if that was true, why did I have so many problems with accepting what my bishop and others in authority told me was the right thing for me to do?

But there was also a further trial, as the pastor, who rarely paid bills on time, refused to grant me the power to sign checks. At first I had the parish book-keeper fill out checks and then would haul the ledger down to the hospital for him to sign. But bill collectors kept showing up at the door. So eventually he just started signing blank checks and told me to have the book-keeper fill them in as needed. So it was not that he didn't trust me (I could have emptied the parish coffers with one of those checks and taken off with the loot!) — it was just that he being the only one to sign meant that he was in no hurry to retire — even though that was exactly what was on practically everyone's mind. Finally, I went down to the diocesan offices to ask the chancellor (the bishop's chief executive assistant) what could be done to alleviate the situation. He told me that was *my* problem because, as he admitted, they had assigned me to that particular parish counting on me to ease the old man into retirement! Not too long after that, a priest friend of mine who was in line to get his own parish, told me that rumor had it that when he left where he presently was, I'd be re-assigned there — where the pastor was an alcoholic. That week I marched back down to the chancery and told the chancellor flat out that I'd refuse any such assignment and that I'd quite had enough of being sent to "difficult situations". He denied they had any such intention in mind.

Nevertheless, by April I was dreaming again of a hermitage some place. But I also appealed to the local MSU Newman Club chaplain (whom I used to help with Friday confessions) to try to intercede for me to get assigned to student work. Nothing happened in that direction, but meanwhile plenty else happened back in the parish. A number of them involved among the most traumatic events I'd ever had to deal with in parish life. Two were murders, one of a woman who lived on the edge of town and whose throat had been slit by an assailant whose sexual advances she had resisted in her own home. The other was of a ten or eleven-year old girl who was raped and killed close to her own home one night by an escapee from the Ionia Prison for the Criminally Insane as she returned from the local Dairy Queen. That last one happened just about the time I was being transferred to my next assignment, but I knew her family quite well. It would not be the last time tragedy struck them in years to come. And then there was the time I was called to administer the last rites to a girl from our parish who died of mononucleosis in the doctor's office just a few weeks before she turned sixteen!

More and more my work in the parish seemed to me to be fruitless. I seemed to be winning friends but influencing no one to the better. People I had tried to help, in some cases for years, only seemed to be worse off. People kept telling me I was "so understanding"— yet I couldn't seem to get them to understand. By November I was getting markedly depressed. I wondered (again) if the personal transformation I sought might be possible if I joined the military and ministered where people were dying and needed and really *wanted* help. I felt overcome by a sense of futility and saw myself in spiritual danger not from temptations so much as from lethargy.

Maybe it was the time of the year or its events. On November 11, my classmate in the Upper Peninsula, Fr. Tom Coleman, our class cut-up, died from cancer. He had tried, back when he was still a seminarian, to help my uncle who had killed himself. Then, on December 6th, we laid Bishop Albers to rest in the plot where I had meditated seven years before that day when he had ordained me a priest.

Yet there was also a question of priestly morale. As Vatican II wound down, there was an increasing exodus of priests from ministry. Up to that time dispensation from the priesthood was almost unheard of. Once, when asked about a priest who had promised he would get a dispensation to leave the priesthood to marry, I advised the woman not to count on it and as much as said that I thought the priest was feeding her a line. A few weeks later I heard over the radio, no less, that the Vatican had decided to open the process up to make it possible for priests who were unhappy in that life to leave it behind and still be good (and married) Catholics. I felt like a rug (or even the floor) had been pulled out from under my feet. My reaction was kind of like "You mean I have to decide that all over again?"

So that final year in Grand Ledge I also decided I must face another problem, that of real friendship with (and not just ministry to) women. There was one in particular, a volunteer in my high school religious education program who had really become a good friend of mine. Tall, articulate, only about five years younger than I, not so much pretty as handsome, and single. I suppose people could not help but notice that we were, indeed, good friends. But I was generally quite careful to make sure that if we spent time talking, it was out in the open where anyone could see us or in a group like a small discussion group I had started with some similarly aged people, both single and married. But it appears some people were already suspicious. One day that winter, when the high school kids had the day off, we'd taken the parish bus (which we'd bought a few years before to haul around the boy scout troop, run a few parish kids to the edge of the school district where they could be picked up for transfer to the Catholic High School in Lansing, and also, in the summer, to gather Mexican "braceros" or field laborers for Sunday Mass) and hauled the kids to a ski slope about 35 miles away to spend the day there. But I had to leave early because of a funeral the next day and rode back to Grand Ledge with one of the parish women who had come along, but had brought her own car because she too had to be home earlier than the kids.

All went well until just after I got back from the funeral home when the bus pulled in. I went over to greet the kids on their return, thanked the bus driver, and was turning on my heel to return to the rectory when the driver said to wait as there was one more passenger — this one needing help. I looked up and there was my friend slowly easing herself off the bus with a badly sprained ankle. So what to do? She said she couldn't drive her stick shift Corvair convertible parked behind the church. So I went across the street, got my car, helped her in, and drove her home to her mother's where I helped her up the front steps and into the front room where I told her mother she'd better send her son, who wasn't home at the moment, over to pick up her daughter's car. But her brother didn't make it over to pick up the car until the next morning. However, some member of the parish who lived near the church parking lot saw my friend's car parked there overnight and jumped to her own conclusions and spread it all over town.

By that spring I was more than a bit worried about my friendship with her as well. I discussed it with a priest friend who, although only a few years older than I was, I considered to be a very wise man. His own opinion was that perhaps I was still a bit young for such a "spiritual friendship" as I had described it. But I also thought I read between the lines the implication of "immature". Perhaps I was, because just before I left the parish that year I let her give me a ride in her convertible right through the middle of town — with the top down. Might as well really give the folks there something to talk about!

Chapter 4

Three vacation trips during those Grand Ledge years also were particularly significant for me. One was a fishing trip up to the U.P.'s "Big Two-Hearted River" where one morning, meditating while my dad slept, I had an unsettling premonition of what life would be like for me once he was gone. He was, in so many ways, everything to me.

Another was a trip on my own to Canada where I drove back far into the forest on a lumber trail to a remote lake, and having launched my canoe, located a trapper's cabin on a little island where I remained alone for about five days. The following week I spent at a cabin with a group of vacationing priests on another island in a bay in northern Lake Huron. The Sunday between those two weeks was the first Sunday I had taken off since I had been ordained. This was partly my own fault, because although we were allowed an uninterrupted two weeks vacation a year, like many of my priest-friends who were outdoorsmen, I generally took one week off (between Sundays) to go fishing in the summer, and saved the other week for deer-hunting season in the fall.

The third such trip was all around Lake Superior, again with my father, begun immediately after Fr. Csaky celebrated his 50th year of priesthood and finally agreed to retire. We'd ended up camping on the shore of Lake Nipigon and we went into the local parish in Nipigon, Ontario, for Sunday Mass. After Mass we called my mother in Birmingham and she said a letter had arrived that week from the diocesan chancery. I asked her to open and read it. It said I'd been assigned to Saint Monica's Parish in Kalamazoo.

Fourth Assignment: Saint Monica's Parish, Kalamazoo

In some sense my assignment to Saint Monica's in Kalamazoo was, in Yogi Berra's famous words "Déjà vu all over again." If not the biggest parish in Lansing Diocese, it was big enough (about 1200 families) to confront me with most all of the challenges of bigness that my first assignment at Holy Redeemer had. There was a large grade school (but not a high school) and a bevy of nuns to staff it, and like Holy Redeemer, the church building was still an auditorium/gym. There were also three priests assigned to the parish: the pastor (who had founded the parish), and another, older assistant, and myself. We also had a full-time secretary-receptionist who during normal office hours answered the door and took most incoming calls.

However, there were also differences. For the first time in my clerical career I was living in a rectory or parish house that had been designed for this purpose and was not just some old house that had been taken over and pressed into service. I actually had my own assigned office up front, plus, farther down the hall, a private study, bedroom, and bathroom of my own. There was also an attached garage with automatic doors. Unlike Holy Redeemer, we had a full-time live-in cook-housekeeper — an elderly lady who was a long-experienced and accomplished cook, but still spry enough to handle most of the house-cleaning jobs. Materially, we lived the life of kings.

However, personality-wise things were far from ideal. The pastor (who had staked out his territory for "his" new parish while still an assistant at an older parish downtown) seemed to consider that he had accomplished his main work in life and seemed to have only scorn for us younger priests who hadn't accomplished all that he had while he was still young. So except for Mass and hearing a few confessions (and signing checks) he seemed expect us assistants do all the work. But looking back on that time now, I suspect that my own interior tensions had started to make me somewhat hypercritical, perhaps envious of my boss seeming to be so self-satisfied. Still, what particularly galled me was that the other priest really wasn't supposed to be a full-time assistant, but rather a resident helper whose main job was being the chaplain of the large state mental hospital. This was, I thought, a full time job enough for anyone and I told him so, and urged him to confront the pastor, who seemed to expect him to do almost as much parish work as I. But he demurred, saying that one reason he allowed himself to be worked that hard in the parish was that it provided a "sane counterbalance" to his "parishioners" at the hospital.

At least my colleague wasn't expected to teach in the grade-school: I was and was asked to take the religion classes, respectively for 5th, 6th, 7th, and 8th grades, at least once a week. This did not include my work with public high school students on Monday nights, and the instruction classes for adult converts, also held one night a week. Now except for 8th grade (and possibly 7th grade in Battle Creek) I'd never been asked to teach grade school religion classes to young children before. Two of my initial attempts to keep 5th graders, especially the boys, in their seats (much less hold their attention) convinced me I wasn't cut out for that job and I went and cut a deal with the principal, saying I'd teach both the 7th and 8th grade classes twice a week if she'd relieve me from the futility of my trying to teach 5th and 6th graders. She mercifully agreed.

But I still preferred to work with high school kids. The last year or so while in Grand Ledge I took a job teaching religion to the junior class at the new O'Rafferty Catholic High School located on the far west side of Lansing, nearly half-way from downtown to Grand Ledge. So I decided to do the same in Kalamazoo. However, the new Hackett High School (for boys), which was located just down the street from Saint Monica's, was fully staffed by an order of brothers who had their own priest chaplain and didn't seem to want my help. Where help was appreciated, however, was at O'Brien High School (for girls) housed in the old Saint Augustine Parish high-school building downtown. So I took on a junior class there. I'd never taught in a segregated school like this before and thought that perhaps, without the distraction of boys around, these girls might be even more amenable to serious study and discussion than would be normally the case in a mixed classroom. Alas, it seemed just the opposite. For the most part, they seemed lackadaisical beyond belief. Though disappointed, I kept up my efforts to spark their interest. But I was beginning to drift in the direction of the belief of one of my former pastors (the one who had finally taken over at Holy Redeemer after my five-month stint as administrator). He was of the opinion that the Church should stay out of the secondary education business because, as he put it, at one point or another most every kid begins to hate school and that he'd rather have them hate the local public school board than hate the Catholic Church. I thought the opinion rather extreme, but I was beginning to see his point, as it seemed to me that the public school students I'd been dealing with on Monday evenings were often much more alive to the challenge of being a Catholic-Christian in the modern world.

Parish Priest

Which brings me to TEC or "Teens Encounter Christ". Back when stationed in Grand Ledge, a classmate of mine whose assignment was to run Christo Rey, the Hispanic parish in Lansing, had imported into the diocese the "Cursillo"— the new weekend revival program that had recently arrived in the USA (from Spain via Cuba) designed to activate (or reactivate) more or less moribund faith. First conducted in Spanish, it was quickly translated into English. It heavily involved peers, especially dynamic personal testimony by laypeople speaking to laypeople, who in turn were divided into small discussion groups. Clergy were asked to be available for sacramental ministry (particularly hearing confessions) but it was laymen (or laywomen in the case of women's Cursillos) who kept the thing moving — and also provided the follow-up.

Another classmate of mine decided that what we really needed was something similar for our teenagers, both those in public and Catholic schools. So a further "translation" was made, this time from the rather revivalist penitential-centered Hispanic style of piety of the Cursillo — heavy on "palanca" (fasting, vigils, etc.), tearful public confessions, and "embrazos" of reconciliation — to concentrating on the sacramental meaning of Baptism and its completion in the self-dedication made in the sacrament of Confirmation. Even though most of these kids had already been confirmed, we found out that most of them had still been much too young at the time to have experienced the full implications of that step and that the TEC program was the ideal means to activate this sacramental completion. Contrary to current trends to insist that Confirmation be administered to younger children, to preserve the traditional order of "the sacraments of initiation"— Baptism, Confirmation, First Communion or Eucharist — what we were finding from our experience in this program was that these youngsters often not only resented having been confirmed so early, but even envied those who still had the choice to make, some of whom did not yet feel themselves quite ready for making that choice.

In any case, with the TEC programs being held in the old nursing students' residence in Battle Creek (the same where my cousin had lived that month or so when she first agreed to come back to

Chapter 4

Michigan) I became heavily involved in the individual confessions-counseling aspect — often not returning back to the rectory in Kalamazoo until very late on Saturday evenings or the wee hours of Sunday morning.

I also organized at least one or two contingents of public high school kids from Saint Monica's to attend TEC — something that was to lead to a great deal more of a counseling burden than I had bargained for at the time. It seems that the dynamics of the program were bringing on, or at least bringing up to the surface, emotional problems that sorely needed attention, even to the extent (as I was to learn later on from my classmate who had started the program) that not only the program, but the diocese itself, was being strongly criticized, and in one case, being blamed as the trigger for one teen's suicide. I knew very well what he meant. Two of the girls from the Saint Monica's group in particular seemed to have real emotional problems, or maybe I should say one of them really did but with whom the other overly empathized. But after trying to get to the bottom of her problem (perhaps too successfully) which in turn triggered a suicidal gesture or attempt (we were never certain but, at my suggestion, the doctor had her stomach pumped out to make sure — and to teach her a lesson!) she needed to be hospitalized for a while for her own good. The psychiatrist who took on her case at first seemed put out that I had been involved at all. But as he dealt with her further he admitted to me that I had proved to show some real skill. My colleague at the parish (the state hospital chaplain) in fact wondered out loud if I shouldn't take over his job, exchanging my teen-age crazies for his adult ones. "No thanks," I answered. Two months serving in such a place and I was sure I'd need to be committed myself.

I really wasn't joking. The fact was that I had decided that I myself needed professional help. Since some of my work with others had put me in contact with the psychiatrist at the local Catholic hospital, I went to talk to him about the stresses and strains I was experiencing, and my almost constant temptation to run away — but not about my long-standing yearning for monastic life or the hermitage (particularly about the latter — not wanting to appear any more crazy than I actually felt at the moment). He wasn't at all surprised, in fact as a somewhat or at least slightly anticlerical Irishman (born and raised, as they say, "on the old sod") he muttered something about my thinking that I'm Jesus Christ — trying to save the whole world single handed. "Exactly," I told him, "that is what they kept telling us in the seminary — that we must be 'other Christs'!"

He suggested that maybe what I needed was not so much a period of "testing" in the contemplative life, but simply a good long vacation, a "sabbatical", perhaps a whole year off. He told me he'd be willing to write the bishop on my behalf, urging just that. He also gave me some pills to take.

By then I was willing to try anything. My regular doctor had also given me some pills to take, but while they helped me relax, they also put me in a mood that scared me — like not just that I didn't care a damn about anything, but even worse, that I didn't give a damn about not caring a damn! Besides that, those other pills would give me a splitting headache. So during the first week of April I began still another letter to the bishop, recounting the whole history of my struggle, but this time leading to a request that I simply be given a year off to find myself.

However, as I continued to marshal my arguments some days later, a disturbing new admission emerged, one that I had consistently avoided before. It was, to put it simply, that I more and more questioned the Catholic Church. It was not that I had any doubts about Christianity as such or the core of the Church's teachings, but that I had serious reservations about the manner of its presentations of those teachings, its perceived authoritarianism, its inability to deal with the "real world", especially the world as revealed by modern science, or to honestly own up to the history of its own past. Or as I was to put it in another draft of the same intended letter (I still hadn't actually sent anything as of April 20th), I had found that my future, as well as that of the Church, was the big question mark. By 1967 the council had ended and already the battle lines were forming. One of the priests of our diocese had persuaded the bishop into allowing him to go for further studies and had rewarded the bishop with a book

Chapter 4

titled *A Modern Priest Looks at His Outdated Church*. Shortly after, the author left the priesthood and the Church and he was the toast of a series of late night talk shows on TV. But with or without the modern ex-priest's help, reactions both for and against the results of Vatican II began to take more definite shape. While still in Grand Ledge, I had been appointed to a committee to help draw up guidelines for the formation of parish councils. And while in Kalamazoo, somehow I had been picked to be part of a symposium discussing ways pastoral ministry might be restructured or reshaped.

At the latter I delivered a paper before a group of priests where I suggested that each region or deanery of a diocese have its own local "pastoral bishop" who could relate more personally to the people of his area than the single diocesan bishop off in a distant city — despite the administrative efficiency of our present system. Why or how I was picked to dream up, much less, to share such ideas is beyond my recall. At the same time I already felt myself to be under special scrutiny when at a priests' gathering in Lansing, the chief doctrinal watchdog of the diocese (the only one who had a doctorate in theology in the whole diocese — other than the one who had just written the book and left) came up to me and told me the bishop had received complaints about me recommending that couples "try using the pill." I had, I explained, but only as a possible means of making the "rhythm method" work, but that they should see their MD about that. That seemed to satisfy him, but now I knew I was being watched. Hence the admission in the letter to the bishop as well.

Before I even sent that letter off, something else happened to me which I'm still at a loss to explain. On April 12th, the day I had started the first draft of that letter, I drove later that morning up the western Michigan coast line towards a town called Pentwater, where I had spent a week or two as a young child with my folks. I stopped my car along the banks of the south branch of the Pentwater River and there a sudden feeling of loss and despair came over me — a feeling that my whole life, especially my life in the Church, was totally coming apart. I fought off the despair by a sheer act of will, reasoning that I was simply emotionally worn out and that my thinking was not to be trusted at that point. I went on to the north branch of the same river, took my fishing rod and reel, and hiked upstream a bit and baited my hook, finding a dry patch of bank to relax upon while I let the spinner and the bait drift slowly in the current. As I wrote it down later that evening in a cottage owned by friends along the south branch of the Pere Marquette River:

> Lately I feel so often like I just want to sort of curl up and die in a way, to get life over with, yet not by dying, not yet. I really want to live alone, away. In a sense I want heaven now, but not a next-life heaven but just peace and calm to be one with all and God . . .
>
> Today by the Pentwater River, half-asleep, death struck me broadside. Everything seemed so unreal, the woods, the stream, the birds, the worm turning on the end of my line. I knew that within the hour I would go [i.e., leave that spot] just as within 30 years or so I could never hope to be there again and it all seemed the same and I both grieved and felt I couldn't care less. I felt like a traitor to evolution, a hireling ready to desert the flock and I didn't care . . . and saw the decision to live on or die so innocently and unobtrusively before me that I was shocked at myself. I had to make no decision. I only wanted desperately to live, to be one with God now and forever — that's all — nothing else seemed suddenly to matter. [Then I added] I find the strongest proof of God in an act of faith — a protest maybe, that without Him and eternity, the whole thing, life, change, death, especially death, is idiotic.

But was that all? Looking back now I can say that the above was the negative (and close to despairing) side of the experience. But there was a positive side as well, one that I was unable to describe back then, but that fit my recollections of the whole episode, or what I might call its positive rebound. I'm not quite sure of the sequence of events, but then, as I tried to describe the rest of the experience many years later in one of my books, pretending on that occasion that it was contained in a passage of a letter from a friend, I wrote:

> I had fallen asleep [on the above thoughts] but instead of waking up refreshed, I awoke with a great sense of oppression bearing down on me. Then all of a sudden — I can't explain it — I seem to have been lifted up, not physically or anything like that, but

it was like I was being cradled in someone's arms, but not those of a tangible or visible person, but by an engulfing, loving presence. At that point time seemed suspended and I realized that dead or alive, it is all the same. I was given to know that we all exist as part of a vast totality within which our puny individual existence means little in itself and yet is infinitely precious in the eyes of this loving being. I got up, walked back to my car and drove to a friend's cabin where I tried to write down an account of what had happened. But all descriptions eluded me. I only knew that in some way I no longer had to "believe" that God exists—I had experienced God first-hand!

During the months that followed that experience, even occasionally during the many years that have followed, I have asked myself if what had happened to me back then was "real" – that is, something more than just a mere figment of my imagination. Certainly, by then, I had studied enough psychology to know that I could have been the victim of some kind of self-induced hallucination. But I had studied enough "mystical theology", for example the writings of Saint John of the Cross, to know also that this was the kind of thing that could be seen as a special grace or favor from God to spur us on to face some kind of test or challenge that still awaits us. Which it is can only be judged in view of the outcome. And in my case, it gave me the will, not just back then, but in occasions yet to come, to keep on living.

More immediately, however, I returned to the parish the next day determined to do something decisive, and after I mailed a further redraft of my intended letter to the bishop on April 21st, received a call from his secretary asking me to meet with the bishop on the 3rd of May.

My notes for that day recall that he agreed to give me an indefinite leave to try out with the Camaldolese Hermits, beginning in August, but no permission to live alone totally by myself. But the second part of my interview — about my "faith crisis" was less satisfactory. Although he admitted the difference between faith and theology, I got the impression that he took me for a simpleton who could be exhorted to belief and who would be better off forgetting about theology and simply concentrate on believing. I noted later that "for me it cannot be that simple: I can believe, but I hardly can take this as a mandate to quit thinking."

The rest of that summer, while continuing my parish routine, I slowly prepared for my departure from parish life, but also to plan to make the most of the year to come, hoping to acquaint myself with several contemplative groups including the Carthusians in Vermont, and a colony of hermits led by a Benedictine priest on Vancouver Island in British Columbia. I was not yet prepared to put all my eggs in one basket. Meanwhile, my Irish psychiatrist also surprised me by not considering my desire for life in a hermitage as "too neurotic". In fact, he said it might fit my temperament quite well. But he worried that the lack of apostolic activity might soon pall. Well, I'd find out about that soon enough. But he was urging me to consider the stay with the Camaldolese hermits as an "extended vacation" not as a certain "new vocation" — at least not yet.

Early in June I wrote the Bishop again, indicating what Dr. Curran had said and reporting that the new Camaldolese prior in Ohio would be very happy to have me come down there after they moved into their new location outside Steubenville in September. Then I added:

> As far as my difficulties in regard to the magisterium [the official teaching office of the Church] is concerned, I have simply chosen to ignore the problem for the time being, taking refuge in the realization that the Church is, after all, a mystery, and that the present state of confusion affects all our minds (including the pope's) and threatened accustomed habits of thought, yet does not change the truth itself both in its essential core and the general direction of its development.

Later in June, during the diocesan priests' retreat, when I stopped by to ask the retreat house director whether one of the Franciscan brothers could give me a haircut, I got my heart cut instead. This priest, a Hungarian-born Franciscan who was a good friend of Fr. Csaky, and was also directing this particular retreat, accused me of "running-away, losing courage, and losing faith in myself." Well, maybe he was right, but I was more in fear of losing faith in the

Church altogether. After his second conference to the priests, which I found encouraging (he was talking about God's grace being sufficient for us) I also somewhat sarcastically noted that he (the retreat director) "would guarantee the grace to suffer all things in the fulfillment of God's will, yet would seem to leave God's will to be found in whatever way the mop flops — provided its not against Canon Law and the Ten Commandments. This I can't buy."

In July I went up to the Stella Maris cabin with my father and my godfather (I had joined the group a year or so before when the membership had been expanded to help pay for some additional land). I told my dad about my impending "leave of absence" (as it was being officially termed). He seemed saddened by the news, reacting much the same as the diocesan retreat master. I was also saddened by the possibility of seeing the Stella Maris property and its beautiful trout stream for the last time after having used it as a vacation spot for so many years and having just recently used up almost all my savings to become a full-fledged member of the group.

On July 20th the diocesan newspaper published the list of new assignments for priests around the diocese and with them announced my going down to try out monastic life in Ohio. My parents were resigned but most of my priest friends were very encouraging. I stopped by Grand Ledge where I learned the news was causing quite a stir — a lot of people there couldn't figure out why I did not replace Fr. Csaky after he retired (not knowing that as a rule pastors were never succeeded by assistants — least of all by one who still had a few years to go before qualifying for a parish in the first place). I also found out that there was an ugly rumor going around that town that I was being "sent" to a monastery for unpriestly misbehavior.

In mid-August however I returned north to Stella Maris for just one more visit and then, in August, set out on my intended swing east before heading down to Ohio.

Looking back on those nine years, what can I say? From the point of view of what I had intended to do — and from what Bishop Albers had given me assurance could be worked out — they were at least four years too long. Were they then, in my eyes, completely wasted?

Not really, I suppose. But still, I could not help, then as now, wonder if our ideas of "God's will" are way too simplistic. True, I gained experience — enough perhaps to give me both good memories as well as bad ones for a lifetime. Among the latter is the regret I feel over sometimes having said things, or reacting to what others may have said, in ways that were insensitive or sometimes really stupid.

That being said, however, parish ministry is, if nothing else, hardly ever boring. But it is also very demanding, and I still, to this day, consider most parish priests that I know (especially today, as their numbers dwindle and their tasks increase) as real heroes, if not outright martyrs. But I also blame the Church itself (meaning especially the leadership in Rome) for this situation. Celibacy is never easy, even for someone who, like me, deliberately chose it — in my case, this quite apart from it being required of priests. And here I'm not talking about sex (regarding which I quickly learned that married men seem to have as much or even more problems with sex than do most priests) as I'm talking about loneliness. In making celibacy mandatory for admittance into the priesthood, I believe the western or "Latin Rite" Church made a mistake, and that it (especially the ordinary people who make up the bulk of its membership) will continue to suffer for it. But this is only one of the issues that more and more began to command my attention as I moved into the next stage of my increasingly long journey of life.

Chapter 5
On the Road

August 1967 began what was to turn out as a major year of change and upset. It had already seen the major race riot in Detroit, of which I'd gotten a quick glimpse of back one morning before returning to Kalamazoo as I skirted the area near Sacred Heart Seminary, where clouds of smoke were rolling up the street from the southeast part of town. By August I was officially "On Leave" and very much on the road. I decided first to take a tour of various monasteries before settling down with the Camaldolese. The first stop (on August 22nd-23rd) was at the Trappist Abbey ("Our Lady of the Genesee"), just south of Rochester in western New York State — the daughter house founded from Gethsemane Abbey during my first year in the seminary when vocations to monastic life, especially the strictly contemplative orders, were at an all time high.

By then, they too had begun to suffer a loss, with a number of monks leaving for a more active life in the world. It seemed already that I was swimming against the tide. But while there, I did get some reassurance from a visiting priest from Vermont who had once been a Trappist seminarian but who had left and become a diocesan priest. He was now thinking seriously about returning to monastic life, and told me — undoubtedly reflecting on his own experience of trying to live a monastic life on his own —"You can't be a monk without a monastery!" Yet at the same time it must have been he who told me about a Trappist monk living as a hermit in Vermont — just where I was headed.

Next stop was to the new Carthusian foundation—the first one in America by this ancient order — high up on the west side of Mount Equinox in southwestern Vermont. I was especially impressed with its inaccessibility, Mount Equinox being privately owned, with a gate house at the foot of the mountain where a private guard had to give you clearance to even drive up the road. Apparently the Carthusians had made an exclusive deal of some sort. There I was to get the advice I'd already gotten so often — to go home and be a more prayerful parish priest — as if I hadn't tried that for nine years! Then I drove eastward a bit to stop overnight at an experimental "primitive" Benedictine community, "Weston Priory", founded by a diocesan priest. The idea behind the rash of these new Benedictine foundations (like that founded by Dom Mercier near Cuernavaca, Mexico) was to return to the original pattern of life established by Saint Benedict back in the sixth century, a monastery populated by brothers (the number of priests kept to a necessary minimum) living according to the Benedictine motto of *"Ora et Labora"* (Pray and Work), where the work included a major dose of farm labor for all but the infirm. No school teaching, parish work, or the like. I have to admit that by then such a "primitive" monastic life had a strong attraction for me despite my scholarly ambitions. But close community life did not.

After spending a few days visiting my dad's younger sister in Burlington, and taking an eight or so mile hike, climbing up the west side of Camel's Hump, a mountain where my great-great grandfather had a partnership in a lumbering operation over a hundred years before and where one could still see the ancient stumps in the now largely re-grown hardwood forest. I signed a visitors' guestbook in a Appalachian-Green Mountain Trail shelter near the top and found a remnant or two of the Army Air Force bomber that slammed into the top of the mountain during World War II.

Next day, after visiting aunt "Billie's" grave in Bristol and stopping by her old farmhouse outside Montpelier, I went over towards Dansville, to see the exclustrated Trappist who lived alone in a hermitage back in the woods. "Exclaustration" means that one is on leave from living in a monastic cloister, much as I was "on leave" from working in my diocese. Although Fr. Bruder was on leave from a Trappist monastery in California, it turned out that he had Michigan U.P. roots and had, like my first pastor, John Blasko, also spent a boyhood in Arizona for much the same reason — a miner father who could find no work in Michigan's Copper Country during the great depression. A small world indeed!

We talked that whole evening while a buck deer, with antlers still in velvet, wandered by his hermitage door. I slept on his front porch and next morning, and after celebrating Mass together, we talked

Chapter 5

some more. His opinion (as a former novice master) was that I'd find the Camaldolese too restrictive and that besides, he thought a "community of hermits" was something of a contradiction in terms, but that a protracted stay with them would both do me and them good — as he felt they could benefit from some of the post-Vatican II renewal fervor that was sweeping the Church. (It seems that year I kept running into people who were impressed when they heard that I came from Lansing Diocese. Apparently we had a national reputation for "being with it" when it came to implementing change!) Fr. Bruder also told me about a few other experimental foundations along hermitage lines. One was in West Virginia and another in Sedona, Arizona, which although he hadn't visited, sounded to him to be very interesting and which he thought might well be worth my looking into. Apparently I took special note of that.

Later that day I drove down to Rumford, Rhode Island, to visit an aunt — the widow of one of my mother's older brothers. She and her youngest son, her daughter-in-law, and I went down to Newport to take in the flurry of activity there as the America's Cup sailing races were in progress and to see again how America's richest families once lived in their extravagant shoreline mansions that served as their "summer homes". It rather reminded me of my mother's remark the first time she saw the yacht basin at Fort Lauderdale, Florida: "Now I know why there are Communists!"

On August 28th I made, what was for me, a very special "pilgrimage". It was to Teilhard de Chardin's grave at the Jesuit novitiate at Saint Andrew's on the Hudson, not far from Franklin Roosevelt's family home at Hyde Park. I was directed to the grave site by the brother who answered the door, but was told there was no room for me to stay at the novitiate overnight. So I ended up sleeping on the ground alongside my car in a small roadside park overlooking the Hudson River, moving under a picnic table when it got a bit drizzly. But the main memory of that evening was a kind of "vow" or promise that I made. It was that I would do my best to spread Teilhard's vision of a Christianity that could come fully to grips with evolution and not be frightened by modern science and that in turn, I was asking for Teilhard's own determination to remain faithful to the

Church, no matter how badly it mistreated him or censored him for this thought. It was a deal that I think has helped keep me loyal ever since, even though there have been many times when people have questioned me (as they did Teilhard) as to how one can remain in an institution that often seems so frightened of the truth.

The next stop was at one more monastery, Mount Savior Abbey, another new "primitive" Benedictine foundation outside Elmira, NY. The place has a spectacular setting high on a bluff overlooking the Mohawk River valley. There I met another priest-monk who had a background in the diocesan priesthood and thus made me a little less uneasy about the experiment I was about to undertake.

Nevertheless, after I arrived at the new Holy Family Hermitage near Bloomingdale, Ohio — it seems to me it was even a day before the hermit-monks arrived at the scene when they moved up from their older hermitage site near McConnelsville — I went into a depression of sorts. I'd been assigned "cell" #6, actually one of ten small cottages arranged in a circle around the site for the still unfinished community chapel, each with a sitting room/study, a tiny "oratory" or private prayer room, plus a small bedroom and bath. The prior, Fr. Charles, an ebullient Pole who had once been, he told me, secretary to the Cardinal Archbishop of Warsaw, said I probably needed rest more than anything else for the time being and urged me not to try to get up for the 3:30 AM office for a few days.

But despite reassurance, and perhaps because of a very poor night's sleep, I experienced again something like the mood that had overtaken me along the banks of the Pentwater River that past April, only this time there was no follow-up moment of grace. Instead there was a deep dark depression, an experience of utter nothingness. I felt the nothingness of not only myself but this time it was as if I was even without hope of survival in God. And with this I experienced what seemed to be two opposite reactions; the thought of suicide and at the same time a desire to flee, to run, to drink, to do anything to avoid the thought of and confrontation with death.

By the next day I seem to have snapped out of it. I was given a chance to do a lot of useful work with my hands. One task was to build a number of board-walks from the individual cells to the temporary chapel (in the community office, library, and kitchen building) over the still muddy and just seeded community court-yard. I also built several tall book stands for the chapel, a housing for the well-pump, and other odds and ends. Fr. Charles was soon to consider me a mechanical genius of some sort.

However, from my journal notes, I see that I still had a lot of other things on my mind. In fact, I had mapped out four areas of study and had resolved to spend the next month reflecting on them taking on one topic per week: first, God; second, Christ, the Church, and the Holy Spirit; third, celibacy and marriage, and fourth, my own vocation. But the arrival of "Father Major", the Camaldolese Prior General from Rome, sort of threw my schedule off. Fr. Del Rio, a jolly old Spaniard with a white beard that made him look for all the world like Santa Claus, but in a white religious habit, immediately turned our attention to what changes might be considered in Camaldolese life due to Vatican II. Very little he assured us. In fact, most of the changes had already taken effect. In the USA they no longer broke their sleep for a midnight office, but instead, like the Trappists, just got up very early in the morning. I was very thankful for that. Second, the priests in the community "concelebrated" the Eucharist together instead of saying individual "private Masses". All this seemed to me to be relatively progressive. But I was also a bit set back by what seemed to me a great fear to change anything else.

A good example had to do with diet. Like most of the stricter monastic orders, the Camaldolese never ate flesh meat. Fish, eggs, and dairy products, however, were allowed, though the bulk of the diet was made up of vegetables, fruits, and bread. However, the young brother who did the cooking one day pointed out to me what seemed to him to be an oddity. The Camaldolese rule allowed a certain amount of wine each day except during the strictest times of fast and abstinence. Now, he reasoned, that might make sense in Italy, but here, where we only took wine on big feast days, why not substitute something even more healthy, like milk. Whether he had actually suggested this to the prior I don't know for sure, but I suspect he had and had gotten "no" for an answer — that the rule didn't allow for it and apparently had no provision for a local superior to use his own common sense. Thus I began to see what was involved in joining an "order" and particularly the hassles over what seemed to me to be trifles during a time that called instead for serious thought. If so, I wanted no part of such squabbling.

In the meantime, as that month's trial came towards an end, Fr. Charles was starting to give me a real pitch as to why I should consider joining them. As to my objection that I'd probably find Camaldolese life too restrictive or too cut off from others, he almost promised that he would make me "guest master" so I could talk more with those who came to visit or make private retreats. But I also was finding the life to be a bit too physically restrictive. I had already taken to wandering through the beautiful woods on the hermitage property, but was told that except for designated times (like Sunday afternoons) this was considered a sign of instability — even though I found it personally a help in a life devoted solely to prayer. I also told him that I needed to travel a bit and see more of the new monastic and eremitical experiments that were taking place (like that place in Arizona and the other hermit colony I'd heard of that was located on Vancouver Island in British Columbia). And finally, I told Fr. Charles about all my "faith and anger" problems — just to cinch my argument as to why I shouldn't, and couldn't, stay.

My strategy didn't work. Fr. Charles told me prayer would fix everything and that there is both the divine as well as the human in the Church, and that it was obvious that I never had a vocation to parish work and that I should stay out of active ministry. He told me I could write books if I wanted and even pursue "an artful craft" to help support the hermitage. All this seemed like a wonderful offer and looking back on it, I still sometimes regret I didn't take up his invitation then and there. But I really didn't feel that my faith difficulties were being taken seriously, neither by Fr. Charles or even by my bishop — whom I had reason to think took it all to be more of an emotional problem than an intellectual one. So, on September 24th I began a long letter to the bishop laying out my case as to why it was time to move on. I stressed the fact that all the hermitage cottages or "cells" were booked for the winter, and for me to continue to occupy one, to the exclusion of someone else who wished to come, would be selfish and dishonest, even if Fr. Charles hoped and prayed I'd change my mind. Instead, I planned to ask the bishop to either allow me to go out to Arizona to reside at the Spiritual Life Institute for the winter, or — and here is what I think I really wanted to do — to simply return to Michigan to live alone at the Stella Maris cabin, living much the same as my new hermit friend, Fr. Bruder, in Vermont. By now, I thought I had earned the bishop's trust.

By the end of September I was back in Michigan, with an appointment to see the Bishop on Oct 3rd. Meanwhile, a priest friend (who was having great problems himself) tried to dun into me (by pure repetition and scripture quotes about "the seed needing to die to itself") the message that I was far too worried about myself and my own needs. He was probably right. But still, I had come this far and was determined to bring things to a resolution. My old pastor in Grand Ledge was disgusted with the bishop for not ordering me back into a parish so that I'd know "God's will"— but which in fact I'd been willing to do, but the bishop too apparently wanted to see me resolve the whole thing, and although he would allow me to return to Stella Maris temporarily, he insisted that I try out the Arizona place as soon as they had room for me — which was to be, as it turned out, late in November.

Meanwhile I continued to work through the topics I had set out to examine more in depth at the beginning of my stay with the Camaldolese. In particular I gave a great deal of attention to just why I had chosen celibacy as my state in life. I recognized, by now, that my reasons for choosing to remain single were mostly negative, not just the fear of having some woman try to run my life but perhaps just as much, an unwillingness to be responsible for others — the same feeling that had made me hesitate, early on, about the priesthood and which made the parish priesthood, or even more, assuming the duties of a pastor, particularly difficult for me. In other words, I remained single, or even went out of my way to vow celibacy, not so much out of idealistic reasons — although I may have persuaded myself of the more idealistic reasons at the time — as I did for less than idealistic ones. Did the bishop detect this? I wondered exactly what he meant when he told me, at our last meeting, that "we must learn to accept our emotional defects as well as our physical ones." I felt that no doubt he was referring to something that the hospital psychiatrist in Kalamazoo had written into the letter backing my request for a leave of absence. So I decided that if this was the case, then the best thing for me to do was to accept this negativity and to allow for it by not pushing for some sort of confrontation that would threaten my emotional defenses. Little did I realize that within a month or two I would have these defenses challenged as perhaps never before.

Nevertheless I did not let this topic or any others worry me too much as I enjoyed a glorious few weeks — Octobers seem always glorious in the North Country — back in the solitude of Stella Maris, a place that I had already feared I'd never see again. Nor was it complete solitude. A few of the other members came up for a few days of partridge and duck hunting. One afternoon's excursion down the river by canoe yielded us several ducks and two magnificent Canada geese. But then, after they left, not the solitude, but the fear I'd never see this north woods paradise again began to haunt me as well as a certain sense of aimlessness, or a sense of futility in trying to map out any definite plans for my life. On Oct 20th, this sense even drove me to trying to write poetry — always a dire sign of some sort for me. This one was hardly more than a "haiku" in length: it read, "October brings me — thoughts of dampness and decay, of finality and resurrection."

But I also made a resolution that same day, among other things, to: (first) finish an article I had begun on "Restructuring the Episcopacy"— apparently growing from the brash talk I'd given in Kalamazoo the spring before; (second) begin an article on "Proofs of God"; and (third) to begin a draft on a book on Teilhard. I also, two days later, wrote a bit in my journal about the role of play or sport (especially hunting) in the process of "hominization". I'm sure Teilhard would have been totally puzzled by the attempt.

I continued to read and write (mostly read) in the solitude of Stella Maris well into the month of November. Two books seem to have particularly impressed me. One was *Truth and Revelation* by the Russian philosopher Nickolai Berdyaev; the other, *A Question of Conscience*, by the theologian and former English Catholic priest

Chapter 5

Charles Davis. They formed an interesting contrast. Berdyaev, a devout Orthodox Christian and exile from the Soviet Union, seemed to me to be both rigidly dogmatic and yet highly existentialistic at the same time. His was a view that emphasized both individual human freedom and responsibility for the corporate future of humanity as well as of the Church. One thing more about Berdyaev reminded me of Teilhard — someone who could be highly critical of the Church, yet insist on playing his role *within* it.

Davis, on the other hand struck me as being a "cop out". Although I understood and could sympathize with many of his reasons for leaving the Church, I could not see where his belief that by leaving the Church he could help reform it was all that plausible. Certainly, as an academic, he would have had to defend his views within any church-affiliated institution and, particularly with the appearance of the so-called theological "mandate" required to teach theology in such institutions, he probably would have eventually lost his job altogether. But rereading his book shortly before his death years later only confirmed my initial judgment. Meanwhile, look at all the influence towards reform that he could have been had he not discredited himself in the eyes of so many by "abandoning ship" — so to speak.

Finally, with the deer hunting season beginning on November 15th — I would have loved to hunt with the rest of the cabin members, but what would I have done with all the meat? — I decided it was best to return to my folks' place for a few days. There my mother confronted me with her distress over my "not finding myself" and challenging me to do what she always wanted me to do — to get married. I'm afraid I was rather abrupt, but I had to admit to myself she was right about one thing — that I was running. We went to see Sidney Portier in the movie "To Sir With Love", and so much came back to mind about that tumultuous year in Kalamazoo! At the same time I was reading Dostoyevsky's *The Possessed* and saw myself reflected in the ineffective and pretentious character Prof. Verhovensky, who liked to imagine he had a gift to give to the world but was reluctant to put it to the test lest he discover he is the fraud that he suspects he is. So I decided I'd best try not to take myself too seriously. So after a few more days of sitting around town, and after a family get-together over in Jackson for Thanksgiving, I set out from there the next morning for Arizona.

I did not keep any records of that journey. But I remember I lodged one night in a motel near Lincoln, Nebraska. The next day I accidentally locked myself out of my car at a rest stop along the Platte River, but was able to reopen it with a wire through a slight gap above the window, so when I arrived in Estes Park, Colorado, late that afternoon, the first thing I did was have a spare key made. I also begged a place to stay at the local Catholic parish church. The next day I made it to the Trappist monastery at Snowmass, Colorado, and stayed there two nights, taking a long hike on a snow-covered ridge between the mountains from where I could look eastward over to the resort town of Vail and its ski-slopes . Then I took a gravel road over a mountain pass and rejoined the highway towards Durango. That night I found the tiny Christ in the Desert Benedictine monastery in Chaco Canyon near Abiquiu, New Mexico, and met the next morning with Fr. Dennis Hines, another exclaustrated Trappist living as a hermit on the property.

Later that day, after a quick visit to Santa Fe, I took a back road over to Jemez Springs, where the Servants of the Paraclete, an order of priests and brothers that specializes in care for priests who "have problems", put me up in their guest house at *Via Coeli* (The Way to Heaven"). I had arrived well after dark, and although I recall them giving me something to eat, I guess most of their "guests" had already turned in. Next morning I was shocked to see how filled the place was. There seemed to be a lot more priests with problems than I ever realized — though at that time I naively assumed most of the problems were with the bottle. In fact, it was not until some weeks or even months later that I first ever heard of any priest being accused of sexual misbehavior with children or even adolescents. With women, yes; but with kids, no. Apparently the Church's ability to hide such deviant conduct, even from many of its own clergy, had become a well-practiced art.

The next day I traveled westward into Arizona along the fabled Route 66. I had to stop at an Arizona Department of Agriculture checkpoint to be inspected for contraband citrus fruit from Texas and upon opening my car's trunk, the inspector was puzzled to see my pair of huge LL Bean brand snowshoes. "What are these for?" he asked. I told him that I was headed to Sedona for the winter and had been advised that sudden snowstorms were not unheard of that far north. He looked at me rather skeptically. Two weeks later a storm did hit, the worst that Arizona had experienced so far in that century, dumping two feet on Sedona and up to seven foot high drifts in Flagstaff along Route 66. The local pastor in Sedona told me I must be a prophet, as I was one of the only two owners of a pair of snowshoes in town.

The Red Rock country around Sedona was spectacular, but the "institute" itself was far less so. If fact it was hardly quite like what I had expected. There was, to be sure, an impressive "Chapel of the Holy Cross" perched on the side of a butte overlooking Oak Creek Canyon — an impressive structure featuring a dramatic bronze figure of Christ on the Cross. The care of the chapel and its gift-shop (since it was a great tourist attraction) had been entrusted to the institute but the institute complex — named "Nada Ranch" (well-named, *nada* meaning "nothing" in Spanish) itself was some five miles away on seven or so acres of sage brush, cacti and a few scrawny trees, with a small collection of rather broken down looking buildings that had served as a movie set in a Walt Disney film titled "The Boy and The Eagle" some years past. The collection of buildings consisted of one small one-floor clapboard "ranch house", another little cottage (occupied by the institute's director), and a rather make-shift "hermitage", a small storage building, and the remains of a small Navajo style "hogan" that had been part of the movie set. A young woman just out of college, but who kept the institute's books, occupied the ranch house, and I was given the "hermitage". It had been recently vacated by an older layman who had fled to Los Angeles as winter was coming — and I could quickly see why. There was no oil stove or fireplace in the hermitage, only a small electric heater.

But I only had to try to keep warm in that place for about ten days or so as by December 12th the director and his assistant had gone their separate ways back East for a long (three week) holiday, leaving me with the whole place — including the oil heated "ranch house", all of which was soon to be inundated beneath 2 feet of snow. I was supposed to take care of all scheduled services at the chapel, receive any visitors, and answer the phone. After getting my little Chevy Corvair hopelessly stuck in the snow I managed to hitchhike down to Phoenix to pick up the institute's new Jeep pickup which the director had left at the dealership for its 1,000 mile checkup when he flew East. I had dressed for the weather in Sedona, which was well below freezing, in my LL Bean high-top rubber-bottom shoepacs, my winter parka, and fake-fur trooper hat. My ride left me on a street corner bus stop on the north side of Phoenix to catch a bus across town to reach the Jeep dealership. As it was in the 60s there down in Phoenix, people drove by looking curiously at me like I had arrived from the moon.

The rest of those first three weeks in Arizona was quite uneventful. As the snow diminished a couple of Jesuits came up from Phoenix to spend a weekend and I got to know a few of the local people who served on the institute's "board". They seemed quite concerned about the future of the place — as well as its reputation. It seems that it already had a reputation as a kind of hang-out for hippies, and in the summer, in particular, as a mecca for college kids — mostly of the female variety. In ultra-conservative, strongly "Birchite", Arizona this was not good. They seemed to hope that I could influence the staff (such as it was) to make it into a more respectably religious-appearing place. So I decided to do what I could, knowing that I really had not much choice, in that my bishop expected me to spend at least the rest of the winter there.

Well, I did try. After Christmas another college girl came back to keep the other one company, and the director managed to find me new lodgings about seven miles away in a large cabin on the west bank of Oak Creek. It belonged to some wealthy friends of his from California. It had a huge fireplace to match, plus a couple of gas-heaters that could be turned on for short bursts of warmth before the carbon-monoxide made you a bit nervous. It was reached by a built up concrete "ford" through the creek, or when the winter-spring run-

Chapter 5

off from up-canyon was too high, by a metal and wood suspension foot-bridge. It was an interesting place to live and work. I wrote a lot, cut and split wood, hiked in the canyons and snow-shoed up on the 7,000 foot high plateau (Sedona's elevation was more about 4,500 feet above sea level), and back-packed to camp out a few times. I also made several trips up to the Grand Canyon, camping one night in the snow in my pup-tent along the south rim. Another priest from Michigan, a fellow Stella Maris cabin owner who was on leave following recovery from a heart attack, came to visit me for a week. We went back up to the Grand Canyon and spent some time on the Hopi reservation, where we witnessed the annual "Bean Dance" at the pueblo named Shongapovi —an impressive and rather moving sight. I returned to the reservation country once or twice more. One trip was especially to survey the ancient Anazasi ruins at Betatakin National Monument. I also visited Monument Valley, and entered a snowshoeing race at the Williams Arizona Winter Festival where I was beaten by a lone cowpoke who had strapped his snowshoes tight to the soles of his boots, the heels as well as the toes — something I had never seen done before.

Among the books I read that winter, and which provoked one of my essays in particular, was Raymond Nogar's *Lord of the Absurd*. Nogar, a theologian of the Dominican order, had distinguished himself by writing, just a few years earlier, a weighty book on *The Wisdom of Evolution*, a book based largely on Teilhard's thought. Although I hadn't gotten around to actually reading that book, I felt that I had a fairly good grasp of its argument, both from its title and various reviews I had read. So this second book of his caught me as something of a shock. Was he repudiating all that he had written before? Eventually, as I wrestled with his argument, which was that evolution was so incredibly wasteful and bound up with so much tragedy and suffering that the idea of a "teleology" (in this case, the notion that there is a divine plan or goal to creation) becomes untenable, I began to wonder if belief in God is not so much a logical or rational conclusion, but rather is a desperate "leap of faith". Could this, for example, have explained my previous spring's experience along the banks of the Pentwater River, as well as its scarier repetition when I arrived at the Camaldolese Hermitage? But then I also came to several conclusions.

One, which I wrote down, was that Nogar's second book was, in a sense, the "flip side" of Aquinas's teleological proofs for the existence of God — that is, that one could argue that the universe is so senseless that nothing (including its workings as revealed by science) can make sense unless we presume the existence of God. Otherwise, nothing ultimately adds up. My second conclusion, which was a question that I did not write down, but which was very much in my mind, was what had happened, in a personal way, to Nogar to provoke such a radical shift in his thinking. Was it some premonition of his impending death?

As for the institute itself, I really didn't spend much time there. I wasn't very comfortable around the place and they knew it. I even wrote the director, during one of his many absences, a rather pointed letter expressing what I thought it would take for the place to be taken seriously, beginning with his more constant presence and by a "horarium", that is, a daily schedule of community prayer, silent time, work time and the like — something that visitors would either be expected to fit into or else terminate their visit. Instead we'd end up with groups of young kids coming and spending a weekend, bringing with them a jug or two of wine, and probably, as the local sheriff seemed to suspect (he paid the place a visit at least once while I was there), a modest supply of "pot". The place was not a spiritually inspiring scene.

Meanwhile, on another trip down to Phoenix, I looked up one of the Jesuits who had visited Sedona back around Christmas to talk to him about all this and what I was attempting to do, and he advised me to consider going on leave from the priesthood altogether to sort things out. This, in the face of the insecurity I already felt about my vocation, I was not prepared to do. In fact, I did just the opposite and attempted to get involved in a few other ministries just to enhance my sense of usefulness and to try as well to help the institute along.

One of these activities was to help at the local parish in "Sedona West" and at a few other places when I could. Another was to substitute teach a few times in place of the institute director in a

Chapter 5

religion class at Verde Valley School, a boarding school for mostly wealthy high-school age kids, both boys and girls, from both coasts. Many of them seemed exceptionally intelligent and I quite enjoyed the experience. It was also the first time I had ever been asked to talk about philosophy and religion to a mostly non-Catholic audience. It made me think a bit more positively about teaching again or even going into it for awhile full time. But as far as actually influencing the institute towards what I thought were very much needed changes, I seemed to be getting nowhere fast. At an Easter Sunday party at the institute, I met a young widowed artist from Montana who had recently joined the Church, taking the name "Michael" at her baptism. She told me that she was headed back to Montana with a young fellow who had run away from home. As for myself, I resolved to leave the place shortly after Easter and to go visit the rest of what I had decided to come west to see.

So I headed out to California on the first of May. I still remember the thrill of the long descent down the mountain near Palm Springs and the glare of green foliage on the broad desert valley floor. Of course it was all due to irrigation, but still, it was the first concentration of really bright green I'd seen in months. I stayed overnight in the back of a bookstore in Santa Monica that was partly run or owned by the fellow who had preceded me in Sedona and who had left before the winter set in. The next morning I went to a parish church near-by for Mass and couldn't believe how restrictive things were in Los Angeles under Cardinal McIntyre. I stayed in the area another night, this time at Saint Andrew's Benedictine monastery in the San Gabriel Mountains, then headed north up the coast on Highway 1 to the other Camaldolese foundation at Big Sur. Despite its trendy and spectacular location, it struck me that there too they were still holding on to the pre-Vatican II church. (Years later I would return and see how wrong I was about that.) I then visited my dad's cousin and his wife at their retirement home in Monterey, then, over another night, crashed with the Jesuits at their Los Gatos location — which kind of made up for the night under the picnic table near Hastings on the Hudson.

Perhaps I should explain, at this point, my financial

arrangements. To tell the truth, I had none. No stipend from my diocese; nothing except what I had in some very modest savings, what I could earn from my services as a priest, and a loan, if necessary, from my folks. So I basically begged for places to stay, or else slept in my car, or on the ground. But gas was very cheap and so was fast food, so I got by. I even had some health insurance, due to the beneficence of some Lutheran-sponsored outfit that catered to ministers who, most having families to raise, were probably worse off than I. Still being only thirty-five years old back then, I don't remember ever worrying much about it (finances or health) anyway.

Just south of San Francisco, I stopped to see my old seminary rector (Fr. Lyman Fenn) who lived in retirement at the Sulpician Seminary at Menlo Park. He told me he was glad I was seeing his native California in the spring when things were green. Rest of the year, he said, it's "golden", which he admitted was a euphemism for being "burnt up". I passed quickly through San Francisco hardly stopping, except to slow down for a quick look at the Haight-Ashbury district that everyone seemed to be talking about during those tumultuous years. Then I drove over the Golden Gate Bridge to head for the Trappist Monastery near Santa Rosa where my Vermont hermit friend Fr. Bruder was still technically a member. But a phone call ahead (I wanted to meet the abbot there for some reason — and it turned out he was absent) sent me back toward the coast via a road along the Russian River where on a detour over a high hill I came across, of all people, the artist I met at Sedona, with her young run-away friend standing by her old pickup with it's radiator steaming away in the wind.

We ended up driving up along the northern California and Oregon coastline together, only "Michael" ended up in my car while two other hippie hitch-hikers rode with her young charge in the truck. We all camped together one night near Crescent City, California (the first time I ever was treated to bulgur wheat stew) where I gallantly loaned Michael my tent while I slept in my car. The next day was a very anxious one for me when the kids disappeared with the truck. I was stuck with Michael, wondering if I'd have to haul her all the way back to Missoula. At the end of a rather hectic afternoon search we finally came across them — seems they figured we'd find them rather than they find us. After bidding her and her run-away friend goodbye and a safe trip back to Missoula, I remember sleeping more soundly that night up on a lumbering trail on a deeply forested hillside in Oregon near the mouth of the Columbia River, not far, I guess, from where Lewis and Clark had spent a rainy winter in 1805. Next day I did the whole coast of Washington up to the Olympic Peninsula, camping overnight by a reservoir deep in the peninsula's rain forest, driving the next day up a mountainside to a closed ski resort but snowshoeing there a bit for exercise, before taking a ferry to Vancouver Island.

The "Hermits of Saint John the Baptist" were located on some property part way up the east side of the island. They were a number of men, most of whom seemed to have been former Trappist brothers – at least there was a pile of old dark brown Trappist brothers' habits in the corner of the main room of the guest house. I stayed there two nights, visiting with the Belgian Benedictine, Fr. Jacques Wenandy, who headed the place. They seemed to be a bit uncertain as to their future as a foundation, earning their livelihood being one of the problems. Several were to hire out as forest fire-tower watchmen. In parting, Fr. Wenandy gave me a printed copy of their rule of life and let me take one of the castoff Trappist brother's brown hooded scapulars as a kind of souvenir — or maybe as a reminder of where the Lord might be leading me. I took another ferry to the mainland, tried to find a gas-stove part in Vancouver, and then headed eastward back to the western edge of the Canadian Rockies then across the Canadian prairies back to Michigan.

I don't remember much of the rest of that trip other than knocking my Corvair's rear suspension out of line on a rough rail crossing in Saskatchewan and that one night I was hosted in an ancient looking little French-speaking Trappist monastery near Winnipeg. The rest of the time I guess I must have camped out.

My first meeting with the bishop when I got home was electrifying, to say the least. He asked me what I decided and when I told him I had not yet come to a decision, he told me that either I reach one soon or he'd decide for me; so I begged for two weeks grace. So two weeks later I went back and told him that I wanted to go to grad school to study theology. He told me that, although he had no need for another theologian in the diocese, he'd extend my leave so I could go to school. He also told me he wished I'd join the Jesuits or the Sulpicians — but regarding the last, since they had been dismissed from their charge in Michigan (the Bishop claimed they had left voluntarily, but I'd heard otherwise); I said that I could no longer see any point in that. He also offered to pay my health insurance (that year the diocese had finally gotten around to arranging some for its priests) but I declined the offer. I had decided I was ready to manage completely on my own, with no obligations to anyone. Besides, I had come to the conclusion that I wanted to try to teach in a secular, or preferably state college or university, much as had the Jesuit, Fr. John Hardon, who had taught at Western Michigan, with great, or as I was to learn later, much too great, success. But that is another story which belongs, if not to another year, to another phase of my life.

Following that second meeting with the bishop, I then retreated north to the Stella Maris cabin just to catch my breath and plan my next move, which was to begin contacting grad schools. But I was there only a few days (just a week or so after Robert Kennedy's assassination) when I received word of the sudden death of one of my cousins. She was only forty years old, a nurse married to a heart surgeon in Neenah, Wisconsin, and the mother of six children, all daughters. She had been struck down by a cerebral embolism. I drove to Neenah where after waking up very early in the morning I wrote a short piece (with Nogar's book very much on my mind) and delivered it at her funeral on the apparent irrationality of life and the plea of Albert Camus' — "If only the universe had a heart!" A number of people, especially some non-Catholics present, had apparently never heard anything quite like it in a church. Their favorable reactions seemed to confirm to me that I was on the right track at last.

Having already received a negative reply from Yale's divinity school, the trip back to Michigan was punctuated by quick stops at Marquette University in Milwaukee, the University of Chicago, and Notre Dame University. At the first two places I was told, like the replies from Yale and the University of Toronto, that I was far too late

Chapter 5

to apply for admission into a doctoral program beginning that fall and that I should apply again for the following year. But I knew I would not be given a year to wait — that it was either begin now or lose my chance.

The head of the theology department at Notre Dame University seemed to instinctively understand my predicament. He said that they could admit me to their doctoral program that fall on a "trial basis" based on my high marks in the seminary (crediting my Bachelor in Theology awarded by Catholic University of America for my studies at Saint John's Seminary as if were the equivalent of a Masters degree) and providing that I took and passed "pro forma" the standard GRE (Graduate Record Examination) test. So on my way home from there I stopped and talked to one of the priests in my own diocese who was in charge of the mission parish at Edwardsburg, just a few miles north of the Michigan-Indiana border and a scant dozen miles or so from the Notre Dame campus. The mission church not only had a small apartment attached, but would also provide me with weekend "work" that would help me pay for my tuition, groceries, and gas. Everything seemed to be almost miraculously falling into place!

I quickly made plans to take the GRE later in July at Michigan State University and secured a manual specifically designed to help one bone up for taking this test, which was designed not so much to give one answers but to hone one's skill on coping with the two or three hours of dealing with questions designed to test one's ability to do graduate level work. I immediately found out two things about my own ability. The questions designed to test one's reading skills were very easy. The questions designed to test one's mathematical skills were, for me at least, very tough. So I began to work very hard at my math, and the harder I worked at it, the worse my results. On top of that, I hadn't been at the task for a week when I received news that my remaining aunt in Vermont, my dad's younger sister, had died of a cancer that had spread much quicker than anyone expected. I very reluctantly decided I could not take the time to accompany him on a long drive east. Nor was I all that certain I'd make it through the GRE, so I also sent another inquiry to a theological grad school I'd heard about, the bilingual Universite' St-Paul/Saint Paul University in Ottawa, Canada, which apparently was looking for students and did not require passing the GRE — just in case.

Yet, in the midst of all this feverish activity, I still found myself longing for more solitude and contemplation and the worry that in opting to go to grad school, that I had (as I then recorded) "allowed myself to be panicked into a compromise, into a meaningless convention." I was also working on a "thesis" as I already termed it, a manuscript I called "Prayer and Process: A Venture into the Theology of Contemplative Prayer Based on an Evolutionary View of Man" (sic) — PC terminology not yet having reared its contentious head.

Meantime I took the GRE test, found the reading comprehension sections somewhat harder, but not impossibly so, than those of the test preparation manual and the math questions seeming much easier than the manual's ones. So I left the test hall somewhat confident I'd had at least done reasonably well. Later on I was to learn that while I had scored in the top 98 percentile in reading comprehension, that my math score was so marginal that I barely passed that part of the test. But as it turned out the whole exercise was futile, as a new head had been appointed for the theology department at Notre Dame and it appears that his first executive act was to throw all late applicants out of the program for that fall — even before they had seen the GRE test results. So almost immediately I tried to write to Saint Paul University in Ottawa but had to resort to a phone call there when the Canadian postal service workers went out on one of their frequent strikes. The school's dean assured me I'd be most welcome. He booked a room for me at the Oblate Father's "Residence Deschatelets" on campus and told me they'd expect to see me in the first week of September. So that was that.

Meanwhile, the storm had broken out over Pope Paul's "*Humanae Vitae*"—the so-called "birth control encyclical". In reflections I intended to possibly share with my bishop, I wrote that while, "because of my training and temperament" I personally tended "to agree with the decision and the reasoning behind it", but that "pastorally enforcing it" was something else. I saw the reluctance of many bishops and many bishops' conferences to press the issue as a sign of an inherent conflict between the doctrine of papal infallibility taught at the First Vatican Council (in 1870) and the concept of "collegiality" as taught by Vatican II. Again I'm not sure if I ever actually sent the letter to the bishop, but the topic of the church's teaching authority, much more than the issue which had prompted this crisis, continued to occupy my journal reflections for many pages (and as it turned out, for many years) to come.

But as for that particular issue, which has driven so many from the Church and which even now still divides it within, I think that the root of the problem has been the Church's (particularly its theologians') reliance on the Stoic tradition of "natural law" reasoning. It assumes that because we are, as Aristotle said, "rational animals", that somehow our rationality (which most philosophers and theologians stress above all) should have full control over our natural drives and instincts (of which bishops as pastors are more fully aware). Meanwhile, the whole problem has been compounded by the "Perfection of means and confusion of goals" which, as Einstein once observed, "...seem to characterize our age."

Looking back now, some fifty years later, that one year that I had spent in so many different places travelling from coast to coast in both directions, was, although rather inconclusive in its final outcome at the time, nevertheless one of the most decisive ones in my whole life. And although Bishop Zaleski had no clear idea as to what the outcome was going to eventually be – nor had I for that matter – I can only be grateful that he was understanding enough, and had enough faith in God, to leave me free to gradually find my own way. Had he "ordered me" back into full time parish work, I doubt that I would have lasted in the priesthood even for another year.

Chapter 6
Back to School Days

Through a mix-up of some sort, I seem to have arrived in Ottawa a few days early, a mistake which gave me a very lonely feeling, even though the "Anglo" (actually Irish-American) dean of students at the otherwise very French Université St-Paul tried to give me special attention the morning after I arrived from the long drive from Detroit. It probably would have helped a great deal if I had immediately found myself among my future classmates, but instead I spent the next few days alone lounging around the grounds of the Residence Deschatelets in the warm early September sun — especially where the east side of the small campus fronted the Rideau River. I had decided I'd better give myself a crash course on the philosophy and influence of Immanuel Kant. The Dean of Studies had decided, since my goal was to equip myself for teaching in a secular university, that my theological curriculum should concentrate on contemporary philosophical underpinnings, and from what I could remember of my college philosophy courses, especially the history of philosophy, was that everything in the great medieval philosophical tradition had begun, at least from the Church's point of view, to unravel with Kant.

To tell the truth, I was rather terrified. The dean had signed me up not only for a course on "Philosophical Problems in Evolution", but also for a course on Ludwig Wittgenstein (whom I'd never heard of) and his philosophy of "Linguistic Analysis". I was also going to follow that latter course with another on the Marxist aspects of the thinking of Jean-Paul Sartre. All of these were being taught by professors from the University of Ottawa's philosophy department, who were housed in the same classroom building as the Université St-Paul. In fact, the whole arrangement seemed to me to be a bit strange and perhaps needs to be explained.

The University of Ottawa was originally a Catholic institution run by the Oblates of Mary Immaculate, an order of priests who were very strong in Canada, especially in the mission fields serving the native peoples in the far north. However, with the growing ascendancy of French-speaking Canadians in the Ottawa area, and Canada's new emphasis on bi-culturalism, it was decided that Canada's capital city needed a truly bilingual and more or less secularized university, which in turn put the theology and canon (i.e., church) law departments in a rather awkward position, especially since these latter were already licensed to award degrees sanctioned by Rome. The solution was to create a somewhat separate institution affiliated with the University of Ottawa, in other words, a theological and canonical graduate school, throwing in, for good measure, a graduate program in "missiology" to specially train those priests and religious who were bound for work in the mission fields. Meanwhile, those clergy who remained as professors in other areas (such as the departments of philosophy, psychology, history or whatever) within the old University of Ottawa took off their Roman collars and sported neckties (as the local joking went) while the crucifixes came off the old school's downtown classroom walls.

Confusing as the setup seemingly was, it had distinct advantages for students like me. For one, courses that I took from U. of O's philosophy and religious studies department could be counted towards a theology degree at Saint Paul's. In fact, my program of studies would result in dual degrees being awarded, a Ph.D. from the University of Ottawa, and a S.T.D. (Doctor of Sacred Theology — which for obvious reasons I now prefer to abbreviate as S.Th.D.) from Saint Paul's as approved by the Vatican in Rome — a kind of "two birds with one stone" arrangement that was unique, as far as I know, at least on this continent. But at the same time, the "Roman connection" afforded another advantage in that Saint Paul's doctoral program was very much styled on the European model, with heavy emphasis on the dissertation and the research that goes into it, rather than on a lot of course requirements or classroom work. And unlike the U. of O's requirement of passing an entrance exam testing competency in French (or in English — depending on one's background), Saint Paul's was content to only assume that by the time one got into one's dissertation research, one would be able to do that research in whatever languages would be necessary, depending on one's topic. Since I was to work for a doctorate in theology, it was expected that I already had some Latin and Greek, along with some familiarity with Hebrew. But, thank the Lord; they did not require me to prove how much of these I remembered through any tests. And as for my competence in French — well, that was another matter I would soon have to face.

Meanwhile, I was amazed to learn that about two-thirds of my tuition was being paid by the Canadian government, but had I not been a priest (or a member of a religious order) the government would have paid a major portion of my living expenses as well! So even though I still knew practically no one there yet, I was already beginning to feel at home.

Yet I was still a bit fearful. Here I was, a Yankee in exile, soon to be surrounded, I thought, by men (and some women) whom I figured would be much younger than myself. I was now thirty-six and at a time when the slogan "Don't trust anyone over thirty" had become commonplace, and as a result, feeling quite middle-aged. I had also set myself a deadline. I was determined to complete my degree work by the end of my fortieth year.

Imagine my surprise when it turned out that there was to be a small, but very noticeable contingent of students at Saint Paul's who were around my age or even older. In fact, I remember one fellow, a Jesuit, who was pressing what we now think of as senior citizen status. As he explained it, the "Jebbies" had just kept him too busy teaching college theology courses all these years, and it was under the incentive of a new lay board of directors at his college that he had orders to either get a doctoral degree or retire. A Ph.D. (or its equivalent) was, just as the dean of studies at the University of Chicago had told me, one's "union card" — either one had it or could forget about being hired. Also there for the program was a Detroit area priest who had been teaching at the seminary where I had been. He too was somewhat older than I, as was a former Air Force chaplain, and quite a few other ex-patriot Americans. There was also a scattering of students from other countries, such as India and elsewhere across the globe.

But I was still nervous. Unlike Notre Dame, which was to have accepted me as having the equivalent of a master's degree in theology from my seminary days, even though technically I only had a Bachelor of Theology in addition to my college B.A., Saint Paul's required that all of us earn a Master of Theology or "S.T.L" (the "L" standing for "licentiate" — the Roman equivalent of a master's degree). This meant that all of us had to be able to pass an exam at the end of the year that might cover any one of some eighty-three theological propositions, ranging from proofs for the existence of God to the power of priests to forgive sin. So my fellow doctoral candidates and I decided we'd better set up some weekly study groups to bone up on all this stuff we'd once learned back in our seminary days but feared we'd do poorly in, particularly when one of the faculty members informed us that about three-fourths of the younger (and presumably more up-to-date) Saint Paul's seminary students, who had attempted to obtain the master's degree rather than simply be approved for ordination, had failed to pass the year before. Later on we learned that the percentage of failures was considerably lower — but by then we were suitably impressed with the school's seriousness. So I also decided I'd better do one thing more — and that was to review some of these basic theology courses by sitting in as an "auditor", that is, not to earn a credit, but simply to brush up on things, and also to get to know the professors a bit better before we faced them one-to-one or filled "blue books" for them as part of our comprehensive exams that coming spring. I even began sitting in on one professor's French language presentations as well as his English language ones. I'd take the notes that he handed out in his English language sessions and try to follow his lectures in his sessions given in French.

I also started tackling the job of learning to read the rest of Teilhard de Chardin's essays in the original French. Some of them had not yet been translated into English, but I started with those that had been first. I bought a small *Larousse French-English Dictionary* and went to work, translating the French word-by-word into English as best I could, and then comparing the results to the published English translations. The reason, of course, was that I was still determined that my thesis topic, whatever it turned out to be, was to be on some aspect of Teilhard's thought. I really still wanted to pursue that topic of prayer and contemplative life from a "Teilhardian" or evolutionary point of view, but in any case, I knew that even if I couldn't speak the language, I definitely had to know how to translate it. I didn't get very far that first year because of all the other distractions — like getting through those comprehensive exams.

And then there were those other philosophy courses I was taking — like the one on "Problems in Evolution" which kept me very much challenged. It turned out that the professor, an American ex-Dominican scholastic who had studied under Raymond Nogar (the same of *The Lord of the Absurd* fame) was also a fan of Jacques Maritain — who had been, of course, with his championing the great aristotlean-thomistic synthesis, a severe critic of Teilhard. And as for the course in linguistic analysis, we had a brilliant professor, who unfortunately, as far as we could tell, was really reading to us the manuscript of his soon-to-be published (and therefore not recordable or reproducible) book in refutation of Wittgenstein's early work — something I think most of us thought to be rather redundant, insofar as Wittgenstein himself repudiated his early work.

This same professor had also tried to talk me out of my fascination with Teilhard and get me into the "process philosophy" of Alfred North Whitehead instead. I tried to warm up to Whitehead, but found his language and style (as a mathematician turned philosopher) forbiddingly abstract compared to the concrete imagery used by the geologist-paleontologist turned philosopher-theologian Teilhard. It also seemed to me that Whitehead's philosophical reasoning was based too much on an analogy to quantum mechanics — something that still (being rather uneducated in contemporary physics) appeared to me to be a questionable theory at the time. Teilhard's speculations, at least, were based on irrefutable science.

New Friends

Early on in my new life as a grad student I began to visit the lay religious organization near Ottawa that I had heard about (from "Michael") when still out West. When one of my fellow students, a priest from southern Ontario told me that the "Madonna House Apostolate", as it was called, was probably the most influential new

Chapter 6

movement in the English-speaking Canadian Catholic Church, I thought I'd better investigate, and another classmate (a priest from Philadelphia) and I drove some 100 miles northwest of Ottawa to a little village called Combermere along the Madawaska River. There we found something that was truly amazing and unique. Here was a community of both women and men (including a few priests) all living a life of poverty, chastity, and obedience, not under formal ecclesiastical vows, but under "promises" made to the community and to God, first for a period of time, and then, eventually, for life. They lived simply and frugally, both from their farming and from donations, and much of what they produced or were given was in turn shared with the poor. Already they had started various missions along the lines of soup-kitchens and medical dispensaries in various cities through out North America and even in a several more exotic locations, like an island in the Caribbean known as Carriacou.

The most extraordinary thing about this group, at least as far as I was concerned, was their leader or foundress, a Russian-born woman whom her community members generally referred to as "the B" (for "Baroness"). Born near the beginning of the last century in Czarist Russia, Catherine Kolyskine had been educated among the elite of Saint Petersburg, was married at a young age to a cousin named Boris de Hueck (he was of partial Dutch ancestry). She was decorated for heroism during the First World War after she served with Russian troops as a nurse, only to have to flee Russia with her husband as the Bolsheviks and their supporters took out their fury on anyone who was connected with the old ruling class. And Catherine certainly was. Her father, of Polish ancestry, had served as an adviser to the Czar. Catherine had some of the Czar's daughters as schoolmates at an exclusive girls' academy in Petersburg. And before she and Boris had escaped (by jumping off a train near the border with Finland) she had lost a number of relatives to the Bolsheviks, and she herself had been shot through the hand by a drunken sailor on the streets of Saint Petersburg.

Catherine and her husband finally made it to England and then to Canada. By then they had a son whom they named George. However, their marriage fell apart and Catherine, with her son, ended up on her own. She eventually got a proper RN's certificate, but soon after found out she could do much better, with her booming voice and exotic Russian accent, on the lecture circuit. She also had many useful connections, especially through the Russian expatriate community in Paris and elsewhere. Then she had founded depression-era settlement houses in Toronto and Harlem and Chicago, causing quite a stir in each place, particularly after she remarried, this time to a well-known Chicago reporter named Eddie Doherty and her own community turned against her. So she and Eddie fled back to Canada, and again, this time to the backwoods of rural Ontario.

By the time I met her, both she and her followers had become something of an institution in their own right. Not only were young people from Canada and the USA joining her group, but some from overseas, as well as some priests and a even a few sisters from more established orders of nuns. The attraction was almost spell-binding for me. All these young people mixed in with older people of fascinating backgrounds. There was the blending of Catholic intellectuality with Orthodox spirituality, liturgies celebrated in both Western and Eastern rites, a life lived in solidarity with the poor, and yet deeply contemplative in orientation. I was to keep going back to Combermere, stopping there for long weekends on my way back to Michigan on holidays, or again in the summer for longer stays.

I also took on a spiritual director, as was the custom there. He was a former Trappist monk, now a member of that community. I would consult him regularly, especially after spending a day or two myself in *poustinia* — the Russian word for "desert" or a "hermitage". These small log cabins, equipped only with a wood stove, table and chair, a cot, a few blankets and a tea-kettle, were scattered around various locations on the community's property, to be used by community members and their guests for days of private retreat. One went there with only the clothes on one's back, a notebook, a jug of water, and a loaf of bread. As for reading matter, each cabin contained a Bible, and that was it — unless one was driven to reading scraps of old newspaper provided for lighting the stove. The "plumbing", as one might guess, like much of the facilities at Madonna House, was an outhouse. And as for the spiritual direction, I was definitely going to need it in the months and years to come. The reasons would soon be obvious.

One of the other people with whom I soon became acquainted was a young philosophy student who had, for some time been a seminarian in the building next door. He had left the seminary program several years previously and married a girl from his home state of New Hampshire. At the time I met him, he was the proud father of a little girl and was about to become a father yet again. He invited me to go out to visit him and his wife, and to share Thanksgiving dinner with them at their little cabin along the Gatineau River near the village of Wakefield, Quebec, some 30 miles north of Ottawa. I was glad to accept the invitation.

A week or so after that occasion, his wife went to the Ottawa General Hospital to have their second child. Things did not go well, and I went to visit her there, in fact, to bring her the sacrament of the sick. The child, a boy, was born successfully, but during the process of recovery she had somehow contracted an infection that almost killed her. What was to have been a very joyous occasion turned out to be a very trying time. However, she eventually recovered and returned home, and I began to visit them now and then. Meanwhile, especially on weekends, I more and more found myself at loose ends.

Yet another person I soon became acquainted with was a nun or (or more properly "sister"—because strictly speaking, all nuns live in cloistered convents) about my age from Western Canada who was also attending Saint Paul's. After awhile we started going out for dinner some evenings and soon found ourselves engaging in long talks about the future of the priesthood, of professional religious life, and of the Church. After several such conversations, something I'd begun to suspect became obvious, and that she was doubting her own vocation and that it was up to me, I thought, to save it. Too late it turned out. She announced she was planning to leave the sisterhood to marry a priest whom she later brought out to Wakefield to introduce me to. At that point he was waiting for his official "laicization" and dispensation to marry. But in a way I was very relieved. For the way I suddenly saw it (and I told her so) it was better him than me. In other words, I cared for her a good bit myself.

By then it had slowly become obvious that I still had a problem when it came to women. Still resolutely determined to remain celibate, at the same time I found myself more and more attracted to female company. Not so much in groups (I'd had more than enough of that in parish work and still plenty of it in my visits to Madonna House) but rather in the one-to-one intimacy of sharing confidences and exchanging insights.

Not that my work as a priest had not involved me in such direct person-to-person relationships, but it was always in the context of professional to layman (or in this case, laywoman), not the kind of exchange that goes on between equals or just friends. This was something almost but not quite completely new to me. But what was really new to me was the apparent freedom to have it develop into something more.

Much of my thought on the matter at this time was soon to be strongly influenced by my reading (and translating) of Teilhard de Chardin's essay "L'Evolution de la chastité"— an essay from the 1930s in which Teilhard expounded his own views on the evolutionary directions that he believed sexuality, if rightly understood, was likely to take. There was no question in Teilhard's mind about the value of religious celibacy or its power to elevate human spirituality to greater heights. This he believed was an aspect of human nature borne out by the history of religions around the world. What Teilhard objected to, however, was what he believed is the artificial segregation of the sexes from each other in order to make celibacy easier, especially during an age when the reproductive aspects of sexuality were becoming more and more problematic. As he saw it, the future value of religious celibacy could not be achieved by ascetic escapism, but only through the deliberate cultivation of the psychological and spiritual power latent in the attraction between the sexes. As he put it, "Man [i.e., humanity] approaches God not as a monad, but as a dyad"— that is to say as people whose full spiritual potentialities as woman or man cannot be realized except under the influence of each other.

I very much bought into this very rarified (and some would say naïve) view of sexuality and recognized in it what I had always been looking for in my relationships with women from way back. Not sex, that is, physical sexuality, but the psycho-spiritual potential contained in the complementariness of women to men or vice versa, or more exactly, between a particular man and a particular woman. Yet, at the same time, I also carefully tried to determine the exact boundaries that such a spiritual relationship demanded. For one, physical expressions of intimacy should be confined to what might be considered proper between brother and sister. For another, too much exclusivity should be avoided – thus any suggestion that one or the other person had exclusive rights over the other's friendship with anyone else. And finally (this from a letter of Teilhard's to a younger Jesuit), always pick a woman who is secure in her own vocation, be it as a wife or mother or professional woman — thereby insuring that you will be at most, only a treasured friend.

As I was to find out, it can't always be as simple as that. In looking back on my thinking at the time, it seems that I was still under that mistaken impression that women, while they generally appreciated affection, were really not so keen on having sex unless it was in their vital interest to do so. And I am afraid that my persistence in this ignorance (indeed, now it seems to have been what I preferred to believe) explains at least some of the exasperation and occasional angry outbursts that were deservedly directed at me. In fact, looking back at all that now, I'm inclined to believe that my enthusiastic espousal of Teilhard's evolutionary views of the future of sexuality served as a convenient cover for what amounted to, at least for me, a celibate ego trip. And for that I owe an apology.

But even aside from such monumental ignorance and self-centeredness, what will happen, as I soon found out, when your friend decides she no longer has a vocation, such as to religious life? Or what happens when another friend finds herself deserted by a husband who has decided that his real vocation is to be married to somebody else? I had already found out how vulnerable I was to the first eventuality. The vulnerability to the second wasn't to happen until about a decade and half later.

However, even then, this new discovery of the psychological

power of sexuality had brought on a renewal of what was still an on-going midlife crisis. I remember that during one of my stays at the priests' retreat house at Combermere being seized with the realization that even if I were to change my mind and leave the priesthood, or even to be married, marriage really would make no sense in my case for the simple reason that I had no desire to have children. And the reason for that was even more radical. It was (and still is) my conviction that Christianity holds out the promise and hope of eternal life, and that this hope is so central to Christian belief that, at least in my mind, to bring children into this world without that prospect of eternal life is irresponsible. And, add to that, if my decision to live a celibate life – whatever the less than ideal reasons I may have had for doing so – in any way continues to strengthen this hope and belief in the prospect of eternal life, then it is my God-given privilege and duty to do so.

Meanwhile I also had a lot of other things still left to sort out. By the middle of my second year at Residence Deschatelets I'd had it with the place. Not that it wasn't handy to school and inexpensive — with plenty of food to eat. In fact, there was, in one aspect in particular, the breakfasts, way too much variation, one morning it being Corn Flakes, toast, etc., the next, no Corn Flakes or toast, but French Canadian lumberjack style meat pot pie. Just try sitting through a two hour philosophy class with that in you while your stomach tries without too much success to find the right acids to digest all that! But most of all, the residence was under reconstruction, and the floors and wall foundations having been poured in concrete, required the use of jackhammers to make alterations. Just try concentrating on theology books amid that racket! So when the second semester of my second year came around, I decided to move out to live in the tiny priest's overnight accommodations that were part of the mission parish at Farm Point, Quebec. The priest who served the parish, an official from the Diocese of Hull (Msgr. Thierry), was glad to have an English-speaking priest help out on Sundays (there were normally two services, one in French, another in English) plus someone else who he could call on when he needed to be away on official diocesan business. And having successfully gotten through my preparation for the master's degree comprehensive exams with the help of that quiet, and the opportunity to take long hikes in the dense forests of the Gatineau hills, I decided to sever my connections with Residence Deschatelets and to move out to the Farm Point Mission when I returned in the fall.

The following school year went by very quickly. With the encouragement of and some coaching by the Rector of the Université St-Paul, Fr. Marcel Patry, I had agreed to attempt a doctoral dissertation on the subject of Teilhard's interpretation of the Pauline epistles in the New Testament. However, when I presented the project before the university board, they were very skeptical as to whether or not the subject had not already been sufficiently explored by other researchers and was instructed to revise my proposal, which I did, only to be told again that my proposal was not deemed to be all that promising. But by then I had already made plans to travel to Paris to do research at the "Fondation Teilhard de Chardin" where most all of his manuscripts, correspondence, etc. were stored, having decided that even if that particular dissertation project was not yet approved, that while in France I would dig up enough material to write a dissertation on one or two other aspects of Teilhard's thought that might possibly satisfy the board – which I found out later had rejected the dissertation proposals of several more of my classmates, one or two of whom had given up all hopes of ever earning their doctoral degrees.

Innocent Abroad Redux

Nevertheless, I was determined not to give up that easily and early in June of 1970 I caught a Caledonian Airways plane (one of two old Boeing 707s owned by the Glasgow Football Club) for an overnight flight from Toronto to London. It was a flight marked indelibly in my memory by two kilted lassies who seemed to spend most of the night trying to sell the passengers fifths of Scotch from a cart that neatly blocked the single narrow aisle and with that, passage to the restroom, and which I hope was not a contribution to the white knuckle landing we made in dense fog at Gatwick airport after circling London for an hour looking, in vain, for a break in the fog over any airport within reach.

After a couple of days in London, where I began my research by visiting the main Jesuit residence in London (Teilhard had done his theological studies at their college near Hastings in Sussex) and a quick visit to the British Museum, I caught a "boat-train" to Dover and took a ferry across the channel to Calais and caught another train to Paris. After a short stay at a place where I'd stayed with my seminarian friends a dozen or so years before, I was able, with the help of my former seminary (and ex-artillery captain) professor and spiritual director, Fr. Michel Baron, to find lodging with the Sulpician Fathers at 6 Rue de Regard, which was just across the street from a place where Teilhard had lived while he was a student at the Sorbonne or was teaching at the Institut Catholique. Since my purpose for being in Paris was to study at the archives of the Fondation Teilhard de Chardin, the connection was even more interesting, even providential, because early on, while living there, I became friendly with a young Mexican theology student. He wanted to practice his English and I needed to catch up on my Spanish, and we were both not very fluent, and especially I wasn't, to say the least, in French. When he learned of the nature of my research, he told me that one of his professors at the Institut Catholique was a Jesuit who had known Teilhard personally and he offered to try to arrange a meeting with him for me.

It was, looking back (though I even sensed it then) the break of a lifetime. It seems that the Fondation Teilhard de Chardin had been feuding with the Jesuits for two decades over the proper ownership of Teilhard's manuscripts. Teilhard had, on the advice of a fellow Jesuit, willed his manuscripts to the foundation which his non-Jesuit friends had set up, fearing that pressures from Rome would result in his writings, most of which were still unpublished, being destroyed after his death. The Jesuit order, on the other hand, claiming that none of their members (living under a vow of poverty) could properly own anything, held that his writings were not something that could be bequeathed (except to the order itself). French civil law, of course, did not agree. So the Jesuits were jealously guarding the little bit they had — which consisted of his private notebooks and precious little else.

Chapter 6

But the good Fr. LeBlond did fix up things for me so that after almost two months of laboriously copying typewritten manuscripts by hand (or smuggling them out of the archives during lunch break and locating a photocopier that didn't cost 1 Franc per copy) I moved to the former Jesuit Novitiate at Chantilly to study Teilhard's personal notebooks from the last ten years of his life. His earlier ones were left either in the possession of his relatives when he was ordered to do paleontological work in China, or had disappeared with his personal effects when he had left China at the end of World War II and the Communists took over before he could return.

The Chantilly place was a wonderful vacation time retreat from the city — and besides, everyone who can leave Paris in August deserts the place. The Jesuit "Centre Cultural" (as they now termed the place once there were next-to-no new novices after Vatican II) was a huge rambling mansion that had once belonged to the Rothschild banking family, with a Jesuit-built dormitory, refectory, and library attached. It was said that the Rothschilds had given the place to the Jesuits out of gratitude for the number of Jews the French Jesuits had saved from the Nazis. Probably they didn't even want to see the place again, for the Nazis had previously erected barracks and dug bomb shelters on the property after Reichsmarschall Herman Göring had made the place into the headquarters for all the western air operations of Germany's Luftwaffe.

My mentor in deciphering Teilhard's notebooks was a Jesuit by the name of Fr. Christian d'Armagnac, who also seems to have known Teilhard some before his death. D'Armagnac had reputedly been in the French underground. But despite his help I was frustrated by French ways. There was a librarian from Notre Dame University in the USA who was busily photocopying all the Chantilly archives, a lot of stuff dating back centuries or so. I talked to him about photocopying Teilhard's "Journals" and he fairly jumped at the chance. So then I went to d'Armagnac, but it was no go. Apparently they were still afraid something would get out that would embarrass them, some further Teilhardian heresy or the like. Later on, I was to run into the same problem when it came to publishing my dissertation. I ended up having to paraphrase Teilhard's journal entries but never directly quote them. (Recently I have learned that those notebooks have finally been microfilmed and that a copy is available to scholars for study at the Woodstock Library at Georgetown University in Washington, DC.)

When I was done with my researches in France, I decided to travel a bit with the few weeks I had left over before my flight returned to Canada. I'd already taken a few weekends off to spend time with my old seminary professor visiting at the ancient Abbey of Fleury where he had spent some time before joining the Sulpicians, and again with him and his family near the ancient cathedral town of Chartres. Two other weekends I spent at Jean Vanier's "L'Arche" community at Trosly near Compiègne near the border with Belgium. Vanier, a Canadian and son of a former Governor General of Canada, had a doctorate in philosophy from the Institut Catholique, but had set aside a promising career as professor and had dedicated himself to the service of the emotionally disturbed and mentally retarded and had begun directing retreats, even while still a layman. I had recently attended one of his retreats that he gave near Ottawa.

Near Trosly there were the ruins of a country home where Teilhard had reputedly spent some time between bombardments at the near-by World War I battle-front. Wandering through the woods near there I could see the remains of old battle trenches. During this visit I became much more aware of Europe's long history of bloody wars, and, I must say, critical of America's readiness to think that every major world problem can be settled by the use of armed force. Even Teilhard, who had heartily embraced the idea that the First World War was "the War to End all Wars", was very skeptical that the Second World War, which he lived through during the Japanese occupation of China, would ever change much unless people themselves and the political structures which served mostly their selfish interests, were willing to change. In fact, I even had joined other American students in a protest demonstration in front of the U.S. Embassy in Ottawa just before I left for France.

In addition to that, while in Paris, I was told by a Vietnamese Catholic priest who had served U.S. forces, that as far as he and his countrymen were concerned, the USA was probably doing more damage than the Communists ever could. When I returned home that fall I let the White House know about it. In return I received a pile of position papers from the State Department explaining how the Vietnamese didn't realize what was for their own good.

After visiting a cousin who was in the U.S. Army and stationed near Mons, Belgium, I stopped by the University of Louvain where I found out that if my dissertation project was shot down one more time in Ottawa, they'd be very happy to take me in there — with no need to take but one more class. This was a relief, since I had left Ottawa without any insurance that my topic (or any of the two alternatives I was toying with) would ever be accepted when I came back. One cannot help but wonder how things may have turned out for me had I been forced to move to Belgium that fall. Instead, after a week spent riding trains in Denmark and Sweden and hiking, boat and train-riding and even hitch-hiking in Norway, and more of the same for another week in Scotland, I caught the "Flying Scotsman" for London, hoping to get off the train for a few hours to visit the ancient city of York. I saw its famous cathedral towers in the distance, but the train didn't even slow enough except to grab a mailbag off a post as it went by. Soon after I was winging back over the Atlantic and seeing icebergs floating on the ocean's surface as we approached the barren coast of Labrador.

Back in Canada

This time I was able to convince the review board that I had dug up enough new material that would make a dissertation on Teilhard's use of the Pauline scriptures truly worthwhile. However, one professor still remained highly skeptical, but went along with the rest of the board, confiding to me that if nothing else, he admired my persistence. By then it seemed that not just a few, but about half my fellow students in the doctoral program had given up after having their projects shot down so many times. Since I would be taking only a couple of courses during this school year and spending a lot more time lining up all my new material for my thesis adviser's approval, I decided to move back out to Farm Point, but learned, to my dismay, that the good monsignor had decided to loan out the residence to

Back to School Days

another student priest, but one who could celebrate the Sunday Masses in both French and English. So there I was back in school, but with no place to live.

Then my young friends out in Wakefield came to my rescue and arranged for me to stay in a ski chalet next to their cabin that belonged to a fellow and his wife who wanted only to use it on some weekends — and that I could bunk at my friends' place if and when that happened. All I had to do to earn my keep was to pay for the fuel oil to keep the chalet warm and to contribute grocery money to my friends, since the plan was that I'd take my main meals next door.

It was great at first. There was a beautiful view of the Gatineau River with a covered bridge spanning it just a quarter mile away. I also accepted an invitation to become a "chaplain" for a ski resort five miles up the road, where in exchange for my services on Sunday morning, I had a year's pass to go skiing whenever I wished. Two or three days a week I went into Ottawa for a class or two or to spend time in the library. The rest of the time I wrote, studied, hiked, or skied, and spent a lot of time with my friends in these picture post-card surroundings. And then everything started to go wrong.

First, my friend came down with mononucleosis and had to be hospitalized. Next, the infamous "October Crisis" hit Canada when the Quebec liberationists kidnapped a few important people near Montreal, murdered one of them, and the whole of Canada was put under martial law. At that point I began serving as surrogate man of the house and courier for tapes dictated by my friend from his hospital bed for his philosophy classes both in Ottawa and a hundred miles up-river in Pembrooke. I remember being a bit apprehensive one gray November afternoon in their VW van, a camper with not much window space and Quebec plates, as his wife and kids and I drove past some embassies where Canadian Armed Forces guards stood with rifles and fixed bayonets. I wondered how we would explain ourselves if stopped and searched. But apparently it was mostly for show. Most of the "Canadiens" I talked to around Ottawa thought their cousins in eastern Quebec had gone nuts.

But that wasn't all. Next, the water line froze up into my chalet, then, as that winter became ever more ferocious, the water line to my friends' cabin as well. We were reduced to melting snow in the bathtubs so that we would have enough water handy to flush the toilets. We hauled spring water from a highway-side spring across the river to have cooking and drinking water. For showers, they went to friends' places in town and I sneaked into the facilities at Residence Deschatelets or in the college building itself (there used to be residential rooms on the third floor before they had been turned into offices). By spring, when the accumulated 3 to 4 feet of snow had finally melted, and the water lines began to work again, I'd had enough of living in Quebec, and so also my friends, who were now expecting their third child and who had to move elsewhere to some other university where he could begin work on his doctorate.

During my fourth year of graduate studies, I would be taking no classes, so I decided to embark on an experiment. My spiritual director at Combermere, who had decided to finish his doctorate in scriptural studies, was due to go to Rome and then to Jerusalem. So I was going to live in his hermitage (which was actually an old farm house) along with another young priest who was seriously thinking about joining the Madonna House Apostolate — much as I already started to consider doing myself. The plan was for me to spend mornings in the hermitage writing my dissertation, while he would return afternoons to be alone while I worked with the community. I would travel to Ottawa and back approximately every two weeks or so to see my thesis advisor, depending when I had another chapter or so done. I also took a week off to travel down to New York to attend a three-day conference at the Riverside Presbyterian Church and Union Theological Seminary. It was sponsored jointly by the American Teilhard Association and another group representing Whiteheadian "Process Theologians". On the way down I stayed again at the Mount Savior Benedictine Abbey near Elmira one night and remember thinking how strange was this womanless community to me after two months of residence at Madonna House. I was more than ever convinced Teilhard was right.

But a week later, shortly after my return to Combermere, everything changed for me again. My mother called me with the news that my father, who was newly retired for about a year, had just suffered a very serious heart attack. Could I possibly come home?

Of course; how could I refuse? I hastily packed up and returned to Michigan, assuring my thesis director that I'd see him every month or so with another chapter or two written at home. As things calmed down at home and my father began his slow recovery, I also arranged to stay, during trips back to Ottawa, with a priest-professor friend of mine with whom I'd made arrangements to stay when things got too complicated in Wakefield the year before. So then began a long period of writing at home, then a summer of writing up at the Stella Maris cabin with another couple of trips to Ottawa, and finally, at the end of Christmas break, my thesis or dissertation defense in front of a board comprised of professors from both the University of Ottawa and Université St-Paul. It didn't earn me any *summa cum laude*, but they did recommend that I try to get it published, as I guess they'd gotten their wish — a piece of work that truly covered new ground, yet, as so many works are, questionable as to be worth ever repeating again. Once I had finished navigating through this academic minefield, I never wanted to see (much less write) another footnote again as long as I live. But that was not a promise that I've succeeded in keeping.

The Aftermath

Now what to do? Actually, I already had a job – well, sort of. I had been approached about the possibility of taking over the Catholic chaplaincy for Lansing Community College, but not sure that was what I really wanted to do — was I earning these degrees just for prestige or to actually teach? So I ended up insisting on working part-time, teaching philosophy for the humanities division of that same college. It was an up and coming, and very attractive looking group of buildings just a block or two north of the state capitol building and just a block away from the cathedral where I had been ordained. I had hardly expected to end up right under the bishop's nose after being told four years previously that he had no use for another theologian in the diocese. And so there I was, even though I had agonized for quite a period while still in school over whether I really ever wanted to return to Michigan, or at least to the Diocese of Lansing. Meanwhile, my father's precarious health had more or less decided things for me.

Chapter 6

Besides that, the schools in Ontario where I also had gone job-hunting were not interested in any more Americans on their staffs, especially since they had lost many of their more prominent people to higher-paying jobs south of the border. Finally, I turned down the possible offer of a college seminary teaching post in Seattle, as the pay was so low that I would have used it all up in just air-fare for two or three visits home. So I felt kind of stuck and gladly took what was offered close by.

That summer I also took a job as temporary chaplain to the mother house of the Sisters of Saint Joseph at Nazareth Michigan, just outside Kalamazoo. It was for the most part in exchange for the help of their French professor in making sure I had accurate translations of Teilhard's writings for quotes in the published version of my thesis, which was now to be re-titled *Teilhard, Scripture, and Revelation: A Study of Teilhard de Chardin's Reinterpretation of Pauline Themes.* The original dissertation was more or less bi-lingual, with my text in English but with all the quotes in the original French.

At that time, however, Nazareth College was undergoing its own difficulties. They had decided to go co-ed after many years of being strictly a women's college offering majors in nursing or in liberal arts. Yet with three other colleges near by (Western Michigan University and Kalamazoo College, and the then new Kalamazoo Valley Community College) things were not going well for the sisters little institution. The sister who had been president of the college up until then decided it was time to step down. So when the president of the congregation (that is, the chief officer of the Sisters of Saint Joseph) told me at lunch one day that they were looking for a new college president and asked me if I'd be interested, I laughed and said that as someone who could barely keep my own check-book balanced she'd have to be kidding. And that was that.

Since then I've often thought about that encounter and wondered if it wasn't one of the big lost opportunities of my life, as I think she was serious, or just possibly so. As it turned out, they did find a new president, a layman who decided that a big new gymnastics and sports building would attract young men to the campus. So they built the gymnasium, but this "field of dreams" plan didn't work. The college folded a few years later and I think back and say, "Well, at least if I had agreed to the job they probably would have saved a lot of money." As one adverse to mixing sports with academia, I would have saved them all that trouble and expense.

Instead, I continued to plug on with my part-time teaching jobs, three years at Lansing Community College, another year, simultaneously at Olivet College (a small Congregationalist College not far from Lansing), helping out at parishes on weekends, and periodically going around to the various state university humanities and religion departments (those that had them) looking for a full time job.

The responses were varied and interesting. Some years before, Western Michigan University had hired the Jesuit Fr. John Hardon as a professor of religion, but had to endure a lot of criticism when Hardon's classes proved extremely popular and Hardon began personally receiving students into the Church. He had also caused quite a stir in the local diocese by by-passing the Catholic college chaplaincy in the process. But I had to admit that Hardon was an excellent teacher, as I had taken two courses from him in Ottawa, and found him to be the best-organized professor I had ever had.

Nevertheless, after that, the staff at Western Michigan University was quite obviously not going to even dare to consider hiring me no matter how much I tried to guarantee them I'd never repeat their ousted professor's evangelistic crusade. But it also seems that "the Hardon experience" had put most of the other state universities on guard. At another state university I was quizzed closely as to whether I'd ever involve myself in pastoral work. I told the department chairman that it would only be in dire or temporary emergencies. The chairman, who was an ordained minister himself, I think, believed me, but it seems no one else was willing to take a chance. At another smaller state college I was told I was ideal for one of two positions that were opening up, but, unfortunately, one call was for an orientalist (Asian religions) and another requirement — not openly stated but, as I was told, understood — was that one of the positions had to be filled by a woman. So somewhat mischievously I wrote down the name of an Asian woman whose name I had found on a theological convention interview list and sent it to the department chairman. I suppose I could have sued on the charge of gender discrimination, but by then I had fairly well figured out what the real problem was and that had I resigned from the priesthood my chances of landing a full-time job at a state university would have been considerably better.

However, I didn't give up entirely. At Michigan's most prestigious university (U. of M.), I was invited to offer a course on Teilhard's thought in evening lectures in a new "program" (but not a department) of religious studies. But this was only on condition that I could raise my own salary with the industrial or other philanthropic powers that be. So I approached the president of Chrysler Motors (who happened to be at that time, a member of my parents' parish) and he tried to work, through his company's philanthropic office, on influencing the university board a bit, and the whole thing blew up in my face. It seems the engineering school was about to hit Chrysler for a big donation and here was Chrysler's representative questioning the board as to why this particular university was the only state university in Michigan that did not have its own full and fully-funded department of religious studies. The head of the program called me at my folks' home and let me know in no uncertain terms that I had really messed things up for him. But still, he managed to keep his job and I had, after all, only done what he had asked me to do, and that was, to quote his own words, "to rock the boat a bit."

Meanwhile, after my father suffered a second heart attack, I decided I'd better move out of the Lansing area and be closer to Detroit, so I took a post as chaplain at Mercy College of Detroit. Another ex-women's college, it had expanded its programs into those which might be much more attractive to men. There I felt rather frustrated by being a chaplain, but not on the teaching staff as such, so that spring I went into the college president's office to resign and was told that their plans were to drop me anyway — in other words, I'd been fired (although I preferred not to think of it that way). My only consolation was that they had decided they could do without a full-time chaplain. (I'm not sure it was because they figured I was irreplaceable or useless — or both!) And as far as I know, I was the last one they ever had. (Eventually, in 1990, Mercy College merged with the formerly all male Jesuit run University of Detroit to become the University of Detroit Mercy, which presumably has solved any problem finding suitable chaplains.)

I also had begun to live with my father at home after my mother suffered a completely disabling stroke that left her paralyzed and speechless. Now added to my duties were visits to a nursing home at least four days a week. I did continue to teach at Mercy College part-time, and began to teach part-time at Madonna College in Livonia as well, conducting courses ranging from philosophy, to psychology, to psychology of religion, to who knows what. I began to realize that if you have a Ph.D. and are still willing to work on the cheap, they will just about ask you to take on anything. At the same time, I also began to think of higher education as a kind of competitive industry where courses and whole programs are designed mainly not to truly educate, but to keep people coming and paying tuition so that teachers and administrators can earn a living.

I think the major crisis came when I was asked by Mercy College to teach a night course on philosophy to a group of Detroit policemen who had enrolled in a program leading to a degree in law enforcement. They were mostly on the youngish side of middle-aged white males, and looking back on it now, given the prevalence of firearms in our society, generally terrified by their work. Trying to teach them any ethics, particularly regarding the use of lethal force against law-breakers, seemed like a lost cause.

I began to realize that not only was I getting tired of this (not of more normal college students so much as the whole academic enterprise) but that I was getting cynical about the whole thing. Not a good sign! Much as I had during my days up in Lansing, I began dreaming of a little cabin in the country some place. Some place just to pray, meditate, write, and live a simple life.

That same winter, during the Christmas-New Year school break, I decided to make an eight-day retreat with the Jesuits at the Columbiere Center outside Pontiac, Michigan. Such retreats are a condensed and extremely intensive version of the normally thirty-day long Ignatian Spiritual Exercises. I had planned to make the thirty-day version a summer or two before in Guelph, Ontario, but the repeated heart-problem with my dad had forced me to cancel that. So now I decided to make up for it. It was, in a way, very decisive for me. And it was not easy. The retreat master, a former philosophy professor himself, pronounced me the "most controlled" (I presume he meant self-controlled) person he'd ever attempted to direct. I knew that, as many people had as much said to me, at different times in my life, that "I lived in my head." The retreat master was determined to break that down with the help of the Ignatian method and I can remember, at least one evening, of practically breaking out in a cold sweat. I now saw my life half-finished and began to wonder what I really had to show for it all. I reviewed my relationships with women, particularly that with my mother, and also began to admit to myself that it was also my ties with my father that perhaps were constricting me even more and that I had been wrongly blaming my mother for this.

In fact, I had gone to a Catholic psychiatrist the year before a few times to deal with this problem, and when after a few sessions, he wanted me to start seeing a woman psychiatrist, I backed away, sensing that she'd soon demolish my excuses or defenses – and who knows what might happen to me after that?

Likewise, while on this retreat, I also realized that I must face the fact that my chances of ever being hired as a full time "Professor" (even if my students occasionally addressed me by that title) or even as a full—time "adjunct" instructor, were practically nil. When I had approached the religion department at Mercy College, figuring that I at least maybe had some chance of being taken on there full-time, the head of that department, a layman, told me frankly that in his opinion, I seemed to be more cut out or qualified to teach in a graduate or post-graduate level school. It turned out that he was also hoping to find such a position as well. I wished him lots of luck!

So while still on retreat, realizing that probably half or more of my life had already passed without my having reached what was, at best, only a temporary goal, I made another decision, and that was to quit teaching for a year, retreat to the north woods for a long winter in solitude, and to write a book. So while I still had hopes of being hired as a full-time professor someplace, I also began to realize that it was probably mostly to be able to say that I had held such a position before I up and quit to do what I really felt called to be doing.

Accordingly, beginning in late summer, as I could hardly wait to get started, I moved back up to the Stella Maris cabin and began to live again, what was, in my mind, a totally new life. Of course, I had interruptions, fall being hunting season and with another half-dozen priest members still being hunters at the time, but once deer season was over I had uninterrupted solitude, except for a twice-monthly jaunt home to see my father and to visit my mother in the convalescent home. And I wrote and I wrote. I set up my typewriter on a table in the cabin's chapel, not too far from the oil space heater, as much of the time I was too busy to feed the fireplace. I wore felt snowmobile boot liners on my feet to protect me from the cold tile-covered concrete floor, and when one pair of liners got cold, I put them on top of the oil stove to warm them up and put on the warm pair that had been on the stove. I ate mostly pancakes, apples, venison chili and Civil Defense Corps "Emergency Crackers"— old soda crackers that had been hermetically sealed to store in bomb shelters during the height of the cold war. And I finished the first draft of my book on *Evil and Evolution*, a book which, I think, shows more passion than anything else I have written in my life. However, I still was not sure what God really wanted from me, especially as long as both my parents were still alive.

Then word came to me that Saint John's Provincial Seminary needed, at least for a year, a part-time theology instructor. At last, I'd get a chance to teach what I'd been at least partially trained for and, this at the school (my alma mater) where a former rector had warned me, some years prior, that the board of directors (the bishops of Michigan) would never agree to my being hired because of "my specialty" — that is, my specialty in the thought of Teilhard de Chardin. The subjects were to be "Christian Anthropology" the first semester and "Christology" the second — both strong interests of mine. I approached the task with enthusiasm. But even though I had been warned by my predecessor, a priest from my own diocese who had landed a job at university out west, I soon found it very troublesome work. Part of it was the range of students. Now that its courses were open to women, there were a few of them scattered through the audience of still mostly young men. But there was an obvious difference. Most of the women, except one who already was an ordained Protestant minister of some sort, were there for a theological education, one that could prepare them for the priesthood, but which was rapidly becoming evident would remain closed to them within the Catholic Church. This situation left something of a chip on the shoulder of a few of the female students, which made for some tensions in the classroom.

Yet this was not the major problem I faced there. The seminarians, with a few exceptions, seemed not all that keen on learning anything that didn't fit with their preconceived notions of what theology should be like. They seemed particularly upset by my throwing theological problems to them to wrestle with — like how to think of the human consciousness of Jesus — rather than just to be able to be content with repeating the answers they thought should be found in the text book.

Then there was one seminarian who was something less than honest. I had asked them to pick topics for a term paper and to let me know what it would be. Several weeks later this particular fellow came to me and asked if he could change his topic. I should have known better by then, but from future priests, I expected better. What he handed in a few weeks later was all too obviously a paper he'd done back in college. I suppose I should have flunked him on that basis, but what real proof did I have? So I just gave him a rather mediocre grade for a mediocre paper and let it go at that. Years later I heard that a certain young priest was causing some problems in the Detroit Archdiocese. I forget exactly what the problem was, but I hadn't forgotten his name.

In fact, one of the things that really made me upset later on, when my appointment was not renewed for the following year and a nun was hired in my place, was that I was never once invited to attend a faculty meeting where these kinds of problems should be addressed and where, if students are unhappy with an instructor, some help and suggestions might be given. In fact, at every other school where I had taught (and by now I could count close to a half-a-dozen) it was expected that all faculty, including part-timers, would be present at faculty meetings. I credited this omission to the fact that seminary faculties, at least on the theological level, have to pass on the suitability of their students for ordination, and that perhaps a part-timer, particularly because he or she is not part of the resident faculty, is not in a position to know everything that one should. But still, I think that even this part-timer could have identified at least one of their candidates as a cheat.

Later that year (1978), on August 12th, my mother died, and not long after, so did Pope Paul VI. My mother's death was for me, something of a relief, partly because during the last six months of her life, after what appeared to be a second stroke, every waking hour was for her a continuous time of trial. Late one night, when I was called out to the convalescent home because they thought she might be dying, I administered the oil of the sick and told her, because the corridor light shining on her eyes was obviously bothering her (they had her out there because her room was being repainted) that she'd better get used to all the light because we've been told there is a lot of it where she was headed. She gave me a big smile. Unfortunately she had to suffer some more months before her release. And while I am highly dubious about thinking of a time in purgatory after we die (how can there be time in eternity or timelessness?) I'm sure that she went through it all ahead of time.

This left me alone now with only my father to think about. For all his anguish over her condition, her absence left a big gap in his life. He began to pester me (or at least remind me rather often) about when we might get started in building a northern or rural retreat center of some sort. I had shared with him my growing idea that small, informal retreat centers with hermitages or *poustinias* available to people for a few days or weeks at a time could be a boon to the Church, and with his love of using tools and making things out of wood (certainly a odd choice for a metallurgical engineer) he was now raring to go. He even called in a real estate agent or two to have the house evaluated so we'd have a better idea of how much we could afford by way of property. We even made several scouting trips together to northern Michigan to look at a few places that sounded promising, and corresponded with a zoning board representative or two in various counties. I'd also taken my father to visit the Madonna House community in Combermere, and he came away from there very much impressed — particularly with "the B", who even doted on him a bit.

Meanwhile, I had taken another part-time teaching job, this time at Saint Mary's College at Orchard Lake, Michigan, a college affiliated with the "Polish seminary" named after Saints Cyril and Methodius. This college also had opened its doors to women — bringing with it something of the same problems, though not quite so severe as what I'd seen at Saint John's, because on the college level, the distinction between the ordination-bound and those who were not was not so evident. And there was a cheater, and again, I believe he was again one of those aiming for the priesthood. But this really didn't shock me, because even when I was back in the seminary, there was always a fellow or two who complained that all he thought he really needed to know was "how to pour the water on the baby's head." It seems that human nature really isn't all that different, whether one is talking about ditch-diggers or future parish priests.

During that spring break my father and I decided to drive to the Washington DC area to celebrate Easter with one of my cousins and his family who lived across the Potomac near Great Falls, Virginia. On the way down, we went out of our way to stop in western New Jersey and visit with a diocesan priest who had started a retreat center very much like what I had in mind — a main house and chapel with little hermitage cabins arranged all around. He gave each of us a cabin to stay in overnight, but before we left, he confided to me that if I was really planning to live in solitude and write on theology and other such subjects, he'd advise me not to get into what he was doing. This was because, in his opinion, that I'd end up spending most of my time counseling and in spiritual direction, and not in what I originally intended to do. I don't think I said anything to my father about what this priest said.

As it turned out, I really didn't have to. We'd only been back home a few days, and I went over to Saint Mary's College to teach my first class after the Easter break when I got a call from my dad that he was stranded on the other side of town with our second- (or really third-) hand International Scout, an aging 4WD machine we'd bought in anticipation of moving out to the country. I had taken our new VW diesel Rabbit to school, so I said for him to be patient and I'd get over to where he was as soon as class was out. So I drove home and over to the garage. The Scout had quit about a block from the garage that he liked to take his car to, but the people at the garage had refused to help him since he didn't have an appointment and the place was full. We got home for a late lunch and afterwards he told me he didn't feel well. I suggested that we go to the hospital to have him checked out. He said he'd go upstairs to take a nap instead, but about twenty minutes later he came down and said I was probably right. So I took him to Beaumont Hospital in Royal Oak (where he'd been many times before) and admitted him to emergency. Then I told him I thought he would be OK and said I was going to drive over to that garage to consult with them about what should be done with the Scout.

But I didn't. Instead I sat in the waiting room reading and telling myself that he really would be OK, but after an hour I got anxious and walked up to the counter to ask how he was, when just then an intern walked out to tell me they had lost him and took me into the main part of the emergency room to show me his body. And — would you believe?— I had even carried the oil of the sick with me. So it seems I had a premonition that this could be the end, and yet, when it happened, I was out in another room denying what was actually taking place! As I see it, it was a case of denial pure and simple, and to me, next to unforgivable. They say that each of us dies alone, whether there are people, even loved ones, standing around or not. But some how I've never been able to forgive myself with that excuse!

My cousin (the one who I considered a brat back when we were kids) but by then a nurse of many years experience, tried to console me, telling me that she felt many people preferred to die alone in order to spare their loved ones the grief of seeing them go. Perhaps, but the only way I can think of making up for it is for myself, when my time comes, to die alone. I pray that God will grant me that wish.

I remember that day, April 19, 1979, was also a day of a partial

Chapter 6

eclipse of the sun. I had carried my camera equipment to school to snap a few pictures of the eclipse between classes. I remember doing so, but I could never remember what happened to the film. Perhaps it is just as well, because even without that record of that particular eclipse, it has remained the darkest day of my entire life.

After that, grief racked me for some time. I found myself getting angry with people; especially those whom I had felt had slighted me in my professional life. But at the same time I also felt guilty, not only for having walked out on my father on his death bed, but for also feeling strangely free to determine my future without regard to any obligations that I had felt toward my parents. Meanwhile I kept a bit of advice from one of my old Cincinnati friends who warned me that, according to Freud, the death of ones father is apt to be the most significant – in my case, traumatic – event in any man's life.

Although I decided not to do anything rash or at the spur of the moment (people were already inquiring about my folks' small, but picture-perfect little Cape Cod style house), I decided on several things. I decided to follow the advice I have often given others after the death of a loved one – which is not to make any big decisions for at least a year. So through the rest of 1979 and the first half of 1980, I continued to live at home and to teach wherever I could. Then when that one year period had ended, I made the following decisions. First, I would rent the house out for the coming winter. Second, I would take a long delayed driving trip to Alaska and back — something my dad and I had always planned to do from the time of Fr. Hubbard's lecture in Cincinnati but for one reason or another had never gotten around to doing. Third, I would go back to the Camaldolese Hermitage in Ohio for a good long stay to see if God was really calling me there. And fourth, I would finally get around to taking a long-delayed trip to the Holy Land. I figured that if I ended up in a Camaldolese hermit's cell, at least I wanted to see these two distant spots on earth before they shut me in for good.

Chapter 7
A Last Fling

Episode One: Alaska or Bust

During the summer of 1980, I began to make preparations for my long journey to Alaska and back. My first job was to convert the little Volkswagon Rabbit diesel 2-door hatchback into a "camper" of sorts. I removed the front right passenger seat entirely and built a plywood platform to extend over the flat space extending from the rear hatch door when the rear seat back was folded down all the way forward to the dash board— enough to provide me with about six and a half by two and half feet of sleeping space. I also built a small folding table that could be set up in the rear hatch to be used for cooking and eating under the protection of the open rear hatch door, and then found a large army surplus mosquito net that could be draped, if necessary, over the whole rear hatch opening, table, stove, and folding stool. Under the extended sleeping platform I stored a hand-winch, trench shovel, hatchet, and various other tools. Crosswise, behind the driver's seat I made space for my rifle, fishing rod and tackle box. On top of the platform was a 4" thick sponge-rubber sleeping pad, and the rest of the space was filled with various other luggage, including sleeping bag, hiking boots, hip-boots for fishing, cameras, maps, books, and various other things. Up front I built a screen to protect the grill and headlights from rocks and gravel. And my neighbors' outfitted me with a T-shirt inscribed with motto "Alaska or Bust!"

Having contracted two local parochial school teachers to house-sit" the place while I was gone, I set off several days before the beginning of the long Labor Day weekend that marked the beginning of the school year and spent part of that weekend at a cousin's summer cabin in northern Minnesota. Then I resumed the journey on Labor Day itself, crossing the border into Manitoba just west of the Lake of the Woods, skirting one side of the city of Winnipeg and heading WNW directly towards Dawson Creek, Alberta, where the Alaska Highway begins. After camping out in a provincial park in Saskatchewan one night (the only night I ever did end up using the huge mosquito net) I ended up staying at the Madonna House Apostolate mission in Edmonton trying to sleep off a nasty cold I'd picked up at my cousin's place. I'd also forgotten that my gasoline camp stove no longer worked (it had given me trouble years before on my return from Arizona) so I replaced it with a small propane unit I bought at a Simpson-Sears store. I also bought a copy of John McPhee's book, *Going to the Country;* his account of Alaska and its people. The men at the Madonna House mission were most accommodating to this sick traveler on top of their usual soup-kitchen clientele.

After several days in Edmonton I resumed my journey, leaving the rolling prairies of Canada's great wheat belt, with its gorgeous "big sky" and little towns, many with onion-dome topped steeples of Ukrainian Catholic or Russian Orthodox parish churches for the sharp rise of the Canadian Rockies whose long alpine valleys cradle the route of the Alaska Highway. My routine along the way was to rise early, say my "office" (the prayers required of clerics each day), celebrate the Eucharist if conditions permitted, brew a cup of coffee, and then drive to the next highway stop which seemed to inevitably consist of fuel pumps, a small restaurant, and grocery, and there eat a large breakfast, fuel up my little diesel, buy a bag of cookies and maybe a can of hash, and set out for the rest of the day's journey, stopping only to take a picture now and then, and then locating a campsite as early as 4 PM, as the farther north I was, the shorter the autumn days were. About half-way up the highway, near Watson Lake, Yukon Territory, just a bit north of the border with British Columbia, I caught my first Arctic Grayling and next day, met a young parish priest in that town who took me out fishing and I managed to catch a huge Dolly Varden trout out of a deep bend in the Liard River. That night I ate a spruce grouse shot by one of the sisters from the local convent when they invited us to supper.

A day or so later I made it up to Caribou Crossing and decided to take a side trip down to Skagway, Alaska, over the White Pass. Along the mountainside road on the steep shores of Bennet Lake I had my first and only punctured tire of the trip, a sharply pointed piece of crushed stone "gravel" piercing my tire carcass like an arrow-head.

A Last Fling

After having the tire vulcanized in tire repair shop in Skagway, I located the local parish, and the parish priest, who was from Indiana, took me to a show being put on at the local high school gymnasium by the crew of a Russian cruise ship. I marveled at the unlikelihood of the whole thing. Here I was, in one of Alaska's most famous gold rush towns, the guest of a priest from Indiana, watching a group of young Russians performing folk-dances for Americans, no doubt under the watchful eyes of their KBG chaperons. Later on, around Christmas time, that priest, who was new to the place, wrote me to tell me that he'd already been spending a lot of time counseling folks who slowly got "cabin fever" in Skagway by December. Even though it is well below the Arctic circle, a mountain on the south side of town leaves the entire town and its valley in perpetual shadow for a major part of the year, and when the road over White Pass becomes snowed shut, leaving no place to view the sun.

This was one of the features of Alaska and the far north that I hadn't thought much about before my trip. McPhee's book spoke about it some, while another book about Alaska, John McGiness' *Going to Extremes,* which I read later, further confirmed the impression. On top of this were the stories and the statistics I would hear about people driven into near dementia, severe depression, alcoholism, violence, and suicide. I had come to Alaska not just on a sentimental journey, trying to imagine my father's presence as I enjoyed the scenery we had both hoped to share, but I had also come up there on as it were a scouting trip, wondering if just possibly I might try to become a hermit someplace up there. Already I was beginning to see that not all was paradise in America's last frontier.

Crossing back up over the White Pass back into the Yukon Territory I stopped by the Madonna House Apostolate mission at Whitehorse and stayed for a day and a half there. One of the fellows at the mission took me out on a tributary of the Yukon River to fish for more grayling, and I found a spot along a river bend where I caught one after another on the same trout dry-fly even while my shadow played on the water's surface. That confirmed my impression of the grayling as being neither a particularly smart nor wily fish. But on the other hand, how many live human fishermen had they ever seen before?

At Whitehorse I took on my first rider, a middle-aged Irishman who was sort of bumming his way from mission to mission, doing carpentry and odd-jobs for his keep, entertaining his hosts with stories and poetry from the "old sod" and patiently sitting on my sleeping platform with his back only partly supported by my rolled up sleeping bag. We drove up the Klondike Highway together, stopping to view the famous Lake LaBarge where "they cremated Sam Magee" and staying overnight at the parish at Campbell River where the priest regaled us with stories of how some tourists, coming up there to see where their grandfathers had spent a few years during the 1890s gold rush, sometimes ran into native (Indian) families who curiously shared the same last names. When we finally reached Dawson City and saw the sights there (like poet Robert Service's little rented cabin) and explored an old abandoned gold-digging dredge, and after bidding good-bye to my Irish passenger, I continued the next day on the "Top of the World Highway" back northwestward into Alaska, this time running into some snow over the mountain pass.

Prompted by a chapter in McPhee's book I then took a side trip about 40 miles to the town of Eagle back down on the Yukon River. Having not planned on this side excursion, I began to worry about enough diesel fuel, but figured whatever gas station was in Eagle would certainly have it. I was wrong. This is where McPhee's book proved invaluable. In it he had described how the town mayor was also the postmaster as well as superintendent of the town's electric generator. So I simply went to the post-office and inquired of the postmaster if he could sell me some diesel engine fuel. That he could, and he invited me directly out back, the generator being practically in the post-office's back yard. He drew five gallons from the fuel storage tank and when he asked for a dollar per gallon (I'd paid about $1.65 per gallon in Whitehorse) and I asked about the federal or state tax, he asked in turn: "What tax?" I didn't argue the point. In fact, except for the US Post Office, the folks of Eagle seemed to have a real grudge against anything the Federal Government might have to say about how they ran their lives, including some signs posted outside yards

A Last Fling

littered with old car, truck, snowmobile and airplane parts, pointedly requesting any government agents to "Keep Out!"

I camped just outside town in a very bear-visited looking small stream-side campground, but to my disappointment, saw no bears. Next day I picked up another hitchhiker near Chicken, Alaska — so named, according to the story, when the town's founders couldn't spell "Ptarmigan". This fellow had just finished a season working on a small, but thoroughly up-to-date gold-mining operation employing a hydraulic sluice. He didn't expect he'd get rich from it however. He probably would have done better working on the North Slope oil fields.

Next day, back on the Alaska Highway, after camping along a road-side lake where a moose came down to drink while I was there, I passed a pick-up truck parked by the side of the road where a fellow was peering through binoculars at a mountainside with his rifle at the ready. I realized that "road-hunting" in Alaska is not so much a matter of slowly cruising back roads (there are so very few of them, unlike back in Michigan) but hunting from the main highway itself. As a friend who had lived up there for many years was to explain, that unless you actually live way back in the bush, or have a lot of money to fly out on hunting excursions, such main road-hunting is about the only kind available to those who live in Alaska's towns.

So too, I was to learn about the availability of land itself. A year or so before my trip there, the State of Alaska and the Federal government had for the most part "triaged" all the remaining non-privately owned land in the state. Approximately one third was to belong to the tribal corporations, another third to the US government, and the final third to the State of Alaska to dispose of as it willed. The state's plan was to make some of its land available through a kind of auction system to those who had lived in the state for at least one year, with prices determined by how close the piece was to the few existing highways or roads. The further back in the bush you went, the more acreage you could get for your dollar. But none of it was intended to sell cheap. In fact, compared to backwoods undeveloped land in Michigan (about $100 per acre at that time), land in Alaska was quite expensive — as was everything else, except perhaps gasoline.

When I finally arrived in Fairbanks I went to the Catholic cathedral residence which also served as home-base for a number of Jesuits who serve outlying missions. I had already written them to tell them I was coming, and had hopes that I might be able to fly up to Point Barrow on the Arctic Ocean over the coming weekend to see what the high arctic and the northernmost point of the United States was like. Unfortunately, the priest who was in charge of that mission could not grant my request as he had been prevented from getting back up there himself for several weeks in a row by bad weather. Instead I was given the chance to fly out to a mission on the lower Yukon River in a light plane to take the place of a priest who was on retreat. The place is called Nulato and turned out to be the farthest up the Yukon River that the Russians had gone with their own trading posts, and a lot of the Athabaskan (Coyukon tribe) natives there had Russian last names.

The day I arrived there was to be a funeral of an old woman who had died well over the age of 100. We buried her, complete with grave blankets and other mementos, in a hill-side cemetery that was just off the edge of the airstrip that occupied a sloping low hill overlooking the town. This was followed by a "potlatch" in a new school hall and gym where we sat on the floor in long rows and ate moose and bear meat and "Indian ice-cream" (berries and nuts in whipped something or other − I think it was Crisco) while the village elders and others gave long eulogies, most of it in the Coyukon tongue. Later that night I sat at the dinner table where the only remaining nun at the mission, a veteran of posts both in the Yukon and Alaska, entertained some of the deceased's visiting relatives, and I listened in amazement to the women complain about the younger generation and how they no longer had respect for the old ways. Later that night I wandered down to the old lady's cabin where a bunch of elders sat around, played cards, and sang traditional songs of mourning, one of which the refrain, I was told, translated into "Now that you are gone, who is to cook the moose?"

Next day, after I had celebrated Sunday Mass for the people, the village mayor and general store-keeper drove me around the village's few miles of road and told me what a tough job he had in trying to keep order, which consisted mostly in trying to keep alcoholic beverages away from the town (it was officially "dry") and to keep all the dogs tied up. He wasn't having much success at either job, but still hadn't given up. That afternoon I took a hike out to the site of the old Russian trading post, equipped with an old 30-40 Kraig (Spanish American War era) rifle that the mayor advised me to carry when hiking out in the bush. I ran into some teenage boys who talked me into shooting off one round at a rock in the nearby stream. They seemed very pleased to meet a priest who could shoot a gun.

That night I was trying to watch some TV (the town post-office was equipped with a satellite dish piping cable TV to the villagers log cabins) I heard a knock at the door and opened it to find a tall handsome young fellow asking to see "the priest". Obviously he hadn't been to Mass that morning or he would have recognized me as being there that weekend to fill in. But I invited him in anyway and we sat down to talk. It was also obvious by then that he'd been drinking, but that is what he'd come to talk about. All his age group, including himself, was a mess because of it, he told me, and he wanted to know how maybe things could be changed. When I seemed to him to be a bit skeptical, he jumped up and pulled up his shirt in front to show me a jagged-looking scar on his belly — the aftermath of having once tried to kill himself with a shotgun. Then when I asked where they were getting all the booze and how much they were paying for it, he suddenly got defensive, but then he calmed down and told me that it came from the Air Force base town of Galena about 50 miles upriver and that it was run to Nulato by snowmobile in winter or by small boat the rest of the year at a going price of about $16 a bottle. I talked to him about the possibility of him and his buddies inviting some AA people to come from Fairbanks or someplace to talk to them. I promised to get him a contact and to write.

Next day I flew out on the mail plane to the airport in Galena, and having time to kill until the Central Alaska Airways plane arrived for the trip back to Fairbanks, I walked into the town, a collection of mostly plywood buildings and Quonset huts strung out along a muddy street. At the one street intersection in town, I noticed the local liquor store, the apparent source of supply for "dry" Nulato. The flight back to Fairbanks that afternoon included what for me — due to the sinus after-effects of that severe cold several weeks before — were two excruciating landings, first at Tanana and then again at Fairbanks, with the small unpressurized two-engine propjet suddenly descending (it seemed almost diving) from about 12,000 to less than 1,000 feet. I told one of the Jesuits at the cathedral residence about my encounter with the young man and asked where I might find an AA contact to get him and his buddies some help. The Jesuit as much as said I was dreaming if I thought what I had in mind could do any good. I also was very disappointed to hear that and even chagrined, when a month or so later I found out, from a cousin, that the fellow who was running that liquor store in Galena was from my mother's home town of Dollar Bay in Michigan's Upper Peninsula.

The day after that funeral in Nulato I had checked the parish books to see if the priest who had flown me out and presided at the funeral before he flew on to his own mission farther down-river had filled out the death registry. I couldn't help notice the number of deaths of men, often very young men, through suicide. So then I turned to the marriage register and noted that very few village girls were marrying boys from that village, and that the few recorded marriages seemed to be mostly to white men from out of state. So then I turned to the baptismal registry and found that most of the babies born in the village were listed under the mother's name with the father designated as "unknown". So I went back over to the convent to talk to the venerable sister about it. She said it really was easy to explain. It seems that most of the local fellows are alcoholics by the time they reach their twenties. The village girls will not marry them knowing they'll end up as battered wives if they do. Those who can leave to marry elsewhere do so at the first opportunity. Those who do not often end up having children whose father remains "unknown". The fellows know this, and having lost any respect for themselves because of it, turn even earlier to drink. A vicious circle all around.

I have gone at some length to relate my experience that weekend because the memory still tugs at my heart and also, because there had been that brief period when I, as an idealistic teenager, had dreamed about becoming a missioner in Alaska, even if as a brother and not a priest. But suppose I had been persuaded, as I was, to become a priest and had ended up at such a mission? Looking back, and cognizant of my own family background, especially on my Irish side, I think I might have lasted at most about five years in any such post before I too succumbed to the "curse". As one of my priest friends who took a sabbatical, and was persuaded to fill in at such an Alaskan mission over one winter, warned me — whatever I did, don't let them talk me into such a post unless I was prepared to spend the winter indoors drinking coffee with no place else to run.

Instead, I was perhaps close to being offered quite another job in Alaska, as the priest who twice hosted me in Anchorage tried to persuade me to stay around a while to meet the bishop when he returned from the lower forty-eight. It seems that the Diocese of Anchorage was looking for someone to take over the task of adult education and, I think, the continuing education of priests. It sounded nice, and even exciting, flying all around to reach the scattered parishes of south central Alaska. But for some reason or other the idea just didn't appeal to me. I knew by then that I was headed very much in a different direction.

The rest of my trip to Alaska, if less heart-rending than the Nulato mission experience, was much more auspicious. I enjoyed fall weather so glorious that, although I've occasionally thought about a return for another trip, I know that, statistically (in a state where any one spot has, I've heard, about a 15% chance of turning out to be sunny on any given day) I could probably never repeat the luck, weather-wise, that I had. I spent four days camping in Denali National Park, where everyday it was sunny, seeing many moose, Dall mountain sheep, and finally, a grizzly bear. I could see the top of Denali (Mount McKinley) practically every time I turned around. Few people, even one Fairbanks resident who invited me to share grilled moose meat supper and who had been to the park on three separate trips and never had yet actually seen the huge mountain, ever had such good luck.

Chapter 7

Not that the weather was perfect through the whole trip. Two weekends spent in Anchorage were both rainy, and I had to go to see an ear, nose, and throat specialist twice to get treated for sinus problems and a damaged eardrum from the result of that one plane flight back from Nulato with its two landings. But a whole week spent roaming and fishing in the Kenai peninsula was under either perfectly clear sky or dramatically fluffy clouds. I did, however, spend a very rainy day in Valdez roaming the site of the disastrous Good Friday earthquake, talking to one of its survivors, and had to wait there another day while the road crews plowed out three feet of snow that had fallen on the pass along the Richardson Highway before I could get back to the Alaska Highway and could resume my journey home. At Haines Junction in the Yukon, I turned southwest to take the pass over to the Chilkoot Valley where the bald eagles seemed almost as common as sparrows at that time of year. I snapped pictures of eagles soaring, fishing, and just roosting like turkeys in trees. When I took the Intra-Alaska car ferry from Haines down to Juneau, a deck hand spotting me taking pictures of the snow-capped mountains and glaciers, and trying to catch some killer whales surfacing, told me I was especially lucky, as it was, as he put it. "the first clear day they'd had on the inner passage all that month so far." It was October 13th.

The next day I flew out to Sitka Island from Juneau to explore the old Russian town and visit the Haida Tribal Museum and heard the same story. By that evening, when I flew back to Juneau, the rain clouds had begun to roll in. It rained all the next two days, one spent in and around Juneau, the next as the ferry took me down the inner passage to Petersburg, Ketchikan, and finally, Prince Albert, British Columbia, where I got off the boat and began the long drive up the Skeena River Valley, to Prince George and glorious sunshine again.

Was I being specially favored because of my resolution to quit my wandering once this "last fling" was over? Who knows? I spent the weekend in Jasper National Park in the Canadian Rockies, visiting all the spots where my folks and I had once visited together back in the summer of 1954. At one place, the mysterious Avalanche Lake, I was shocked to find all the water gone except a single stream flowing through the middle of a dry lake bed, a phenomenon that happens rather regularly when there isn't enough winter snowfall to produce enough spring run-off to back up water behind the lake's porous rock-rimmed outlet. But that probably explained why my dad and I had to paddle our canoe for several miles up the full length of the lake to where the river entered it before I finally hooked and landed a large rainbow trout. I also took the dead end road up to the foot of Mt. Edith Cavell and it seemed to me that the base of its famous glacier had receded markedly from where it had been in 1954. Signs of global warming? Now it seems so.

The next night I camped out alongside a river near the northern border with Banff National Park, visited the Valley of the Ten Peaks again, and then, instead of heading out eastward towards Calgary, decided to double back and go a bit southwestward through Yoho National park before reentering the USA, this so I could go through Glacier National Park where again, my folks and I had traveled, but in the reverse order on that trip, a quarter century before. I definitely was back on a sentimental journey as I was finally heading home.

The rest of the journey was uneventful, except after an extremely windy night that had my car shaking as I camped out on the plains of eastern Montana. I got caught in a heavy snowstorm the next morning, but not so heavy that I wasn't able to plow on (I let a big truck break the way ahead of my little VW), and drove across most of North Dakota the following day. Then, after stopping to see another of my Minnesota cousins, I drove along the north shore of Lake Michigan and was overcome with the feeling that, despite having seen some of the most glorious scenery in the whole world, I was now returning to where I really belonged.

How explain this? It is hard to say, but I think we grow up with various visual clues or something that makes us either feel at home when they surround us or restless when they are absent for any long period of time. I know, on the one hand, that I feel a bit uneasy with completely flat land. The skies may be magnificent, but a horizon that just appears to disappear into nothingness leaves me feeling empty and rootless. On the other hand, mountains, no matter how majestic or spectacular, sooner or later leave me feeling intimidated and hemmed in. I had found this out particularly in Arizona where if I didn't get out of those canyon lands or deep valleys at least once a week and see the horizon at something close to level with me, I began to feel antsy and confined. But perhaps even more it had to do with color. After both the dark mountain rocks and dark growth (evergreens) of the western mountains or the pale lichen and tundra of Alaska and the bleached prairie growth of the west, the still-bright colors of the mid-west's autumn hardwood forests almost brought tears to my eyes. And although I was soon scheduled after a week or two back at Stella Maris to resume my wanderings, I somehow sensed that already I was truly back at home. This time I had been away from home for just about two months.

Episode Two: The Last Chance Hermitage
Early in November I made my way down to the knobs and valleys of the coal county of southeastern Ohio. The reason was quite clear in my mind. If I was to take up a life of solitude, the best and most proper place to do it was, I felt, within the confines of an established order like the Camaldolese Hermits, where the long tradition and full church sanction of their life made this strange vocation, even if not fully understandable, seem commendable and acceptable in people's eyes. So I had an agenda very much in mind, and that was, after spending at least two months there, to make a decision as to whether or not to apply for admission and if accepted, to return for good after disposing of my own belongings, particularly my parent's house after my return, the following year, from the Holy Land.

The Prior, Fr. Charles, knew this, so he decided to treat me as if I were a regular member of the community. Instead of a room in the guest house, I was given one of the regular hermitages to live in. I got up at three in the morning each day to take part in the daily recitation of the psalms and readings of the divine office in the chapel. I concelebrated the Eucharist each morning with him and the other ordained member of the community, and which was attended by several others who were either not yet or didn't intend to be ordained. I ate their same meatless diet, took part in community work (usually performed alone unless requiring more than one hand) and generally lived the life of a Camaldolese hermit monk. And I really took to it.

A Last Fling

Not that there were no problems whatsoever. One week, early on, I do recall going through something of an emotional crisis, but I ascribed it more to what I was still recovering from the year before. The only difference between me and the other monks was that it was understood that I could occasionally drive into town for two or three purposes. One had to do with the final preparation of my book *Evil and Evolution* before I handed it over for a final typing (which required a trip or two to the Steubenville College Library and a trip every week or so to the local post office to mail each chapter as it was finished). The other purpose had to do with getting the required immunity shots in preparation for my trip to the Holy Land. These latter (I think there were three of them) took me through the industrial town of Weirton, West Virginia, across the Ohio River from Steubenville and up a long hill on the other side of town.

What to say about these two months lived under the Camaldolese rule, except to say that when they had ended, with even the last week spent in complete solitude, I was reasonably sure that, if they would have me, I was willing to join. Although I sensed that I might occasionally chafe a bit under the physical restrictions, or even question a bit why something was done this way rather than that, I felt I understood the requirements of living in community, even if a community of hermits, enough that such restrictions would be for me no big problem. To me, the pluses by far outweighed the minuses. Fr. Charles told me he would write the Prior General at Frascati, outside Rome, and I spent that final week in solitude, I guess praying that God's will be done. I then returned to the Detroit area, picked up my plane ticket to Israel, packed my bags (two of them, a duffle bag stuffed with clothes and a camera bag) and drove to Ossining, New York. There I stayed briefly with friends, arranged to park my car on the grounds of the Maryknoll Mission Society just up the road, and a day or two later caught an Alitalia Airlines 747 out of Kennedy Airport headed for Israel via a few days' stopover in Rome. There, as soon as I arrived in the big city from the Leonardo DaVinci Airport, I was jostled by a band of Gypsy or Roma (what else in Rome?) children who lifted my wallet. Not an auspicious beginning for my third trip overseas!

Chapter 7

After securing lodgings for the night at Saint Susanna's (the American parish in Rome) and reporting my stolen wallet at the district police station (where there seemed to be a whole line of people reporting the same) I took an electric-powered train out the next day into the Aubin Hills south-east of Rome to the town of Frascati, famous for its wine and the Papal Summer Villa (and the Vatican Observatory) at Castelgondolfo not too far away. There, on the side of a high hill, was the motherhouse of the reformed branch of the Camaldolese Hermits of Monte Corona, certainly one of the very smallest religious orders in the whole Catholic Church. It consisted of a collection of about a dozen or so little hermitage cottages behind a wall, and adjacent to them, on one side a headquarters building with its offices, kitchen (and I suppose a library) and then across a courtyard from headquarters, a rather large stone guest house and between them, the entrance to a rather cavernous stone church. Both the church and the guest house were constructed, in contrast to the plain lines of the other buildings, in definitely high renaissance style. After the rather cozy simplicity of the new buildings of the hermitage in Ohio, I was a bit taken aback by this definitely elegant, but dated, style. I decided that those two rather pretentious buildings must have been the gift of some rich count about 400 years back and that the poor reformed hermit monks (who themselves had become reformed because they thought the parent organization up near Florence had become compromised in its lack of simplicity) just couldn't say "No".

Unfortunately, the big church also dwarfed the small community. I suppose there were about eight or ten hermit monks assigned to the mother-house at that time. The Prior General, Fr. Michael, turned out to be an American. One of the community was Japanese. I already knew that among other members of the order were French, Spanish, Polish, and of course, Italians. So while very small in number, the Monte Corona Camaldolese were refreshingly international in scope. The next day I wandered around some on the grounds with its orchards before meeting with Fr. Michael. He turned out to be very friendly and unassuming, but also disarmingly frank. He relayed to me much of what I was afraid that Fr. Charles had written him, which was that while I was serious and intent, and probably a good candidate for solitary life, that my inclinations and needs were too intellectual to fit in well with the restrictions of Camaldolese community life. Then Fr. Vincent added, kind of as a consolation prize, that now having seen their headquarters as well as having experienced life at the hermitage in Ohio, did I not also realize that their life was one more of penance and austerity rather than one of real solitude? He suggested that I'd be much better off seeking to become a hermit all on my own under the provisions that would soon be promulgated in the new Code of Canon Law. Under those, I could have the best of both worlds — as much solitude as I craved, yet the freedom to carry on with the studies and projects I felt were important to my life.

Well, so there I had it. The answer was, even if politely and helpfully put, a definite "No". Was I upset? I don't believe so, because I really wasn't all that surprised. But still I was perhaps a bit disappointed. My pride would have been much more pleased to have them begging me to join and my own caution making me think twice. Early the next morning I returned to Rome and caught my plane to Israel. I was to return to Rome only once more, in 2009, when I attended a week-long conference on Darwin and evolution at the Gregorian University.

Episode Three: The Holy Land
The plane, which left late that afternoon after exhaustive security checks (I suspect that at least one of the checkers was an Israeli security man rather than Italian) winged out over the heel of Italy's "boot" and soon had us winding over the snow covered peaks of Crete and soon after that, over Cyprus just as dark fell. How tiny the Mediterranean World, the world of our classical cultural origins, seemed! And then within the hour, a quick descent into Lod Airport, near the ancient site of the Philistine City of Lud that long preceded modern Tel Aviv. Then there were more security checks as we disembarked and claimed our luggage in the airport terminal. I arranged for a ride in a kind of station-wagon type cab with an Israeli businessman or two, and after the driver dropped them off on the western outskirts of Jerusalem, I had a bit of trouble trying to explain

Chapter 7

to him, as he spoke little English, just exactly where I wanted to be dropped off, as I too had little to go by other than the name of "The Ecumenical Institute for Advanced Theological Studies" and the name of its location known as "Tantur", a hilltop south of Jerusalem. I had no street name or number to go by. The people at the institute seemed to assume everyone knew where it is. As it turned out, it would have been much simpler to say "Take me to Gilo" — but on the other hand, since the beginning of the shooting "intifada" — mentioning Gilo, an Israeli "settlement" on confiscated Arab land, recently the target of much sniping from Hamas and other Palestinian insurgents, a cab driver might not be willing to go there at all.

It also seems I was rather badly overcharged. The cab displayed near the top of its windshield a tinted decal kind of sun-shade marked with the name of a popular cigarette called "Gitanos" – the Spanish word for "Gypsies". I tried to joke with the driver a bit about that. After my experience upon my arrival in Rome perhaps I should have said nothing. Maybe I gave the driver ideas. By then it was about 10 or 11 PM. No time to hassle over price.

Next morning I awoke to the blast of a muzzarin's early morning call to prayer, the first announcement that I was truly in another world, perhaps having been even carried back into another point in time — except that the call didn't come from any really close by mosque, but was carried on the wind from a distance which at the same time betrayed its electrical amplification. For all I knew, the muzzarin was still sound asleep at home while a mechanical timer was busy making sure everyone else couldn't sleep. Then, as the sun actually came up, I looked out my window and there was a fellow in long Bedouin robes, wearing a kafiyeh (the standard Arab men's scarf headdress) tending a flock of sheep busily munching on the grass around institute's olive trees. Yes, loud-speakers or not, I truly was in another world.

"Tantur" as we generally called it, was, and still is to my knowledge, a rather unique place. Whether Pope Paul VI thought up the idea himself as a result of his trend-setting pilgrimage to the Holy Land in the early 1970s, or whether he was put up to the idea of promoting an ecumenically sponsored theological study center by other parties, I'm not sure. But the Holy Cross Fathers at Notre Dame University in Indiana eagerly took him up on the idea with the help of land offered by the Knights of Malta, an international organization of Catholic laymen of prominence (and no little wealth). This hilltop which was named "Tantur"— because it was said to resemble somewhat a certain style of Palestinian women's headdress — and which was the location of a pilgrim's hospice midway between Jerusalem and Bethlehem, had been rebuilt into a modern complex of rooms and apartments to house scholars and their families. It had a modern kitchen and dining room, chapel and well-equipped library and beautiful grounds which, on a clear day during the dry winter season when I arrived there, afforded a view across the Judean desert all the way to the shining waters of the Dead Sea in its deep trench to the east. The grounds were not all that spacious, but still big enough to afford a brisk walk. A low wall separated the grounds on two sides from the main road and the branch road up to Gilo, and on two other sides from old olive groves and, as I was to discover to my surprise some weeks later, a small group of hovels — almost dug-outs, really — occupied by a few Arab refugee families. Just to the south down the road to Bethlehem was an Israeli checkpoint, a rather ominous sign that although technically still in Israel proper, we were sitting on the edge of the occupied "West Bank", that check point designating the crossing of what was known as "The Green Line". Just past that was the entrance to a shrine called "Rachel's Tomb", which although no archeologist believes has any real claim to being the place of the patriarch Isaac's wife's burial – the allusion to Rachel being buried somewhere near there coming from a misreading of Matthew's Gospel – nevertheless the location is a popular pilgrimage site for Jews. Accordingly, IDF (Israel Defense Forces) soldiers were usually to be found there standing around or sitting by a big machine gun atop a building across the street.

This, of course, was the picture I saw repeated over and over again. The "West Bank" territory was to all intents an occupied country. Things for the most part remained relatively peaceful, at least back then, but everywhere Israeli troops were to be seen. On any bus trip into or out of Jerusalem, especially if one were riding one of the

Chapter 7

day-time Palestinian busses (they weren't allowed to run at night), one might expect to be suddenly stopped and boarded by IDF soldiers and checked over, and asked for an identification. One American seminarian I knew of (the seminary I had attended, and later had taught at, was then sending its students over there for a semester) was ordered to get off or get up in one of those searches and refused, producing his US passport, much to the soldier's chagrin. What bothered me most was the fact that all this was being done with soldiers carrying US-built M-16 assault rifles. Why did they not at least carry Israeli-built Uzi submachine guns — a much more lethal weapon in those close quarters? Why did the USA keep getting visibly dragged into all of this? Having arrived in the Holy Land with a great respect and admiration for Israeli courage and progressiveness, I soon found myself increasingly sympathetic to Palestinian complaints and what now appeared to be Israeli arrogance.

Nevertheless, we all attempted, I think, to remain non-political. This was, after all, an ecumenical institute, one which not only brought Catholic and Protestant scholars together, but as was hoped, eventually Jews and Muslims as well. There were in fact, a few Jewish scholars who came and lectured. In fact, they were easier to talk to than the Greek Orthodox, who feeling that they alone were the legitimate representatives of Christianity in that part of the world, seemed to treat most other forms of Christianity, including the Orthodox from other parts of the world, with some disdain. One Greek lay theologian came to talk to us, but admitted that if he had been a cleric, he would have been in deep trouble with his church.

The Muslim connection was even more tenuous. One day, talking to a young Melkite (Greek Rite) Catholic theologian, a layman from Galilee, I remarked how I was disappointed to not find any Muslim scholars at the institute. He remarked, rather curtly, how that could never happen, because they (the Muslims) "worship another God." I right off told him that I thought that was a ridiculous attitude and that if anyone could do it, it is people like him, growing up among them, who must try, and that if he could not understand them enough to initiate some dialogue, how could such dialogue ever begin to take place? Next day, at the mid-morning coffee break he came back up to me and said my words had him tossing a good part of the previous night and that yes, I was right. He must try to do something about this. I was very pleased to read, a year or so later, in a mailed newsletter from Tantur, that at least some efforts to dialogue with Muslims at the institute were now being made.

One other thing I did while there may have also raised a few eyebrows. Sundays, we held an ecumenical prayer service or liturgy at which other Christians were generally invited to receive Holy Communion. This of course raised some scruples, especially on the part of those who believed in the real (and not just symbolic) presence of Christ under the forms of bread and wine. When it was my turn to officiate, I planned things rather carefully. I decided to invite an ordained Lutheran friend and an Anglican priest from Canada to "concelebrate" with me, believing that their beliefs on the subject were close enough to mine to justify such a concelebration (besides I had done the same in Michigan on a few occasions at the Lutheran monastery — Saint Augustine House, outside Detroit, something the officials of the Detroit Archdiocese knew took place quite often and never raised a fuss about). I explained during the homily how I decided that if we cannot do this here of all places, then what good is our being here together in the cause of unity? I then added, as the Vatican II Council pointed out, that the Eucharist is both a cause of greater unity as well as a celebration of what unity already exists. I also pointed out that from Saint Paul's First Letter to the Corinthians, we can deduce three basic requirements for receiving Holy Communion: first, that we are baptized; second, that we are sorry for our sins; and third, that we recognize the special presence of the body and blood of Christ and that we don't have to agree entirely on how this presence comes about — only that it is something real. However, just to make sure that the Catholics present would be certain that I was in charge, I decided to celebrate the Eucharistic Prayer in the Latin — and later got kidded a bit about that. But I'm afraid that the four Benedictine monks from the monastery of Montserrat near Barcelona who formed the library staff at the institute were a bit scandalized, having been previously impressed by my getting up early most weekday mornings to celebrate the office and Holy Eucharist with them, and this in their native Catalan (which I didn't find that different from my bad Spanish).

Probably the greatest influence on me during those months was the presence of William Johnston, a Jesuit from Northern Ireland who had spent most of his priesthood in Japan teaching at Sophia University in Tokyo and who was an expert on both the English mystical writing known as *The Cloud of Unknowing* and on Christian-Buddhist dialogue as well. I kind of took him as my spiritual advisor, sharing a lot of my ideas and aspirations, and we also became good friends as well. One day we managed to arrange a trip into the Judean desert east of Bethlehem together to visit the hermitage caves in the cliffs above the Kedron river and close to the ancient Monastery of Mar Sabas — once the home of the seventh century theologian Saint John of Damascus. Actually, Johnston and I split up for the day, he heading upstream from the monastery and I downstream. He had better luck finding solitude than I did. A Bedouin herdsman discovered me and we had a long wordless visit, he sharing my canteen of water and both of us comparing each other's prayer beads — though later on a couple of his kids kept pestering both of us as we waited for our ride back to Tantur. Although we tried not to bother the few monks there, we were so entranced by the setting that a few weeks later we persuaded the institute to set up a small bus excursion to the place so more of the scholars could see it. The monks (the were Greek Orthodox but one was from Australia and much more friendly) graciously opened up the monastery to show us around, including the chapel at Saint John of Damascus' cell and the martyrs' cave chapel where about forty monks were burned or suffocated by Persian invaders in the eighth or ninth century. The only sour note on this occasion was that the women scholars or scholars' wives that came along on the excursion were not allowed to enter the precincts.

We of course went out on many institute sponsored excursions, especially on weekends. Among them were trips to Engedi, Masada, Qumran, Jericho, the Negev desert, Lashish, Gibeon, Megiddo and the whole region of Galilee. There were few major archeological sites we did not see. Then of course there was our participation in the various rites of Holy Week, two of them that year, since the Orthodox Holy Week and Easter were a week later than the western one. I was especially entranced by the rites, and particularly the chants, at the Armenian Orthodox Church of Saint James. Many of us marched in the gigantic Palm Sunday procession from Bethany over the Mount of Olives down into the Kedron Valley to the impressive "Beautiful Gate" on the east side of the tall wall surrounding the Old City. This is the one really big annual event where what Christians remain in the Holy Land – and their numbers continually dwindle as they emigrate, seeing little future for themselves in their own homeland – turn out en masse. Even *The Jerusalem Post* that year estimated that at least 10,000 had turned out for the procession.

A group of us also went by bus one Sabbath Day (Saturday) on a trip to Ramallah and up the side of Mount Gerazim to witness the annual Samaritan Passover sacrifice. Descendants of the Samaritans gather from all over Israel to pray and witness the slaughter of a number of young rams and their roasting over open fires by nightfall. It was a curious and in its own way, impressive sight. All these men in long robes and turbans, but oddly enough being watched by their families, with most of the Samaritan women wearing the latest fashions and high heels. Our Israeli bus driver, on the other hand, packed a pistol in his belt, just in case there was trouble.

One thing that struck me most about Middle Eastern religion, particularly Islam and more traditional forms of Judaism, is the way that women seem to be relegated to the back seat as it were, that is, to side balconies, behind screened off partitions, etc. These seem to be, compared to western, especially Christian churches, very much "macho" religions and defiantly kept that way. Is this why there is so much rivalry between Jews and Muslims at present? If women had more prominent and public roles, would there be this antagonism? And, on the other hand, are the men's egos so fragile that if women took a more public religious role, would the men give up on religion altogether? After several months in this supercharged religious environment one cannot but wonder about that.

Several weeks before Holy Week and Easter, many of us went on what had to have been one of the most unique experiences the

Chapter 7

institute had to offer — a one week camping trip in the Sinai. Guided by an Israeli nurse who was working on her doctorate in the History of Religion, we rode in a six-wheel drive (or maybe it was ten wheels with three axles) Mercedes truck that had plain bench seats arranged crosswise across its flat bed, but with a high canopy that served as a luggage rack overhead. Up there were stored sleeping bags, air mattresses, food containers, and our duffle bags. Beneath the truck bed were two large water tanks, and a rack holding propane tanks for the main cooking stove. Most of the men in the party were assigned jobs like tossing down the luggage from the top of the truck (or catching it) when we stopped to camp overnight. My job was to set up the cook stove, and then unroll a long hose to connect it to a propane tank a good distance away for safety's sake. Although we stopped along the Red Sea's Gulf of Elat to go snorkeling among the coral reefs and took a good long warm-up hike in the rugged hills facing the sea before our truck ventured inland, the night-time temperatures were quite brisk. Riding on the back of an open truck was a rather cool experience, even in mid-day. Most of us wore an extra sweater or two beneath a wind-breaker. A lot of us men wore the kafiyeh, finding the Bedouin Arab head-dress ideal for the occasion. Most of the women bundled up in blankets and scarves.

Our main destination was Mount Sinai (Mount Horeb) now known in Arabic as *Gebel Musa* (the Mountain of Moses) and its famous monastery of Saint Catherine. At one time, it was the custom of pilgrims to hike up the mountain before dawn to experience the sunrise. But after the UN had succeeded in dividing the Sinai to keep Israel and Egypt apart after the final settlement after the Six-Day War, Israelis or Israeli-sponsored tours were not able to camp or stay overnight on the Egyptian side. To get there we had to pass through three checkpoints, first an Israeli one, then a UN post, and finally, an Egyptian one. All this could no longer be done except at specified day-time hours, which precluded an early-morning start for the climb. Instead, we started the long hike, a fairly gradual climb of about three thousand feet up a camel or donkey path, in late morning, spending perhaps only a half-hour at the top, and then, on the way back down, sidetracked down a steep footpath to an overlook to the monastery far below from a narrow gorge said to be the site of the prophet Elijah's silent encounter with God — "not in the mighty wind . . . not in the earthquake, not in the fire . . . but in the murmur of gentle breeze" (1 Kings 19:11-12).

Truth is, that like many pilgrimage spots in the Holy Land, the exact location of the events so narrated remains a matter of conjecture. Gebel Musa or Mt. Horeb is not the highest peak on the Sinai Peninsula, but before the days of modern surveying techniques, or the advent of accurate altimeters and, most recently, GPS receivers, this particular mountain appeared to be the highest, and was therefore assumed to be "the place". After all, wouldn't God naturally pick the most spectacular setting for giving the Ten Commandments? Certainly God was not to be outdone by Cecil B. DeMille! As for the monastery itself, it had been there since at least the fourth century and is still occupied by Greek Orthodox monks. All of us, even the women for a change, were allowed a peek into the monastery church.

After returning to what was then still Israeli-occupied territory (a year later, as a result of the Camp David Accords, all of the Sinai was to be returned to Egypt) we wandered the next day south-eastward into a remote valley with some of the most fantastic scenery on the face of the earth. Each of us was encouraged to wander off to some remote spot — but not too remote lest we become lost — alone to meditate for several hours. Among the curiosities I found were small quartz-like stones, like marbles, perfectly round from being rolled, for who knows how many millennia, by the relentless desert winds. But the strangest place of all was a low plateau, or we'd call it a "mesa" in the American southwest, containing a cluster of small freestone (unmortered) oblong huts with tiny doorways, barely big enough to crawl through, all of which openings face to the southwest. One thinks immediately of tombs, but archeologists have never found any trace of human remains. One also thinks of the early Celtic monks and their "beehive" style stone churches and hermitages. Was this the site of some ancient monastic community, one where the monks were literally entombed in their cells? Or are we here dealing with something that even predates Moses or Abraham — like the rock megaliths I saw on the Golan Heights, huge flat stones balanced roof-like on two smaller upright stones half-buried in the ground. Such prehistoric structures are found in various places from western Europe and the British Isles, to North Africa and even as far East as Japan. Prehistoric tomb-markers, primitive shrines, or merely very permanent shelters? No one seems to know for sure.

Another strong memory — and there are so many others besides telling, like those of my first and only camel ride and a nighttime picnic cooked by Bedouin tribesmen — was a rather cool exchange I had with our Jewish guide. She had ordered the driver to stop by a house-size sandstone rock outcropping in the middle of a large sandy plain. There had been a fence erected around the rock to keep the curious and the inveterate initial-carvers from defacing the face of the rock which contained many ancient graffiti. The place had been a trail-marker and probably a camp spot for pilgrims heading to Mt. Sinai from Jerusalem from early Christian times. Among the short prayers and religious symbols were of course, many crosses of all shapes and sizes. But then she proudly showed us the tracing of a menorah — the seven branched ritual Hebrew candle-holder — proof that there were Jews who also made this pilgrimage in ancient times as well. But then she commented on one variety of cross with which she was not familiar — more or less like an even-armed Greek cross, but with each arm terminating in three short rays, rather shaped like crows-feet. I took her aside and told her that I had recently been reading a book on the Christian archeology of Palestine and it was exactly this shape of cross that the author believed was unique among early "Jewish-Christians". The response was a stony silence. I guess it was not taken to be a rather helpful comment, to say the least. But I also think that silence said a lot.

What that incident told me is symptomatic of the modern Israeli oblivion to the fact that many, if not most of the "Palestinians" whose possession of the Holy Land long predates the state of modern Israel are not all descendants of medieval Arab invaders or of modern Bedouin tribesmen (although undoubtedly many are — as well as of European crusaders, indeed, I even saw red-headed blue-eyed Palestinians in Bethlehem) but are rather the descendants of those

Jews who happened to become Christian quite early on and many of whom had remained so to this day. True, they have for the most part become assimilated into Arab culture over the ages, and no doubt many eventually became Muslim. But as any ethnologist can tell you, rarely, if ever, does a native population of any land completely disappear. (In fact, I have since learned that geneticists can find no significant differences between the Jewish population of Israel and the near-by "Arab" countries, such as Jordan and Syria — except that many of the Jews show some mixture of European DNA.)

On the other hand, just as the bulk of Ireland's population is not racially Celtic, even though their culture early on became so, or Russia's population is predominantly Slavic, even though the country takes its name from the invading Vikings, known to the Slavs as the "Rus", the bulk of the Holy Land's population, now being shoved aside from their own country, were probably not even Jewish to begin with. Instead, they seem to have been the descendants of the Canaanite peoples whom Joshua and his successors (if we can believe the Bible) were supposed to eliminate, but who were more likely first made vassals of the Hebrew invaders then eventually became Jews themselves. In any case, most of the residents of these West Bank towns looked more stereotypically Jewish — that is, of Semitic stock — than the recent Jewish immigrants from Russia that I saw riding on the buses from Jerusalem toward Gilo — many of whom looked about as Jewish as I look Chinese!

Still, of course, we are really talking here more about religious identity than we are ethnicity or cultural identity. And this concerns me greatly, as the problem that confronted me during my whole stay in the Holy Land kept bringing me back to the mystery of the true identity of Jesus. I must confess that from that first daybreak there when I awoke to the amplified call to prayer of a muzzarin, the one question that began to cross my mind over and over again was what sense can the average Jew or Muslim possibly make of the Christian claim for Jesus — that he was the "Son of God", not just in the sense of being God's chosen servant (the "*ebed Yahweh*" as the author of the "servant Songs" in the book of Isaiah puts it), but as the actual incarnation of divinity, truly God made man. Being in the actual land

Chapter 7

where all this was supposed to have happened was for me more of a challenge to my beliefs than it was any real help. I was overcome by the literal concreteness of that rocky and troubled land, where one can see houses and walls containing hollowed out stone blocks pilfered from the ruins of Herod the Great's fabled system of aqueducts, where one can gaze (as at Jericho) at the foundations of a tower built at least 10,000 years ago, and where, at the "Dome of the Rock", today devout Muslims pray beside the rock outcropping that was believed to be the place where Abraham was ready to take Isaac's life but which eventually became the site of the great temple built by Solomon, and later rebuilt by Herod the Great.

In the face of all this, what are we to make of the wandering preacher from Galilee, a wonder-worker (among many claims of similar wonder-workers) who attracted a following for a few short years and then was ignominiously crucified by the Roman occupation force for which the execution of troublesome Jews was practically a daily event? To be living in the tiny country (hardly any bigger than the state of Delaware) among a population which for the most part (the Holy Land was once about 30% Christian, it is now, due mostly to emigration, only about 2%) to be getting along quite well in their religiosity without any reference to Jesus — except for the money that Christian pilgrim-tours bring in — was for me, rather disorienting, to say the least.

Or perhaps I should say that it challenged me to set a new course, a new "orientation" taken in a quite literal sense — a turning toward the East — in my theology. It determined me to embark on a project of trying to understand Jesus first of all as a human being and only then, after I had begun to understand him as one of us, to try to figure out in a totally new (new at least for me) what it might mean to say he was, or still is, "the Son of God".

However, at this stage, that project was only beginning to take shape in my mind. There were many other distractions as my stay there drew towards an end. There was still the problem of finding a publisher for my book on *Evil and Evolution*. Fairleigh Dickinson University (Associated University Presses) was still willing to publish it, even though having taken nearly six years to get my dissertation into print — at one point they had lost track of the manuscript when a typesetter had taken ill — they were willing to let me out of my contract to seek a more popular publisher. Other people at the institute had still other suggestions.

Then there was the question: where would I go when I returned to the USA? Not that I didn't plan to return to my parent's home, once my house-sitters moved out at the end of the school year, but then I planned to sell the place as soon as I could dispose of most of its contents. I decided to send a letter to all the members of the Stella Maris group direct from Israel so that they would have it well before our annual cabin business meeting in June. So I put it directly on the line. Either they could give (or rather "loan") me some space on the property that we all owned jointly, or else I would be resigning from the "Stella Maris Club, Inc." as our organization was officially called. This latter course would involve them having to pay me back a sizable portion of my original investment which I would then use to help purchase land elsewhere. It would be up to them.

Finally, I took two more weekend trips up to Galilee. One was with a small group of the people from the institute who wanted to return there with some relatives who had recently arrived for a visit. We rented a small bus that took us not only back to some of the more usual Christian tour spots (like Nazareth and Capharnum) but also to the Haifa area and along the ridge of Mt. Carmel where we visited a small Carmelite monastery at the supposed site of the prophet Elijah's contest with the priests of Baal (but not the riverside where he had their throats slit) and then, on the promontory overlooking the Mediterranean and the city of Haifa itself, the Carmelite shrine of Stella Maris ("Star of the Sea") — the place where it was believed that Elijah was when he prophesied the coming of a torrential rain that was to end a record drought.

The second trip I took all by myself. A Dutch priest, an expert on the eastern rites, had come from Galilee to the institute one day to lecture to us on early Palestinian and Syrian Christian liturgies. When we learned that he was running a "laura" — a kind of community of hermits on a mountaintop in Galilee, I asked him immediately after his talk if it would be possible to make a visit to his place. It was a

Chapter 7

weekend or two later when I took a bus from Jerusalem to Nazareth, then caught a rural bus out to a village called "Deir Hanna" ("Deir" being Arabic for "monastery" or "convent" and "Hanna" being "Ann") and walked up a long path up the side of Har Netofa, a low mountain whose eastern slope looked out over the Sea of Galilee. Galilee is very different from Judea or even Samaria to the immediate south of Galilee. Lush and green, particularly then in the spring, and from that mountain top, one could see all the way across Lake Genneseret (the other name for the Sea of Galilee) the site of almost all of Jesus' early ministry, and on up farther toward the northeast, the snowy slopes of Mt. Hermon.

The laura itself was a collection of a few small wooden buildings. I was given a room in their "guest house". There was no electricity, but if I do recall, they had a water system of sort which was replenished periodically from a well by means of a gasoline engine-driven pump. The chapel was most unusual, a subterranean cave more or less on the top of the mountain (and not on its side where one would expect caves to occur) and was entered through a small stone structure that stood above ground. It was, if I recall, rather damp. Resident at the place was its founder, another priest (a Trappist monk from the USA), and an older nun from someplace in Europe, and one or two others who were probably on retreat or just visiting like I was. The American monk asked if I would be willing to go out and harvest some of last autumn's vetch from the pasture with a sickle and seemed a bit doubtful I could handle anything like that until I told him what my plans were on return to the states. Then he seemed to take me more seriously and we seemed to get along just fine. But later, that same day, when I was working out in that field, which was right on the top of the mountain, something curious happened – not just once but several times. A single Israeli (but again American built) F-16 fighter-jet would come along, flying almost below my elevation along the south side of the mountain, swing around its eastern end and then head off toward the northwest. I figured it was practicing, if not exactly low-level flying at that elevation, at least it was performing a maneuver that would confuse the big radar installation we saw on a previous trip along the Syrian border with the Israeli-held territory on the Golan Heights.

Well, I suppose it was partly that, but not exactly practice. Upon my return to the Jerusalem area later that week, I read in the paper that the Israeli Air Force had been making air strikes into Lebanon to rocket and bomb suspected terrorist camps and strongholds. On the way back to Nazareth, our bus had to crowd the shoulder of the road as a big IDF tank-carrier (a specially designed truck with a low flatbed trailer) came from the other direction with the real thing on board. As it passed us, it blew a tire and the people on board the bus all practically jumped out of their seats, apparently thinking a bomb had gone off. It was just a few months later that the Israeli Army marched into Lebanon in a campaign to occupy the whole southern half of that county — an operation which the Lebanese now claim cost about 14,000 civilian lives. What I had been seeing that weekend was part of the "softening up" process plus the beginning of the deployment of forces for an impending and bloody invasion.

My memories of my final journey into beautiful, pastoral Galilee are now marred forever with the memory of those ominous signs. If it had turned out, as it did, that I had been in the Holy Land in one of the mostly peaceful interludes during what has now been, as I write this, after some forty-four years of almost constant conflict, it only underlines what has become all too obvious by now. As one priest, a Jesuit from Egypt who was visiting the institute, answered when I asked him what he thought of Israel, told me: middle easterners see it as just the latest in a whole series of western colonies. Only this time it is not France, or England, or later the Italians (in Ethiopia) or the Nazis (in North Africa), but America that is the real culprit — the arm behind the Israeli fist. Should we be surprised that September 11, 2001 happened?

Episode Four: An Egypto-Greco Detour

Because of a time-limit on my round-trip plane fare, I left Israel a week or so before the semester's official closing to spend some time in Egypt and Greece before returning home. Egypt was a long day's bus ride through the Gaza strip down to the border and its checkpoints, with a long wait as passports were checked. We arrived at the edge of the Suez Canal just after sunset, and after a motor-launch took us across the canal, continued on for about another couple of hours in almost complete darkness until we entered Cairo, now one of the largest cities on earth. I had the name of a pension quite close to the bus station, and it was adequate for the night. On the next day, I made it to the Jesuit "College" — a boys high school where I was given a room with a very high ceiling overlooking a very noisy thoroughfare close to the main train station. On the next floor, downstairs, were classrooms and in the hallway, some cases with geological specimens — ones that I suspected were collected by Teilhard about seventy years before when he took his students out in geological field trips into the deserts flanking the Nile.

After finding my way a bit around Cairo, and its environs and sights (the Giza pyramids, the Cairo museum, and much less known, the Coptic Church Museum of early Christian art) and learning to read real Arabic numerals off car license plates which have both the real ones (the bus routes were marked only with these) as well as our bowdlerized version of the same, I felt confident enough to start off on side trips.

The first of these took me a couple of hundred miles south upriver to the ancient temple city of Memphis and its modern (well semi-modern) counterpart, Luxor. I took a fancy overnight air-conditioned sleeper train, which only increased the heat shock when I arrived in Luxor. Cairo had been bad enough, but Luxor was like a furnace by midmornings. I was staying at the Latin rite Church mission, run by the Franciscans, and it was definitely not air-conditioned, although they did have a few fans. I promptly became quite ill with the heat, but still managed to make it over to see the tombs in the Valley of the Kings and to spend another day exploring the vast ancient temple complex of Karnak. I also managed to eat at least two meals as a small Nile-side restaurant that served a very tasty bread and some good beer or cup of tea.

Finding beer readily available in a predominantly Muslim country was something of a surprise. But it was also something of a surprise to find out how visible Christianity is in Egypt as well. The ancient Coptic (late Greek slang for "Egyptian") Church claims to have been around since the days of Saint Mark the Evangelist, and despite the almost overwhelming prevalence of Islam and the Arabic language (which replaced the ancient Egyptian language in all but the Coptic Liturgies) this ancient Christian Church is not about to go away. In fact, it is quite prominently present, with Christians being among the highest percentage of the well-educated, many in the government civil-service. While at most only about ten percent of Egypt's population, Christians seem to be far more influential than their numbers might suggest. And, as I was told, the Coptic Church has been undergoing something of a modern renaissance, learning from not only western religious outreach programs, but even reviving many of its own ancient traditions, like a fervent monastic life. While in Egypt, on at least two occasions, I was befriended by Egyptians who upon learning I am a priest, proudly announced that they were children of parish priests. One young fellow, a college student I met in Luxor, even tried to persuade me to go to his home village with him to meet his dad. I frequently saw Coptic priests on the street, often bearded, wearing long black cassocks and a small round black "pill-box" type of hat, and with a black leather cross braided into a rather intricate pattern I've seen only in Egypt. Coptic churches, many seeming to have not just one but two cross-topped towers, often stood in the center of small towns prominently close to mosques.

I had planned to travel further south to Aswan, but after talking to the college student who warned me that Aswan was even hotter and damper (with all the evaporation from the impoundment from the high dam) than Luxor, I decided to head back north again. This time I took a non-air-conditioned day-train so I could see more of Egypt along the legendary Nile. The valley consists of an almost constant succession of small towns or villages one after another, each surrounded on three sides by farm fields, and on one side by the Nile, with an occasional large town now and then. All this is squeezed into an incredibly narrow strip of Nile River Valley bounded by often steep rocky cliffs on both sides beyond which there is mostly desert stretching both to the east and west. And as I had already found out, despite the proximity of the desert, the river valley has a climate akin to a steam bath. And it was not even summer yet.

Chapter 7

The second trip was northward, to the famous sea-coast city of Alexandria. The Nile River fans out into its large delta just north of Cairo and thus presents one with a totally different landscape from the narrow valley to the south. Here flat land stretches almost as far as one can see. There are many canals, and even occasional lakes and swamps. And when one reaches Alexandria the change in the climate makes it obvious why the Greeks, and later the Romans, made it the capitol of their political, cultural, and commercial activity in Egypt. I suspect that Saint Mark himself was never much tempted to travel upriver or inland once he landed at this beautiful sea-side metropolis, for that is what it was, even in his day. I stayed there however, for only a day or so to see some of the ancient ruins before I returned to Cairo by a totally different route along the edge of the western desert so that I could visit the ancient monastery of Saint Marcarius in the famous *Wadi Natrun* — one of the earliest sites of Christian monasticism.

To get there I took a bus from Alexandria to a place that resembled a kind of run-down truck stop, where I was able to get word to the monastery and a monk came out in a Land Rover to drive me some miles westward where the great monastery's high outer wall, pierced by numerous small windows made it look almost like a ship sailing on a sea of sand. The monks were most happy to receive a Roman priest house-guest and ushered me to a cell (really a little apartment) with a window overlooking the monastery's inner court yard. There were several freestanding buildings there. One was the main church. Another was a kitchen-bakery. Another I took to be the main monastery headquarters building. All these were more or less modern. But near the very middle of the complex was a rather large, but most compact building that almost resembled a fortress, with hardly any windows. This, I was told, was the original monastery building housing the church that went back to Saint Marcarius' own time — nearly sixteen centuries ago. It looked like a fortress from the outside because it had to, as it was also intended to be a place of refuge from desert marauders and others bent on doing the monks harm. And apparently this was not a totally uncommon situation, as periodically monks living as hermits far out in the desert beyond the monastery fell victims to criminals or raiders of one sort or another.

Another feature of this ancient building was that it had separate chapels designed to accommodate monks from various ethnic backgrounds so that they could pray together and listen to the Scriptures being read in their own native languages, even if they all gathered in the main church for the "synapsis" or Eucharistic rite. In other words, there was a kind of gracious ethnically-ecumenical atmosphere working here in the Egyptian desert long before this kind of thing came into vogue with the simultaneous translators employed by UN. How or why then did this church find itself cut off from most of the other Christian churches as far back as the fifth century only to be recognized and to some extent readmitted to quasi-intercommunion status in just the past few years?

This could be a long and complicated question, one which I cannot go into depth here. But just let's say it has to do with the problem I was having in the Holy Land, the one having to do with rediscovering the humanity of Jesus and reintegrating it with the doctrine of the divinity of Christ. Despite its legendary founding by Saint Mark, the reputed author of that document that most scripture scholars today believe was the very earliest of the four Gospels, the church emanating from Alexandria was a church that emphasized, above all, the Gospel of John and its ethereal picture of the almost super-human and nearly totally divine Christ. In Alexandrine theology, the humanity of Jesus seems to have been, at best, a kind of cloak or suit of clothes hiding the invisible presence of God. This is the kind of theological shortcut that Catholic and Orthodox Christians take when they speak of Mary being "the Mother of God" (it was Cyril of Alexandria, who had championed the "*theotokos*" title for Mary at the Council of Ephesus in 431) or when we speak of "God dying on the Cross." All this seems to have been taken quite literally by the Alexandrians — except, in the latter case especially, we must ask who or what it was that really died?

So troubling was this issue that when the council of Chalcedon, in 451, tried to distinguish between and yet assert the two natures of Christ, the human and the divine "without commixture or confusion", the Alexandrine Church refused to accept the formula, and from then on was condemned by the rest of the Christian world as believing in a Christ who was some kind of divine-human amalgam consisting of a divine person with a human body. This "monophysite" (one-nature) or "miaphysite" (mixed or combined nature) view sets them apart from most of the Christian world. Some say that it was politics that caused this to happen — other breaks already having taken place between the dominant Byzantine Church (allied closely with the transplanted Roman Emperors reigning from Constantinople) and other Christian regional churches anxious to protect their autonomy. All these could very well have been real reasons for the split. But on the other hand, of all people, the Egyptians I met seemed to me to be the last kind of people who would pick a fight with anyone just to be contrary to or assert their independence from the rest of the world.

Greece, a short hop by plane from Cairo to Athens, seemed very different. Not that the Greeks were not also friendly and hospitable, but in Greece one is in a whole different world. So old and yet so vibrant, with its stony landscape and rugged mountains pockmarked with ruins and yet its towns and cities seeming to jump with a modern beat. I visited most of the usual touristy places, the Parthenon, Delphi, the Corinthian peninsula, and took a quick overnight cruise to the islands of Pelos and Idhra (Hydros) where I took a dip in the Aegean and ate squid and drank distilled plum brandy and visited an ancient hilltop temple and a tiny whitewashed church and monastery honoring a local saint. A day, and almost a missed plane later — due to not being all that quick at reading the Greek alphabet on bus signs — I caught another airbus to Rome's DaVinci airport and transferred to the Alitalia plane home. Sights recognized or even seen for the first time to and from Israel from 30,000 or more feet were the Adriatic "heel" of Italy, Mt. Aetna, the north side of Corsica, the area around Nice, France, the southwest coast of Ireland, the northeast coast of Newfoundland, Prince Edward Island, the southwest coast of Nova Scotia, the Maine coast, and the shore areas near Boston and the Connecticut shore of Long Island Sound. And a good part of this, some 5000 miles worth, on that one last long day! But by then I was quite weary of travels and anxious to get home, and to get on with my new life.

Chapter 8
Details, Ideals and Reality

It was now early June of 1981. Ronald Reagan was back to work after having been shot and the pope was recovering from his wound. Having suffered enough from the clammy heat in Egypt, I skipped the CTSA (Catholic Theological Society of America) convention in Cincinnati and headed straight home to dispose of most of my parent's home furnishings and sell off their house. It was a big and often heartbreaking job, one that forced me to make a lot of difficult choices. I made a number of trips north to the Stella Maris cabin; the first of these to meet with my fellow cabin members and to decide on a site for my hermitage cabin and what financial and legal steps would be needed before undertaking such a project. Although there were forty acres in the back of the club property that they were willing to sell to me, getting electricity back there would be a very expensive proposition. Nor, except for a swamp that flooded some springs, was there much of a view, and having no mineral rights on that piece, there was no ability to stop the State of Michigan from leasing it and waking up some morning to find a drilling rig set up in one's front or back yard. Eventually it was decided that the hermitage cabin would be located just out of sight of the main cabin at a spot about a quarter mile downstream on the edge of the bluff overlooking the river, even though, due to a large bend in the river, the actual walking distance between the two cabins would be only about 300 yards.

Financially, the understanding was that I was to pay the taxes on the twenty-three acre piece of the Stella Maris property that included that location and was bounded by parts of two quarter-section lines (on the east and north, and by the river to the west and south — about half of this piece being wooded conifer swamp. This way the tax bill on the hermitage could be kept separate from the taxes on the rest of the property which we all shared in common. There would also be a quit-claim deed on my cabin, as well as a provision in my will, that when I kicked the bucket, the place would become the property of the Stella Maris Club, free and clear.

More trips north were made that summer for hauling up stuff I would need for the coming winter, including my woodstove to heat the main cabin while living there and some tools like chainsaw, axe, wedges, and splitting maul for gathering firewood and beginning to prepare my cabin site. The most memorable of these trips was in August with the old International Scout pulling the trailer loaded with tools, office equipment and some other things, including the old fuel oil tank that was to contain my backup diesel fuel. The Scout kept stopping just about every twenty miles or so and I had to sit and wait about five minutes for whatever it was that was causing the problem to change its mind and allow the engine to start up again.

By September the house had been sold, through the instrument of a "land contract", to my young friends, the daughter of our local parish organist, and her husband, a funeral home director — an arrangement that sometimes made me feel a bit creepy as to where my main income would come from for the next seven years. By October 17th the house was empty and I was overwhelmed by the feeling as to how much "something" which I couldn't quite name in my life was "now entirely over and gone". As I wrote in my journal that night "In some ways I feel like a man without a country all over again." When had I felt that way before? And then I headed back up to Combermere, Ontario, with more things to dispose of and to see my friends over at Douglas who were expecting still another child.

One thing really began to bother me while I was there in Canada — enough that I filled several pages of my journal pondering it. It had to do with, as I put it, my "growing wealth". Here I was, on the verge of finally beginning to live as a hermit and yet finding myself the sole heir of my parents' savings and the recipient, over the next few years, of the total value of their home. How should I handle this? One plan, which I was to suggest to the diocesan priest retirement fund director, would be, after building my hermitage cabin, to hand everything over to them and from it to be paid the same as any retired priest, along with medical benefits and other insurance. As it turned out, for some reason or other they were very cool to the idea. I hadn't worked long enough in the diocese to be included under such a plan. So I told them to simply keep what I had earned by way of retirement funds as a donation — which wasn't much, since the program had only started after I had begun to teach.

I'd also had begun to feel guilty about all this money and income, despite the inflation rate (interest rates during the Carter presidency had reached unprecedented heights and even now they had only begun to slow a bit). Another thing that bothered me was the amount of taxes I was paying: the inheritance tax that Reagan was only later to abolish had taken a hefty chunk out of my inheritance. But even more, I opposed the military uses to which these taxes were being put. One of my cabin buddies, Fr. George Zabelka, had been an Army chaplain during World War II in the Pacific theater, and although he was to serve for years after as a reserve and state National Guard chaplain, he suddenly, late in life, had become an almost rabid pacifist. He made a pilgrimage back to Hiroshima which he had first seen within a month or two after the atomic bombing. At that point and for years after, he had seen that as a horrible, but necessary, step to end the war. But now, a quarter century later, George was crossing the country and later on, even Europe, on a "peace pilgrimage", speaking and writing on resistance to all things military. George and I had long discussions or arguments, he contending that all true Christians, whether as individuals or organizations, and hence, by inference, all Christian society, must be ready to "turn the other cheek". I, arguing that while I believed that pacifists had a vocation to raise our consciousness to such ideals (I had already had a paper published in the U.K. in *The Teilhard Review* on this topic) I felt, as did Teilhard, that civilization could no more do without armies to keep the peace between nations than individual communities could do without police.

Yet what I also believed (and still do) is that in no way can the use of nuclear weapons, or even the deterrence threat of using such weapons, especially strategic nuclear weapons (the multi-warhead

ICBM, etc.) be morally justified. I simply could not see this as in any way allowable under the Catholic "just war" theory or doctrine. While the accidental killing of civilians ("collateral damage" as it is now called) seemed to be an unavoidable by-product of modern warfare, it seemed to me, as it still does, that the deliberate targeting of whole cities, of whole countries more or less, simply on the excuse that such warfare might seem so unthinkable as to make its actual occurrence impossible, is not only foolish but profoundly immoral and irresponsible – even if it seemed to work. Accordingly I was really torn up over how to avoid contributing to such terror and I had resolved to somehow reduce my income so that as little as possible tax money would go to the federal government.

First, I decided to start giving some of it away. Not enough to feel much of a pinch myself, but enough, through charitable tax write-offs, that my contribution to the federal government would be minimal. Some money I gave through my folk's parish Saint Vincent de Paul Society to a family in need. Somewhat more I gave to a nearby Catholic college (oddly enough one of the colleges that I thought had intended to hire me a few years back) to provide scholarships to two young Palestinian girls whose school-teacher father had been thrown out of work by the Israeli occupiers. And while in Canada, pondering this affluence problem while staying with my Madonna House associates who lived in a real state of evangelical poverty, my near-by friends up there asked me if I could help them get by temporarily by means of a modest loan for some months. They also promised me the going rate of interest — which seemed fair enough to me. Perhaps it was a mistake. But with all my newly inherited money and a conscience problem over it, what could I say? Returning to Michigan and settling down for the winter at the Stella Maris cabin, I then began to clear my cabin site and pour over my possible cabin designs.

Yet this too presented me with problems. The one-room log "poustinias" I'd been using for retreat days in Canada did not seem very practical for year-round, rest-of-one's life, use. My Ukrainian rite hermit friend up there had one with an upstairs and downstairs, even if he didn't have indoor plumbing or electric power. Since I had already become dependent on an electric typewriter and had long since found out that study by kerosene lamp seemed a sure road to blindness, I decided that I might as well have a refrigerator and electric cooking stove. So that added up to at least several rooms. And then there were all those books and tools. In sum, I ended up with not just a two-story cabin but a three-story plan, consisting of a basement containing a workshop and book/file room, a main floor containing a combined living room, kitchenette, and office space, a bedroom with a couple of closets, and a small bathroom. In the cabin loft space would be a chapel flanked by some under-the-eaves storage space. It seemed a very good plan to me, one that even had some symbolic aspects, with a basement space for physical labor, a main floor office for mental work, and a loft for the life of the spirit. Besides, I figured that having the chapel upstairs would guarantee some warmth on cold winter mornings as the woodstove on the main floor warmed up. A ceiling fan would be used to drive some of that heat back down to the main floor later in the morning, and a drip-feed cabin type oil space-heater in the basement could help even the temperature out overnight in mid-winter, prevent pipes from freezing, and help keep the main floor warm.

Now all this was easy enough to fit into any standard cabin plan, such as those pre-fabricated by a local log-cabin company nearby. Although I wished I had the time and the equipment to harvest logs and prepare them myself, I had promised the Stella Maris group that I'd do my best to be out of their way by the following year. So I decided to go with the "sill and post" type of log construction using short white cedar logs (none longer than 8 ft. — the standard crosswise truck hauling size – spiked in between vertical posts wherever a door or window, or corner was needed. Everything came supposedly pre-cut to size.

Still, I was not to be content with one of their standard plans. Instead I wanted to incorporate the latest solar heat technology as well. Accordingly, I designed a floor plan that would have an offset in the southwest corner of the building to allow for a basement level (since I was building on the edge of a bluff) solar greenhouse, once that would supposedly sluice warm sun-heated air, through registers in the floor, to the living room level, while sucking in air into the greenhouse through register openings on the basement floor. When I had the basement dug that spring and the foundation put in, I had the mason build that inner wall of the greenhouse with thicker concrete blocks and then fill up all the openings in the blocks with poured concrete. All the better, I thought, to retain the heat from the winter's sun. I also carefully calculated the slope of the greenhouse's outside wall for maximum exposure based on the sun's elevation in mid-winter at latitude 45.07 degrees N. All this ended up giving the front end of the cabin (facing west toward the river) a curious lop-sided appearance, one which I decided, aesthetically speaking, needed to be offset by a lop-sided appearance in the other direction on the cabin's back (east or driveway) end. I also decided that the west or river-facing end of the cabin should have a projecting or "prow-shaped" west wall, one that would enable me, while sitting in my rocking chair, to look upstream and downstream without even turning my head. All these fancy plans gave me the feeling that I was a veritable Frank Llyod Wright of cabin designers and gave the poor cabin log fabricator, I'm sure, the fits. It also should have given me, within a year or two, a bit more humilty when I discovered that all my fine plans for a solar green house somehow contributing to heating the cabin in winter turned out to be a complete bust. I seem to have forgotten that anything farther north than 45 degrees is already more than half-way to the North Pole. Eventually I was to reconfigure that greenhouse into a screen-porch and storage area and as a place to park a gasoline-powered generator for when the "Top of Michigan" rural electric co-op lines fail during storms.

Meanwhile, some of my other mistakes began to catch up with me. Late in December, my friend from Canada, the one who now had five children and had needed a small loan earlier, came to see me – this time about a much larger one. It seems that he had invested, along with another college teacher, in an old business building in a nearby town with the object of renovating the building into several small shops with an apartment or two above.

Everything at first had gone fine. They'd gotten a loan from the local bank, but now, half-way through the renovation, before they had any income to show for their investment or work, the local bank, a branch of a very large Canadian corporation, had switched managers and the new one had recalled the loan. Could I help — especially if guaranteed repayment within three years along with the same going rate of interest? I guess I gulped and said, "Well, I guess so" or something like that. At least this would relieve me of my worries of what to do with my extra money. With most of it gone for the time being I'd have much less weighing on my conscience and still be repaid in the end. Nor did it occur to me back then that there might be something unchristian about the whole idea of my accepting interest on a loan from someone who at that point I still very much trusted, and genuinely liked, especially since it was his wife asked me for anything (it was she who asked for the first loan). So how could I refuse? Besides, he promised to be back when I was ready to add the roof to my cabin, a big job I dreaded but which he had, in his summer log-cabin renovation business, done many times. And thus I parted ways with approximately one-forth of my inheritance.

Not that I was left penniless, although paradoxically, my next big trip was completely free. There was still an invitation to a so-called "God Conference" I had received while back at Tantur the spring before. So the day before Christmas I drove down to Jackson to spend Christmas with relatives and then the day after flew from Detroit to Honolulu and then to the island of Maui. There the Unification Church people (generally known as "Moonies") had gathered some two-hundred people from at least thirty-three countries and we were lodged and entertained at the posh Wailea Beach Hotel for the first of their "New ERA" conferences on "God: the Contemporary Discussion". There we exchanged papers, and responses to papers, and dined — but not wined — unless you paid for that yourself. We were also given tours to the old whaling port of Lahaina and a trip up to the top of the extinct Haleakela volcano, from which we could see across to the snow-topped summit of Mauna Kea on the big island, where today are situated some of the world's largest astronomical telescopes.

When the conference had just gotten started, someone discovered that Fr. Hans Küng, the Swiss Catholic theologian who had already raised quite a stir among Rome's doctrinal watchdogs, was staying at the next hotel down the line. He was in Hawaii to give some talks at the University of Hawaii later that week. They invited him to come over to the "God Conference" but he demurred, saying that he was in enough trouble with Rome as it already was. A few days later, when I was back in Honolulu, thanks to my friend Fr. William Johnston, I received an invitation to a party held by one of the university's faculty members at his own home. There I had a brief chance to talk to Küng and he asked me what I was doing and when I told him I was trying to live like a hermit off in the woods and write theology he looked at me with a rather bemused expression and said, "Maybe that is what I should do."

I learned or observed something else of great interest at that meeting. One hears constantly of how religions divide and how a more philosophical and detached academic approach is the key to ecumenical understanding. Yet what I observed at that meeting seemed to me to demonstrate just the opposite. Ecumenically inclined theologians and religious people seemed to have great respect for other's beliefs and were generally more anxious to adopt an irenic tone to their discussions, seeking to find a common ground among their many diverse views. In contrast, the professional philosophers reveled in their differences so much so that if they couldn't find a substantial disagreement in their positions they seemed genuinely disappointed and then inclined to attack each other on the ground of their methodology. Perhaps this is all meant to be part of the academic game, but it seemed to me that these men all too often appeared to be grand-standing their own intellectual acumen more than really searching for the truth. Perhaps it was only a particularly prickly group of philosophers, those so unrecognized that they stooped to attending Moonie-sponsored conferences all expenses paid. But it definitely gave me something to reflect on when I still occasionally long to indulge myself in academic pursuits.

Details, Ideals, and Reality

On the way home I stopped in San Francisco and visited friends of my folks who had retired in San Mateo, and also drove down to Monterey, despite damaged roads from a violent rainstorm, to visit my father's cousin, the retired army officer and his wife whom I had first visited in 1967. They had, predictably, aged quite a bit. This was only my second visit to California and on the way home the plane crossed over the north end of Lake Tahoe, the Nevada desert, Utah's Great Salt Lake, the south side of the Grand Teton Range in Wyoming, and then over the Black Hills of South Dakota. But such immense spaces of nothingness in between! Between Lake Tahoe and Salt Lake! I remember thinking that it would be weird country to drive through, and a some years later, after doing so, I swore I'd never drive that stretch of God-forsaken-landscape by road again. When I got home it turned out that the same storm that had ravaged California had dumped about two feet of snow on my nearly three-quarter-mile long driveway and that being too much for the old International Scout to handle, had to hire a logger from down the road who had a small bulldozer to reopen my way back in.

Breaking Ground

Just before noon March 21st, the first day of spring, I walked around a few remaining snow-banks and with a compass and a home-made transit (a camera tripod with an old rifle scope attached), plotted the exact directions of the four points of the compass and the rough outlines of the excavation for the cabin's foundation. I paid a visit to the Montmorency County building inspector and applied for a building permit, while the inspector, a transplanted Louisiana Cajun lumberman, cranked open his office window to expectorate some of his chewing tobacco.

My neighbor and I cut a swath through the trees about 200 yards long by about 20 yards wide for the installation of a power line and a few weeks later the excavator dug a foundation hole and by May 22, 1982 (I marked the date in fresh concrete by the basement doorway) the footings and floor had been poured. Two weeks later I had basement walls and a tall — really tall, so tall the mason was worried and braced it with angled wooden props — double flue chimney. It sat on angled iron beams spanning two block pillars, another one of my nifty ideas which would enable me to clean both flues without climbing up on what was to be a very steep-pitched (10/12) roof.

By early June a big truck arrived with all the logs cut to size. Plus another truck from the lumber yard with all the floor joists and over-rafters — the local building code requiring double roofs — aboard. My neighbor (a local high-school science and history teacher) and I then set to work. The main floor supports went in first, followed by a sub-floor of plywood. Then we carefully set up and braced all the posts or planed vertical logs that formed the uprights at each door and window opening, and at each corner of the walls. Then the real work began.

Each log had to be spiked into place with large spikes which are square in cross-section, but twisted in a spiral pattern. They are not easy to drive into place and almost impossible to remove once driven in, even in a soft wood like white cedar. But this was not the worst. It turns out that the spikes that were supplied were six inches long rather than the usual five inch ones. A standard hammer just wouldn't do the job. I'd bought a heavier hammer but it would barely do it either. Instead I ended up using a short handled sledge hammer which delivered such heavy blows that my friend had to sit on the logs to keep them from bouncing out of place while I pounded away. And suddenly that summer it also got very hot. We'd start work as early as we could and generally quit by three in the afternoon. We'd just be too exhausted by then to go on. So my neighbor would go home to rest and I'd collapse for an hour or so in an old Avion trailer I'd bought to sleep in and in which to store tools, then go back to work on my own. One day, when I was working alone putting up spruce log beams to support the loft, I slipped on a step ladder rung and one of the beams came down and hit me a glancing blow to my head. Luckily I was wearing an old US Navy "pith-helmet" as usual to shade me from the sun. It was only made of cloth-covered cardboard and flew off my head as the log bounced off it and onto my shoulder. But it saved me, I think, from a real concussion. I've had great respect for hard-hats — even fake pith-helmets — ever since.

Securing the main tie beams across the main room space was something of a thrill as well. For the occasion I got out my great-grandfather's brace and bit set to drill the large holes that were required for the long bolts that would tie the beams together. After that, the ridge pole and the log rafters had to go up. We were now into kind of a high-wire act stage of the construction, and my friend, who didn't take to climbing high up very easily, ended up mostly handing me the ceiling boards while I tacked them into place. So I hired another friend to help speed things up. These ceiling boards and other paneling lumber were of tongue and groove cedar milled on a water-powered saw mill on Silver Creek near Epsilon — over near Petoskey — probably the last such water powered mill in Michigan. The fellow who ran the place (and who worked alone) also supplied me with tongue and groove pine planks for the floors. One morning, just as we were finishing the inner ceiling board part of the operation, I was up on top of the roof and my neighbor was down on the ground below. I had an electric "skill saw" in my hand and was about to trim the ceiling boards along the eastern peak of the roof when my right foot slipped on the morning's dew and both I and the saw started to come down the steep roof. Luckily, I had strung a strong nylon rope from one end of the ridge pole to the other and had fastened myself to it with another nylon cord around my waist. The saw fell all the way to the ground, but the rather stretchy nylon safety line arrested my fall about two-thirds of the way down the side of the roof. By then I was beginning to have second thoughts about lofty beams and steep snow-shedding roofs, but it was way too late to change my plans.

Then my friend from Canada arrived with his whole family to save the day and within about eight days we had all the 2x8" over-rafters, insulation, roofing plywood, and roofing shingles in place, only this time I stayed on the ground most of the time. By now it was near the end of August and my school-teacher friends, both from here and Canada, had to go back to their work. Another carpenter friend came for a day to help me set in place all the

Chapter 8

windows — very heavy ones, all being triple pane. Another retired carpenter friend, a fellow everyone called "Harry Cook" although his real name was Jerome Marcenkowski, wanted to donate something, so I told him he could build me two stairways, a regular one to the basement, and an open, log supported one to the loft. A few years later I was to conduct Harry's funeral after he suddenly died of a heart attack in Alaska where his son lived. I had been called in suddenly from a meeting of priests elsewhere and was a bit distracted. When I went to use his name in the prayers of final commendation, for the life of me I couldn't remember his real name. I hope he has forgiven me that, as very often when I climb those stairs to pray, I remember "Harry's" kind gift to me — plus his remonstrance over why did I use pine (which dents so easily) instead of fir for the flooring, plus my asking why he didn't advise me to do that before I ordered the lumber from Silver Creek.

The rest of that fall I worked mostly on my own, laying flooring, building partitions, putting up paneling, installing sinks, plumbing, and with the help of another fellow (the brother of a priest friend who knew what he was doing) the electric wiring. I also installed my trusty little wood stove so I wouldn't freeze during the late fall and early winter afternoons. I bought an old cabin space-heater from a second hand store. It seems to have been one from the McClougth Steel owned hunting camp that was bought and dismantled by the State when it acquired the "Green Timbers" property to add to the Pigeon River State Forest. The stove itself was made in Beaverton, Wisconsin. That was the town where, I finally learned from my father, the year before he died, that a jury composed mostly of local farmers had decided my grandfather deserved prison for what had gone wrong as a result of the crash of the stock-market a year or two before I was born. My grandfather was pardoned on his deathbed by the state Governor. This family tragedy also explained what always seemed to me to be my father's excessive attention to the most minute details of book-keeping — a trait that unhappily I, a highly unsuccessful perfectionist, have never acquired.

I finally moved into my cabin on "Candlemas Day", February

Details, Ideals, and Reality

3, 1983. The move wasn't entirely voluntary, but rather a necessity of not freezing to death. I had already moved the woodstove there to use during the day. But around the third week in January, the oil tank for the space heater at the main cabin had run dry. Meanwhile, the installation of two new pipelines (one for oil, one for gas) along the county road had torn up this sand and gravel route so badly that even four-wheel drive vehicles were getting stuck. No way could I get the fuel oil company to come out to refill the tank. So evenings I was trying to re-warm the big cabin using the fireplace and by placing a kerosene lamp near my feet as I ate supper. I stood it for just about a week. So with partitions barely finished, and not nearly enough finish on the newly-laid floors, I moved myself and my remaining gear up to my new home as soon as one coat of finish on the floors was dry.

If I have rattled on at length about this building project, I suppose it is because in some way it symbolizes, or more than that, it is one of the few tangible accomplishments of my life. To live in one's own house, especially one built as much as possible with one's own hands, gives, I think, a certain satisfaction like nothing else might.

Back when I was first discussing my plans with the Stella Maris members, one of the senior priests in our group, newly retired at the time, wanted to know why I couldn't just settle to live in a "trailer", that is, a mobile home, as he did, in a mobile home park in the town where he had last been a pastor. I also remember reading about how Thomas Merton's abbot, when he finally gave him permission to live in a hermitage rather than the monastery, suggested they park a trailer out in the woods for him. At this suggestion, despite his years of pleading for this permission, Merton balked. It was not his intention to live in a "tin can". No doubt the abbot really was questioning Merton's — who was known for his rather mercurial temperament — ability to persevere. Although I still owned such a "tin can", later parked out on the back 40 where I occasionally used it as a "poustinia" for a day at a time, I understand Merton's dismay. The reason is that, as I see it, a hermit or anchorite must "stay put" if his or her vocation is ever to bear real fruit. Perhaps it is only a play on words, but I also think that an "anchorite" (from the Greek, *ana-choros*, someone who is set, or lives apart or removed from the rest) needs to be "anchored", that is, not easily moved. If according to one of my authorities, a community of hermits is something of an oxymoron, so too is an anchorite who lives in a cabin on wheels!

Which leads me to my second great construction project — the composition or drawing up of a rule or plan for my life.

Living According to the Rules

Canon 603 of the Catholic Church's then new 1983 edition of the Code of Canon Law only specified two things for those called to the "eremitic" or "anchoritic" life: first, that they "devote their life to the praise of God and the salvation of the world through a stricter separation from the world, the silence of solitude and assiduous prayer and penance" and, second, that to have this life officially recognized by the church, that "he or she publicly professes the three evangelical counsels, confirmed by a vow or other sacred bond, in the hands of the diocesan bishop and observes his or her own plan of life under his direction."

Given this bare outline, I then proceeded to draw up a "plan of life" based on the above more or less broad outline, first of all incorporating most of the more specific rules for priests belonging to the Discalced Carmelite Third Order or "Secular" rule — something I had already undertaken while still a seminarian many years before and had tried to keep, more or less successfully, during my up till then twenty-five years in the priesthood. Featured in this rule is an hour of "mental prayer" or meditation each day (generally broken into two periods, morning and evening), abstinence from meat on Wednesdays and Fridays, (plus Saturdays during Advent and the vigils of some major feasts on the Church and Carmelite calendars). These seemed like hardly onerous practices, at least in the pre-Vatican II church. Then there are the vows of obedience, poverty, and chastity to be lived according to one's state of life — the latter of which of course, for priests of the Latin rite, means celibacy.

Details, Ideals, and Reality

However, all this seemed too vague for me. What I felt I really needed was a daily "horarium" or schedule, specifying my time of rising each morning, starting times for the various "hours" of prayer, rules about the frequency of trips to town, receiving visitors, etc., etc. To do this, I eagerly employed my recently acquired toy — a Kaypro IV desktop computer, whose primitive CP/M software included what was then a very sophisticated word-processing program called "Word Perfect" which was designed by an academic and featured automatic paragraph numbering and indexing in the European style (e.g. 1.3.5, etc.) and easy footnoting capability. My idea was to organize my "Plan of Life" by numbering each paragraph or rule as corresponding to one of three levels, making a distinction between general ideals, more specific rules, and, lastly, the most detailed directives or "observances", and footnoting especially those details that I felt might need future adjustment.

A good thing that I did. Planning ones life down to the last detail might seem like fun for control-freaks, but, despite my tendency in that direction, something told me that my life, as actually lived, might demand some adjustments, particularly when it came to keeping a vow of "poverty" — something that already seemed threatened by my having spent nearly $2000 on my new computer and printer. I'm not sure, but I suspect that perhaps my "Plan of Life" was possibly the first computer generated rule in the history of religion. I could imagine Saint Benedict spinning in his grave!

Still, despite the fun this effort afforded, I did have some more theological qualms of conscience. Very much conscious of Martin Luther's critique of professional religious life and its obsession with rules (in turn inspired by Saint Paul's critique of the Old Testament "Law" as threatening Christian liberty) I also wrote an introductory chapter to my plan in which I tried to evaluate the role and function of such a plan of life. I also tried to incorporate some of these insights into an article I wrote for the Discalced Carmelite quarterly *Spiritual Life* — an article which resulted in a number of letters from others, especially those trying to persuade a bishop to give them official approval to become a hermit or anchorite. Unfortunately for them (many of them former nuns with no established means of support) I had to tell them that the first rule is not to ask a bishop for financial support. My second piece of advice was to be prepared to run into a lot of suspicion, even if they had a means of support. As person who wants to live off in the woods all alone is bound to be considered eccentric. Despite Canon 603 of the new code, getting ecclesiastical approval for such eccentricity is going to be an uphill battle.

Finally, my last piece of advice was more of an observation than anything else: that probably the only reason I was ever able to get this official permission or approval was that I was already a priest and they couldn't figure out what else to do with me. As my bishop had already put it, he couldn't figure out why an academic like me would want to live off alone in the woods — but nevertheless, that he trusted me. Nor did he require a "novitiate" or further period of trial, as by then I'd already been living this life for about four years, during which I'd been in fairly regular correspondence with him. When I had doubted myself in one letter, he replied that he was at least certain my call was not to be in a parish. In view of the repeated requests made to me in the years to come, especially to fill in for resigned, ill, dismissed, or otherwise absent parish priests, at least on weekends, Bishop Povish's opinion, even though he urged me to put myself at the local bishop's disposal in this way, has been a constant reassurance. But most of all, his reception of my vows, pronounced and signed before him and some close friends gathered in the side chapel of Saint Mary (Our Lady of Mt. Carmel) Cathedral in Gaylord, Michigan, on October 3, 1984, made it all official. Unfortunately, it did not turn out to be all that clear-cut or simple. Life never is.

Reality

For those first several years, and even for some time after my status became official, I did go out, practically every weekend, to fill in for sick or absent priests throughout the Diocese of Gaylord. Some weekends I put up to three hundred or more miles on my car when the assigned parish included a "mission" church at some distance from the parish itself. During one period, which lasted for some months, I was practically, for all intents and purposes, the quasi-official "sacramental minister" to a farming community some thirty-five miles away after the pastor became disabled and was replaced — to the extent a priest-pastor can be replaced — by a lay administrator. Later on, that administrator's place was taken by a deacon, one who, for an ex-plumber, was a rather good preacher, but who, as a married man, was (as long as his wife still lived) forbidden the priesthood.

If the Church's rules on these matters had bothered me before, now they began to bother me more than ever. When I had first moved north, I made two requests of the local diocese. One was that, as a trained theologian, I would like to be considered as a possible theology instructor in a program to train local men for the diaconate. I stressed what I saw as the present desirability of having such a program – something that the former bishop of Gaylord's group of consulters studying this same question recommended. But I also spoke of the strong need for the continuing theological education for those who were already deacons, as there were already a handful of them who had been ordained elsewhere and had moved to Northern Michigan. This would be needed in order to advance these men to the priesthood once the people in Rome finally got around to facing reality — that is, that without a married priesthood, or at least a priesthood that was open to married men — that the Church will be in for very bleak times. But for various reasons, among which were the sensitivities of women (who remain barred from ordained ministry in the Catholic Church) even a program for the formation of deacons, was completely shelved in the Diocese of Gaylord, not to be considered again for some twenty years when the shortage of priests had become even more desperate.

The other request, which I actually made twice, once back then, when I first came north, and repeated again when still another bishop took over the local diocese, was that I become officially attached or "incardinated" as a priest of the local diocese — even while remaining officially a "hermit". Both requests were turned down by the local diocesan Board of Advisors, even though the local bishop as well as my own bishop in Lansing felt that this was the logical thing to do. Apparently the board was happy enough to have me around to "fill in" when someone got sick or the like, but having a priest living off in the woods as a "hermit" most of the time, even if financially provided for, apart from any diocesan retirement plan, was just too unusual, or perhaps, unsettling. I can't say I blame them. To me, under the present conditions, parish priests, often greatly overworked and too often suffering from diminished morale, are real heroes, even when their performance leaves much to be desired. Why shouldn't they be suspicious or even resentful of my contemplative leisure, especially when I've invoked the contemplative's privilege of not being obliged to serve in pastoral ministry (see Canon 674)?

Nevertheless, as understandable as this reaction seems to me, it in turn left me increasingly resentful, both of universal as well as local church policies, and as I had to increasingly admit, suspicious of church discipline and even doctrine itself. Some of this suspicion began to show up in my sermons and homilies. At one point I had even drawn up my own "syllabus of errors" — that is, a rather lengthy confession of my own difficulties, ranging from doctrinal issues such as the Trinity (at least as articulated in the usual "person" and "nature" terminology — it still sounded, especially after my experience in the Holy Land, like "tritheism" to me) to disciplinary matters, such as the rationale behind clerical celibacy. The local bishop, in response, assured me that he didn't think of me as a "heretic", even when I wished to point out that according to Canons 750 and 1371, if not outright punished, I should at least be barred from the pulpit. (In 1998 Pope John-Paul II added even further sanctions to these two Canons, apparently to try to insure even greater conformity to official Church teachings.) Apparently I figured that, if nothing else, this would insure that I be given the solitude I increasingly sought.

Nor was I even consistent when it came to this. In the late 1980s I had begun work on a full-length book to flesh out some of those ideas I had played with earlier back when I was teaching, particularly the idea of applying Viktor Frankl's psychological dynamics to James Fowler's analysis of the "Stages of Faith". The result was that Paulist Press published, in 1990, my little work titled *Faith: Security and Risk.* In it I repeated the sharp distinction (borrowed from theologian Wilfred Cantwell Smith) between faith in the gospel sense of a loving trust in God and belief as an attempt, in language, to articulate the reasons for or shape of that faith. In other words, faith is an attitude or attribute of the heart. Belief is a mindset or conviction in our head. Formulas of belief, that is, doctrine, are only halting attempts to point to what is beyond such articulation. To paraphrase Cardinal Newman, "a thousand difficulties" (in regard to our beliefs) "do not add up to one doubt" (against faith). Apparently, at least to the local bishop's mind, my "difficulties" which I tended to see as doubts, did not outweigh his need to have someone, no matter how unsuited, in the pulpit each Sunday.

And of course, my problem is that, having used these distinctions in my book, I can hardly plead that my own analysis can't be applied to myself. If when I was a child, I thought and believed as a child, I should now (especially after writing a book on the subject) know better when it comes to reaching out to those who are still unable to make such distinctions. In fact, I even volunteered to do parish workshops on the subject — providing I could limit myself to one weekend a month. But after giving a few (to parishes whose pastors were looking for a chance for a weekend off — none never stayed around to hear what I had to say!) I gave up on the project, especially after one pastor told me that he didn't want his people stirred up and having to seek his advice.

So my next attempt to insure my solitude took a much more drastic form. I simply decided to isolate myself physically by taking my car out of service for extended periods of time. Several times during my first five years in solitude, I had been without a car when my rapidly aging Volkswagen developed major mechanical problems and had to be left in the repair garage for several days or even a week at a time. Its absence at first caused a kind of quiet sense of desolation that considering my calling, was not all that bad. I began to wonder: do I need a car at all?

Prudence and some close friends, however, persuaded me that being 24 miles from town, and 6 miles from the county bus service, made it risky for me not to have one. So I traded in the VW (or gave away—it being on its last legs or wheels) for a used Jeep Cherokee, one which served me well for 15 years on the road, and which still sat out in the woods for a few more years – until the clutch gave out – near my cabin wearing a set of chains guaranteed to get me out of my half-mile or so drive way in all but the very worst of storms. But still finding myself entirely too mobile, I began to take the Cherokee off of insurance for a month or two at a time during the winter, hitching a ride to town with my nearest neighbors two miles down the road or asking them to pick up my mail and some groceries when convenient. It worked out rather well. At least folks, including the local bishop, seemed to have become convinced that I was really serious about my "hermiting" and even respected me for it. In fact, despite having picked up a newer used Jeep to replace the old one on the road, I was tempted to sell the newer one and do exactly the same with the older until it deteriorated beyond repair.

However, this would not mean that I would never travel. During the period I have written about in this chapter, I did manage to take a few more trips.

One was a rather spectacular trip to Korea and Japan for several weeks in August 1984, thanks again to the "Moonies"— to another "God-Conference" in Seoul with a side trip to the ancient capital of Kyöngju plus ten days in Japan (thanks to the hospitality of the Maryknoll Missioners and Northwest Airlines stopover arrangements) touring the famous Buddhist and Shinto sites in Japan, including Kyoto, Nara, Ise, and the Nikko National Park in the mountains north of Tokyo.

In June of 1986 I took my new used 1985 Jeep Cherokee – camping in the back of it most of the way – to the Catholic Theological Society of America convention in San Francisco, revisiting the Black Hills, the Big Horn Mountains, Yellowstone, the Grand Tetons, and Yosemite on the way out and visiting Crater

Lake, Oregon, and climbing Mount Saint Helen in Washington State on the way back and then a month or so later driving east to New England to visit my elderly aunt in Rhode Island before she died.

According to my "Plan of Life", I still am allowed to take a theological convention trip and one shorter vacation trip (or try to combine the two) once a year. If the latter is a separate trip, it is usually to the Lake Superior country in the fall to camp a few days on the "Shores of Gitchiegumi — the shining big sea water" of Hiawatha's land. A change of perspective now and then is good, even for the hermit's soul. But an even bigger and much more unsettling change of perspective was already in the works.

The Test

When one enters into the life of solitude, as the early desert fathers knew well, one enters into the realm of the demons, but that realm is not so much in the emptiness of the desert, but rather in the depths of the self. Merton, during his short life in his long-awaited hermitage, soon found this out first hand, in his agony over his hospital "love affair" with "S" (a still unnamed nursing student from Cincinnati). Merton's biographer, Michael Mott, quotes brother Patrick Hart, Merton's secretary, as pointing to Merton's hermitage as the place where, at least figuratively, Merton "sweat blood".

My test in this regard began much less suddenly, in fact, only as a culmination of nearly twenty years of friendship. I have written previously of my friends in Canada, particularly of the couple who befriended me almost from the beginning of my studies in Ottawa, who became my neighbors along the Gatineau River in Quebec, who visited me several times in Michigan, and whom I continued to visit in my many trips back to Ontario, especially after they moved to a location not far from Combermere, where I almost yearly traveled to meetings of the Madonna House Associate Priests.

On one such visit, I rejoiced to see the photos of their celebration of their twentieth wedding anniversary, celebrated with a renewal of their marriage vows after what had been, at best, a rather rocky marriage from the start. As I related before, he had left the seminary to marry her. When I first met them they had one child (a golden-haired daughter) and were soon to have their first son. Eventually they would have two more boys, and finally, one more girl, who was less than a year old when they brought them all with them when they came to help me finish my hermitage roof. Although a college philosophy instructor, he had much experience in salvaging and rebuilding old log cabins, and as part of the process, adding new roofs. Seeing this family of seven thrive, despite their difficulties, had been, for almost eighteen years, one of the joys of my celibate life. Indeed, as I have already related, I had invested not a little of my financial future in their success.

Yet I also knew there were still problems. Although he was a rather charismatic and creative personality, he was also, like many such people, somewhat impulsive, particularly when it came to his relationships to women. I remembered, at least on one occasion, trying to explain, if not seeming to defend, to some extent, his infidelities to his wife, reminding her of what her own studies in psychology had to say about such inclinations in gifted persons like her husband. But on another occasion, when they were here visiting me, I also remember making a pledge to her, one which, although carefully qualified, I took most seriously. To explain it, I must tell the reader more about her background.

She had been, in effect, raised, at least partially, by a priest. Her mother, who by then had four children, had been forced to separate from and then eventually divorce, her alcoholic husband. Bereft of any support, her mother was hired by a priest cousin of her ex-husband to be the secretary at his college chaplaincy. This kind priest saw to it that her mother and the children were housed near by, and that the children, each in turn, received a college education. Often sharing meals with them, and acting as counselor and disciplinary figure to the children, "Father Bill", as the family called him, was truly like a real "father" to them all. And although I had not yet met the man, I envied his chance to spend his life working with college students.

In the meantime, my friends' own marriage seemed to be going from bad to worse. Telling me of their troubles when they visited me in Michigan on one occasion, I went so far as to pledge to her, even while hedging my pledge with caveats based on my different, non-pastoral vocation, to try to be, if worse came to worst, for her family as much as possible what Fr. Bill had been for hers in her childhood. I really never figured having to face up to that promise.

As it turned out, their twentieth wedding anniversary was the prelude to a tumultuous break-up occasioned by his twenty-fifth high school reunion back in New Hampshire, where he met up with his recently divorced old flame. Shortly after, he ran off with her, leaving Canada for good and even changing his name. I learned some of this as a result of a call I made when I wondered about their silence over the winter holidays. The rest I learned from her first hand when I drove to eastern Ontario posthaste after getting the bad news.

There were several factors at play here. For one, she was a blue-eyed red-head – a trait that seems to have cast a spell over me as far back as I can remember. But this time it became evident to me as soon as I arrived there, but especially when I had to leave a few days later, that in some sort of a cumulative way, that I was in love with her (something even that my mother suspected years earlier, back when she had urged me to leave the priesthood to find someone to marry). In addition, realizing this emotional tie, I wondered if, or even how much, my attachment might have contributed to their breakup, even while I thought I was struggling to keep them together. And then, finally, I wondered how much my large loan to them, very little of which had yet been paid back, had added to the pressures, especially the financial pressures, that I suspected were partly responsible for my friend's flight to a new, start over-again life, in the USA. To pay off the loan he had even offered to give me title to some vacation property he had bought (rather impulsively) in Colorado, or even to the old log cabin he had rebuilt on property next to their place in Canada. But I had refused both offers, instead allowing him to postpone repayment, or even offering to forget the principal altogether if he could pay me some interest to help with my present living expenses.

What to do? For one, I made frequent calls to her and even a special trip or two to see her and her children (at least the two who were still at home) and spent long hours talking to her and trying to help her cope with her abandonment. I also made another special trip to spend a few days talking to him when he returned there to spend a few days while she (as a social worker) was called to testify in a trial in British Columbia. Oddly enough, I could not get angry with him, being still captivated by his own personal charm!

Finally, since I had already hinted at canceling their debt in exchange for their helping me, if necessary, in my old age, I assured her that she no longer need consider she owed me anything, but, at the same time, I consulted with a Canadian lawyer to see what, if anything, I could recover from him. But the lawyer — who turned out to be quite familiar with my friend's reputation for financial wheeling and dealing — gave me little hope that I could do anything in Canada that wouldn't hurt her as well, and I feared to press further in the USA lest his support payments for his children became more erratic than they already were.

Still, despite the apparent disinterested character or even seeming nobility of these intentions and actions, I have to admit that I was, perhaps for the first and only time in my life, really "head over heels" in love – although figuratively speaking, I think it would make more sense to say "heels over head", since common sense seems to have had little to do with it. Despite my many friendships with women in the past, I had never experienced anything like this before. I was, quite literally, "heart-sick". I had, from the viewpoint of an outside observer, long tended to agree with Freud's diagnosis of this state as resembling an attack of neurosis. Now I knew so first hand. I was both elated and miserable at the same time and even began to suffer some pains that sent me to my physician who deemed it wise that I be given a EKG and a cardio-vascular stress test. Although I seem to have passed that, I definitely was under stress. At first I even found myself writing poetry to cope with my emotions — again, at least for me, a really bad sign.

On several occasions, when two of their older children were married, I was present and took a minor part in the ceremonies.

Both were of course times of great stress with both of the parents present, and me trying to help keep the peace. But I knew that deep down, I had to make some decisions myself. He seemed to be hinting that he'd be quite happy to see me play the Fr. Bill role, while she had made me promise I'd do nothing to help arrange a church "annulment" of their marriage, to which I agreed, telling him that I could not possibly give any testimony that would not reflect unfavorably on him. But after one of their son's wedding, I visited him (I'll call him "R" at this point) and his new wife in the states, then returned to Canada to ask the abandoned wife a big question — would she expect me to leave the priesthood to make good on my old promise? As a rather traditional Catholic, she angrily dismissed the notion, and although that seeming rejection hurt me in one sense, I was greatly relieved.

The reason I had to press that question at that point, even though it was a very stressful time for her, was that I was soon planning to take an additional, and even more irrevocable step into solitude at the time. The "vows" I took in 1984 included the obligation of religious poverty, but up to now took no specific form of implementation — other than my giving away what I thought I could spare to various charities. But the way that things had turned out, due to some bad investments, including this very big, but only partially repaid loan that I had made to them, I could see myself ending up destitute in my old age. So I had decided to approach the local bishop with a plan similar to what I had proposed to the Lansing Diocese, but in the former case, as part of the priests' pension plan. It was an offer to hand over all my capital assets (mostly from my inheritance) to the local diocese in exchange for a monthly living allowance. My offer to Lansing had been turned down by the pension board. (Since then, however, after turning 73, the Diocese of Lansing finally decided to pay me a partial pension plus the supplemental health insurance supplied to retired priests.)

This time I decided to make a similar offer to the Diocese of Gaylord, despite my request for incardination to that diocese having been rejected. But this time it would be under the form of an independent "Hermitage Trust Fund", one which would be legally bound by state law to lend support to anyone else approved to live this form of life after my death. Meanwhile it would pay me no more than the poverty line maximum for any current year. My medical insurance would remain, for the time being, whatever the government provided. And although this same money would have probably gone a lot further for my support in Canada (plus much fuller medical benefits even as a "landed immigrant" up there), in setting up this legally binding "irrevocable trust" here in the states, it was, in effect, entering into a much more permanent "marriage" to my chosen state of life than the Canon 603 vows or promises could be, at least in terms of civil law. All I wanted my friend's first wife to do was to be fully aware of what I was doing and, I hope, never hold it against me. As it turned out, while all this was happening, one of her close friends, a fellow counsellor and co-worker in the Ontario social services was dying of cancer. So eventually she married her friend's bereaved husband. A year or so later I visited them and they had just finished building a new home and seemed quite happy – much to my relief – although I found it rather strange that their new place was next door to the rather large log cabin that "R" had built for her and his family. Not only that: that new home is between the old place and the small log cabin he had once offered to give me to repay that large loan.

However, before I took that final, closing step limiting my future options, I felt I had to do one other thing, and that was to fully examine my own motivations as to how and why I had propelled myself into this peculiar form of life. To do so, I decided to review a book once recommended by Thomas Merton to his novices at Gethsemane Abbey, Karen Horney's study of *Neurosis and Human Growth*. I had read the book once before, greatly impressed by her insights, and underlining at the time all the passages that seemed to apply to me. Now, some ten years later, I had decided to not only reread it, doing more underlining (but with a different color pencil) but also to write a synopsis of what she said and a commentary as to how it might apply to me. What it told me, at least as I interpreted it, was that by taking this final step I would be going ahead with what in her estimation would be exactly the wrong thing for me to do, that is, by withdrawing from normal life in the world, submitting to whatever was most neurotic in my personality, rather than fighting back by conforming myself to a more "normal" way of life. But instead, as I saw it, this final step would present me with the challenge of confronting my "demons" head-on. It was, for me, a truly irrevocable leap of faith.

Cosmic Distractions

Other than this renewed determination to pursue what I saw as my vocation, something else came along my way to alleviate my more human pain. Originally I had excluded from my approved rule or plan of life any presence of a television set in my hermitage cabin. Instead I would travel to friends' houses or my neighbors to view any big events like the pope's visits to the USA or the outbreak of a war. But I soon sensed that this was an imposition, particularly when it turned out that my friends were less interested in some things I found very compelling. Accordingly, when another friend presented me with an old black and white TV set after I had been several years without one, I experimented a bit by watching a few of the more informative programs on public (PBS) television — the only station I could get with any clearness with only a "rabbit ears" antenna.

One of the first programs I watched was a "Nova" series science program about amateur telescope making. Having for the most part finished with any major construction at my place, I found myself intrigued by the idea of making my own telescope, not because I was much of an astronomy buff, (I had watched a few comets, turned out to see occasional meteor showers, and eclipses when they occurred — nothing much else) but because I wanted the challenge of building my own instrument. So I ordered some parts, like a ten inch parabolic mirror and during the some six months it took to have that order filled, bought a small spotting scope and a book or two on astronomy. What I saw — some dozens of galaxies or other "milky ways" — with even this small telescope amazed me. When I had finally finished the much bigger reflecting telescope, about ten months later, I began to keep records of dozens of other such sightings. And what I saw, began to blow my mind — particularly my theological imagination. Now I began to realize what it was that the Church found out was so dangerous and upsetting in the thought and findings of Copernicus and Galileo. It really wasn't that their claims seemed to contradict the Bible — which obviously they did if one insisted on reading it literally. Rather, what these scientific pioneers unveiled was the true immensity of the universe and the paltry place we humans have in it. To peer into outer space, providing you take the time to understand what you are seeing, is quite liable to turn your own personal universe upside down. And when that happens, all other concerns, even all other loves, can sometimes recede into seeming insignificance. People have often accused religion as being dangerously "alienating". Believe me, astronomy can be even more so. Love of God can at least command love of others. Fascination with the stars alone can too easily lead, if we are not careful, to complete indifference to what takes place on this puny planet. And as I found out, perhaps to my chagrin, is that it even has a way of relativizing ones otherwise deepest concerns. But in terms of the emotional shape I was in back then, it was a God-send to me.

On the other hand, when astronomy, or more broadly, cosmology (the study of the origins, nature and future of the universe) is combined with theology, it becomes absolutely mind-blowing. It has (at least as some of Galileo's ecclesiastical critics vaguely sensed) a way of shattering all our previous theological conceptualizations. The idea of a God who has created a whole universe solely for us seems ludicrous, even if we still hold that He sent Christ for our salvation (whether the rest of the universe needed any such remedy may be completely beside the question).

Then there is the question as to whether or not what we consider to be the universe is only one of a series or simultaneously one of many. All this to be pondered, and yet, from my own experience, one can attend dozens of theological meetings without seeing any apparent acknowledgement that Copernicus or Galileo, much less Einstein, Hubble, or even Lemaître (the priest-scientist who first proposed what has been dubbed the "Big Bang Theory") ever existed.

For me, as a theologian, my exposure to cosmology via astronomy via telescope-making has been a kind of personal initiation not unlike the experience of having fallen into love. One can scientifically analyze the subject and all the rest, but until one has experienced it, one really has no real grasp of what it all means or might mean. Until that happens, it all remains an abstraction, with no real impact on ones life. God is love, Saint John tells us, and one who does not know love does not know God — at least the God who is love. So too, God is the creator, and until one grasps, at least in some small way, the immensity of creation, once cannot begin to grasp the immensity of God.

Put these two notions together, the immensity of a God who is purely self-giving Love and you have, I think, theological dynamite. If it is only through love that we can learn to overcome our individual self-absorption, then, I would suggest that it is only through a cosmic sense of God's immensity that we will ever learn to overcome the collective short-sightedness and self-absorption that bedevils all of us.

Chapter 9
Hermit or Heretic?

In one of the collections of stories about the famed "Desert Fathers"— the early monks and hermits of third to fifth century Egypt, — is one about a strikingly tall and rather dark-skinned hermit known as "Abba Moses". Most likely of Sudanese or Ethiopian origin, this particular Moses was easily recognizable, even in the rare times he might be seen in a gathering of his fellow hermits.

In any case, as the story goes, a visitor from the city came out to the desert looking for him, but apparently wasn't sure if he had found the right man. So he asked him where he might find Abba Moses, and Moses answered by asking in return "Why would you want to speak with that heretic?" Put off by that brusque reply, the would-be visitor left Abba Moses alone.

We don't really know if Abba Moses held any heretical opinions or not, or whether this was merely his tactic for getting rid of people who were attracted to curiosities. But in an age when much controversy still raged among Christians, especially regarding the true identity of Jesus (was he truly a human — albeit one fully imbued with the Holy Spirit — or was he an angel or even God himself appearing as if in human clothes?) it is quite possible that Abba Moses, like many others among these highly independent desert dwellers, did hold some strange or even deviant ideas. We do know, for example, that the monks of Egypt were highly sympathetic to the ideas of Origen, the third century Alexandrian theologian, some of whose beliefs regarding reincarnation and universal salvation (that in the end, even Satan would be saved!) were eventually condemned.

I have related this story because if there is any truth in it (that is, about Abba Moses and many of his colleagues having suspicious or quasi-heretical ideas) it may shed some light on the position that I have gradually found myself in. In other words, my solitude is not just one of physical or emotional apartness, but extends to the theological realm as well. Perhaps it is the freedom of living in solitude, without the burdens of teaching people in conformity to a catechism or preaching to a congregation whose grasp of Church teachings remains for the most part on that basic level. So maybe there is something about solitude that tempts a hermit to become something of a theological free-thinker and, if so, perhaps I've gradually succumbed to that temptation, although my goal, from the start, has been to explore new ways to understand and, hopefully, to deepen the Christian faith.

But first, let's try to pin down more exactly what is meant by the term "heretic". It is said to be derived from the Greek word meaning to pick or choose, the implication being that a heretic is someone who treats the Bible or the Church's teachings as something like a theological smorgasbord, picking the items that attract one or best agrees with ones own tastes, and passes by or refuses to accept what does not.

Strictly speaking, at least according to the Catholic Church's official 1983 edition of *The Code of Canon Law* (Canon 751), "Heresy is the obstinate post-baptismal denial of some truth which must be believed with divine and catholic faith, or it is likewise an obstinate doubt concerning the same." The same canon then goes on to distinguish heresy from "schism" (leaving the Catholic Church) and "apostasy" (leaving Christianity altogether). But as the previous chapters I think have amply illustrated, while I may have been tempted at times to become a schismatic, in no way have I ever contemplated apostasy. In fact, you might say that my efforts as a theologian have for the most part been concentrated on defending and promoting Christianity in an increasingly unbelieving world.

However, when it comes to the understanding of what is meant by "obstinate" in the above definition, there seems to be a division of opinion. Many theologians and even canon lawyers, appear to understand the word as if it means "contumacious" or "contemptuous". If so, I don't think that either term applies to me. But if "obstinate" simply means "stubborn" or "persisting", well, in that case, it certainly applies to the facts and the principles that I have sought to apply when dealing with these facts.

Chapter 9

The facts that I'm talking about range between two orders of existence, or maybe might be described as a spectrum that has two extremes.

On one end are those facts that exist in the physical realm, observed and tested through what is called "the scientific method" and generally accepted by the scientific community or network of scientific specialists (physicists, geologists, biologists, etc.) around the world.

At the other end of this spectrum, at least as I see it, are the long-standing religious beliefs. Although these beliefs may vary widely or may even be outright opposed, they are nevertheless "facts" in the sense of something that is fixed or established in people's minds. If anyone doubts that, I would suggest that they travel to the Middle East. And of course, the same could be said of those who are hard-core materialists, who refuse to admit that anything exists except that which can be detected by the physical senses and subjected to the scientific method. And then, in between these two extremes in human thought, we have the whole spectrum of opinions, ranging from philosophical systems, psychological theories, and various political arrangements, and almost anything else you can name.

Basic Principles and Their Applications

Given this vast array of facts and opinions, there are several principles that I have relied upon as a theologian. The first is quite simple: it is, as Saint Bonaventure said back in the 13th century, that there are two sources or "books" of revelation, the Holy Scriptures and, as he put it, "the Book of Nature", and that if we truly believe that God created nature, then we must to equal attention to both.

The second follows from the first, although Saint Augustine articulated it as far back as the 5th century. It is that if the Holy Scriptures seem to be contradicted by clear and consistent reasoning, then it is probably a sign that we have been misinterpreting those scriptures or understanding them wrongly.

The prime example of my putting these two principles to work can probably be best seen in my first two books, the first of which was my doctoral dissertation, which was eventually published under the title, *Teilhard, Scripture, and Revelation: A Study of Teilhard de Chardin's Reinterpretation of Pauline Themes.* Why that "Reinterpretation" in the subtitle? It is because the Jesuit priest Pierre Teilhard de Chardin, as a geologist and paleontologist (the latter being someone who is an expert on ancient forms of life), found himself forced as both a Christian and a scientist to pay equal attention to the writings attributed to Saint Paul as found in the Holy Scriptures as well as to the "Book of Nature" as he found it, so to speak, written in the rocks.

So having become something of an expert in Teilhard's way of thinking, the natural thing for me to do, indeed the only thing, it seemed to me, that I could do, was to apply Teilhard's basic insights as to how nature works through the evolutionary process, and to try to address the problem of evil and suffering, which I, and many others, have always considered to be the greatest obstacle to belief in God. The result was that winter back in the late 1970s when I temporarily quit teaching to live alone at the Stella Maris cabin and wrote the first draft of what was eventually published as my 1984 book *Evil and Evolution: A Theodicy* – that latter word a technical term for any philosophical or theological attempt to reconcile the existence of evil and suffering in the world with belief in a good, just, and especially, a loving God. But it also, although I didn't seem to realize it or at least I didn't let it bother me at that time, eventually launched me into the situation of finding myself to be obstinately, although not contumaciously, a heretic.

First, to accomplish the aim I had in mind I had to dispose of what I felt were the misguided efforts to solve the problem of evil, among them being not only ancient pagan ideas, like the Chaldean and Babylonian beliefs in two gods, one good, one bad, at war with each other, but also what is believed by many scripture scholars to be its Old Testament derivative, where Satan (symbolized by the snake in the Book of Genesis story) becomes the biblical stand-in or replacement for that evil god. But this in turn means that I also had, in effect, to not only sideline the whole Original Sin account as we find it in the Book of Genesis (which I see as a mythical expression of the evolutionary baggage embedded in our DNA), but with it, the belief in angels and their nefarious counterparts, devils and evil spirits of all sorts. After all, if God created us through an evolutionary process, with all its randomness and chance, suffering and failures, and all the other messiness in having material bodies, just to eventually result in free creatures like ourselves, how justify all this if God could have taken a shortcut like simply creating purely spiritual beings who could instantaneously decide their fate for themselves? Faced with this dilemma, it has been something of a relief to learn that a number of scripture scholars today, even within the Catholic Church, consider that belief in such purely spiritual creatures was not originally part of the Jewish faith or system of belief but was another incorporation of a pagan idea that the Jews were exposed to during their exile in Babylon.

But of course, disposing of angels or devils brings further complications. For one, it not only calls into question the whole Original Sin story, but in addition, much of the theology of redemption that began with Saint Paul's analogy of Christ as "the second Adam" (Rom. 5:12-21) sent to undo the damage caused by "the first Adam" and which reached its zenith with Saint Anselm's famous 11th century answer to the question of "Why Did God Become Man?" — an answer that has been a mainstay of Western Christianity (both Catholic and Protestant) ever since.

Not only that, this in turn raises questions about the human nature, or more specifically about the knowledge, of Jesus who, if we take the gospel accounts at face value, seems to have believed that both angels and devils existed — indeed, he made the expulsion of the latter from unfortunate souls a major part of his public ministry. Or was he just going along with people's ideas or expectations in order to get his real message across?

This last question, in turn, brings on another question, it being how accurate are the Scriptures, particularly, in this case, the gospel accounts? This is, of course, a question that has long vexed Christian scholars, especially during the past few centuries ever since Hermann Reimarus' thoughts on the subject were first published back in 1774. This began a debate that has continued ever since despite Albert Schweitzer's attempt to summarize what ever progress that had been made in his landmark book on *The Quest for the Historical Jesus,* first published back in 1906. And the debate has continued with the Vatican's own "Pontifical Biblical Commission" even weighing in back in 1964 with its own guidelines on the subject – which have, for me, become a third general principle that I have begun to employ along with those first two mentioned above.

According to this group of Catholic scholars, three levels or layers of tradition can be discovered in the composition of the gospels. The first level or layer is what the writers of these documents believed to be the actual words and actions of Jesus as witnessed by his disciples. The second layer is the summary statements or proclamation (Gr. *kerygma*) of the good or saving news, such as the announcement that "He [Christ] suffered and died, and rose again on the third day." And lastly, there is the third layer, the one that accounts for there being four written gospels, and not just one: it is the distinctive approach taken by each writer to present the gospel message in language or concepts designed to address a particular audience – for example, Matthew's obvious attempt to appeal to those of Jewish birth or background, with his frequent use of quotations from the Old Testament. This is in sharp contrast to Luke's efforts to explain Jewish customs to those pagans for whom Judaism was another, and strange, world.

But this analysis by the Pontifical Biblical Commission in turn brings other questions to my mind. For example, if the two stories that we have about the birth of Jesus in Bethlehem differ significantly in details, and the earliest accounts of the origins of Jesus (Paul's epistles and Mark's gospel) seem to have ignored those two stories entirely, while the latest account (John's gospel) barely alludes to them, then the question might be raised, how important is the Virgin Birth story to Christianity to begin with? Should the prophecy (in Is 7:14, with the Hebrew *almah* meaning "young woman" being mistranslated into Greek as *parthenos* or "virgin"), and which defies all the laws of genetics, have ever been made an article of faith to be included in the official Christian creeds? Or how about many of the "nature miracles" (walking on water, calming storms, multiplying loaves, etc.) related in the gospels, which even the highly acclaimed Catholic scripture scholar John P. Meier has to admit are at least exaggerations if not mostly legendary to begin with?

Thus the problem, as I see it, is whether or not most of this what seems to be third level material really needs to be taken seriously, except perhaps as acting as an obstacle rather than an incitement to faith. This is not a question of rejecting the belief that the authors of Holy Scriptures were divinely inspired, but simply asking if had they been writing to convey the same message (what Jesus actually taught and its summary in the "good news") to the world today, would they have used much of what the Biblical Commission admits is third-level material, most of it peculiar to this or that particular author or the tradition using that evangelist's or other author's name? In addition, if there is such third level material contained in the gospels, must we not also relegate to that same teriary category much of what we find in the various epistles and other biblical books – again, as a prime example, the development of the Original Sin and Atonement doctrines from Paul's depiction of Christ as the "new Adam"?

Yet examples like that raise another problem, which I would describe as the "shock-level" or disruptive effect on those who have never faced up to the difficulties such questions raise. Thus, the need to consider the other, more subjective, side of the whole subject of faith and belief.

Is Faith Really the Same as Belief?

As I mentioned in an earlier chapter, according to the landmark study produced back in the 1980s by theologian and psychologist of religion James W. Fowler, there are at least six, maybe even seven, more or less distinctive stages of faith, ranging from the basic trust of a small child to the sophisticated understandings of a theologian to a final stage of simple union with God characteristic of a saint or mystic. In between are stages where everything tends to be taken literally (fundamentalism), another stage where people for the most part believe whatever their friends and neighbors believe, and periods of questioning, doubt, periods of recommitment, etc. Wondering why this happens, I decided to write my own study on the subject, using psychiatrist Viktor Frankl's model of psychodynamics as a key. Famous for his best-selling *Man's Search for Meaning* and the definition of religion as being "the search for ultimate meaning" that he gave in another book, I came to the conclusion that the arrest or blockage preventing people from advancing to a higher stage is the fear of the risk or of the uncertainty that the higher stages of faith demand. The effect of this demand for absolute certainty is the same as the false goal of achieving happiness. As Frankl said over and over again, happiness can only *en*sue, that is, come as a by-product of something greater than ones' own happiness. So I came to the same conclusion when it comes to what amounts to the confidence or security provided by faith. The goal must be God, not one's own security. Hence the title of my 1984 book *Faith, Security, and Risk: The Dynamics of Spiritual Growth.*

However, in the process of writing that book, I also came across a paradox which I found somewhat disconcerting back then but which has become more and more clear and marked in my thinking ever since. It is the contrast between *Faith and Belief,* first stressed in a book by that title written by a Canadian theologian named Wilfred Cantwell Smith. In his very scholarly study, Smith pointed out their close association — in fact, in both Greek and Latin there is only one word that can mean either faith or belief. But they are, in fact, two different things. The first, *faith,* in the sense that the gospels use the word, is basically an allegiance or trust, or again "confidence". It is, we might say, a matter of the "heart." The second, *belief,* or more often, a whole set of beliefs, are reasons that we construct in our minds to try to explain and bolster the strength or certainty of our faith. Beliefs are something like the hull or shell of a seed that encloses or protects that germ or source of new life that we call "faith". In other words, belief – as well as the study of religious beliefs that we call "theology" – is, as the hippies once put it, mostly "a head trip".

Chapter 9

Now, despite that distinction between the two, one might think that the more faith one has the more solid are ones beliefs. But in fact, it seldom works out, at least for long, that way. What generally happens is that the more a person's faith seems threatened, the more fanatical and inflexible his or her beliefs tend to become. This explains a lot of the biblical fundamentalism that we run into, even here in the USA. It also explains the Islamist fanaticism of groups like ISIS, the Taliban, Boko Haram, and other similar groups in the Middle East and elsewhere. In fact the very name of the latter group in Africa is said to mean the equivalent of "Down with Western education!"

Yet, if a weak or threatened faith explains rigid adherence to certain beliefs, is the opposite equally true? I think a study of the spiritual masters indicates that more often than not this is exactly the case. Take, for example, the maxims of Saint John of the Cross, the great 16th century Spanish mystic and theologian of the spiritual life. He is famous for his teaching about the "dark nights" experienced by those advancing in the life of prayer. The first, the most well known, is what he called "the night of the senses", by which he meant the puzzling growth of aridity or lack of feelings of consolation or joy that, to begin with, accompany beginners in the life of prayer and contemplation. The reason for this, according to this master's teaching, is that God is testing a person's sincerity. Have they entered the life of serious prayer just to feel good or are they really intent on drawing closer to God? But what is less understood and probably much scarier is "the night of the soul". What did he mean by this? How can our souls fall into "darkness"?

If we need to have this explained to us, I think one can find more than just a hint in his short "maxims" found at the end of most collections of his writings. One of them in particular reads: "To come to the knowledge of the all, desire the knowledge of nothing." And its corollary is similar: "To come to the knowledge of that which you have not, you must go by a way that you know not." Much the same is said about having or possessing anything, or being or becoming anything as well. By "the all", he meant God. And by "nothing", he meant everything else — including all the consolations, assurances, and beliefs that we once relied upon. It is as simple, and as difficult, as that! The more we rely upon our own minds, our thinking, and our beliefs, the more stubborn becomes our resistance to God. God can only be approached and possessed through pure and, one might even say, "naked" faith – that is, stripped of all our own ideas of such faith and love. Everything else is a barrier.

This is nothing new. Four centuries earlier, the great Franciscan, Saint Bonaventure – the same theologian who insisted that we read both books of revelation – had this advice for theologians such as myself who would seek union with God.

> We must suspend all the operations of the mind and must transform the peak of our affections, directing them to God alone. This is a sacred mystical experience ... If you ask how such things occur, seek the answer in God's grace, not in doctrine; in the longing of the will, not in the understanding; in the sighs of prayer, not in research...

In this Bonaventure was only echoing the most famous Christian theologian of all, Saint Thomas Aquinas, who, shortly before the end of his life underwent a mystical experience. After it happened, he told his secretary, Brother Reginald, that compared to what he had just experienced, all that he had written, and Reginald had so diligently copied, was about as worthless as "straw"! Poor Brother Reginald – to be told this after all his (and no doubt my own) diligent pen scratching!

Does this mean that theology and all the hard work, debates, and even outright accusations and condemnations that theologians have traded over the centuries have all been useless? I hardly think so. But to understand what I'm saying about the importance of theology and arguments over doctrine, you have to consider their basic function. They are, much like Saint Paul's explanation as to what the "Law" (the *Torah*) was to Jews, a "pedagogue", that is, an instructor of children to guide them to *something* higher. Or, to use a more contemporary comparison, we might think of religious instruction as being something like the training wheels a parent fastens to a bicycle until the child gains enough experience and sense of balance to be allowed to attempt to ride the bicycle without this extra assistance. Hence the concern that teachers be orthodox, that is to say, that they have the correct or, literally speaking, "straight" teachings. Otherwise, their teaching could turn out to be as useless or even as dangerous as training wheels set at an oblique angle, or at the very least, more of a hindrance than a help. Or to use that "ortho" prefix again in more technical but contemporary context, one expects that a dentist who is an "orthodontic" specialist knows how to install braces that will insure that children grow up to have their teeth arranged correctly enough not only to eventually give them a pleasing smile, but even more important for their future physical health, a correct bite for the rest of their life.

The importance of all this – both of traditional teachings as well as of the mystical or experiential element of religion – can be seen from another angle as well as comparison given by the French evolutionary philosopher, Henri Bergson. Most famous for his 1907 book *L'Evolution créatrice* ("Creative Evolution"), which eventually led to his being awarded a Nobel Prize in 1927, another landmark book by Bergson emerged in 1932. Its title in English was *The Two Sources of Morality and Religion.* In it, Bergson, again thinking from an evolutionary standpoint, compared the advance of human ethical or moral standards and religious practice and teaching to a staircase leading us forward and upward beyond the more primitive stages of the past. But much like any flight of stairs, there are two basic elements: first, and most obvious to our eyes, are the vertical "risers" that take us upward at every step. But secondly, and more fundamental, there are the horizontal "treads" or flat platforms that give us the stability necessary to take that next upward step. Religious tradition and the moral codes taught as part of them, Bergson reasoned, are like those "treads" – an absolutely necessary starting point for any inspirational advance or movement upward, one that is usually initiated by an inspired prophet or mystic who challenges the existing tradition to move to a even higher plane or level than in the past. Or if the word "mystic" sounds too esoteric to you, consider this: the priest-paleontologist

Hermit or Heretic?

Teilhard de Chardin, whose long-suppressed writings eventually forced the Catholic Church to at least begin to face up to the challenge of evolutionary thinking, once admitted that "Mysticism is the highest form of research." So, if we are to follow the logic of Bergson's thinking, just as this same process worked through history in the past, so must it be in the future if the human race is to survive.

One example of this involves confronting a problem that has very much vexed me since I finished – or at least thought I had finished – writing a book which I titled *Einstein and the Image of God* (subtitled *A Response to Contemporary Atheism*) in 2015. In the process of writing that book I again zeroed in on the problem of evil in the world as being the oldest and most persistent obstacle to religious belief. How can people reconcile all the evil in the world, especially the suffering of innocent children, etc., with the concept of a God who is supposed to be good, or who is even described as in the First Epistle of John as being "Love"? I had, as mentioned above, even written that book on theodicy titled *Evil & Evolution* back in the late 1970s. But what I have learned since then is that what bothers most people, at least those who have grown up within a culture largely formed by the Judeo-Christian religions, and who claim to be or are on the brink of becoming atheists, is not that problem of evil in general (as if that were not a problem enough!) but even more specifically the evils, or certainly what we now think of evils, that were attributed to or even commanded by God, that is, if we are to believe much of what is written in what Christians call the "Old Testament". For example, take the famous story of the siege of Jericho where, according to the account given in the Book of Joshua, after marching around the town for seven days blowing their horns – and no doubt displaying their swords and spears – the walls of Jericho miraculously came tumbling down. Then we are told that the Israelites proceeded to slaughter the whole population (with the exception of Rahab and her family), just as they had been commanded by God to do, sparing not man, woman, and child, and not even their livestock. Does the archeological information that we now have, which indicates that none of this ever happened, make any real difference if we keep claiming that this sort of behavior is what was condoned or even commanded by God? How are we to deal with this?

Examples like this, I think, very much illustrate what is eating the heart out of religion today. To put it bluntly, the evolution of human sensibilities and ethical reasoning have already gone beyond that violent past, even if our weapons of mass destruction are capable of the slaughter of innocents far beyond that ever imagined by the biblical authors. Yet we still contemplate, too often, with almost diabolical calmness, the possibility of using such weapons if worse comes to worst. As Einstein once lamented, after the first atomic bombs were used, and seeing the devastation that they wrought, and we began designing even more powerful nuclear bombs, "Everything has changed but our thinking!" The question is, when will we decide to change our thinking and how?

The first step, I believe, is that we have to become "heretics" by making choices, picking and choosing what to retain from the traditions of the past and what to reject. This is what Einstein, and his philosophical hero Baruch Spinoza some three centuries before, both did, rejecting the picture of God portrayed in the Old Testament of their Jewish past. And both of them, Einstein as well as Spinoza, were denounced as being atheists because of that, even though both insisted that they were not atheists. Likewise, both of them were attracted to the figure of Jesus, even though both of them avoided becoming Christians – apparently because they did not see organized Christianity as having followed the teachings of Jesus as it claimed to do. Apparently this same attraction to Christ was also true of Bergson, who is said to have considered becoming a Catholic before his death in 1944, but refrained out of a sense of responsibility to show his loyalty to his Jewish colleagues who were being rounded up and slaughtered by the Nazis.

And it was because of this same realization, unfortunately a score of years too late, that the Catholic Church was forced to admit at the Second Vatican Council, that the Church had been too often complicit in the tendency to blame Judaism, and hence all Jews, for the death of Jesus and on that basis add to the discrimination that had been practiced against them. If this was not entirely the case from the beginning of Christianity, it greatly increased by early in the 4th century, when Constantine and his successors began to relegate Jews to ghettos and, with all that, came the marginalization, and ultimately the hatred that resulted in the 19th century pogroms culminating in the 1940s holocaust.

Such collective repentance and official change of attitude, if not of doctrine – although the supposed guilt of the Jewish people was never an official teaching – was not the only thing. Most of all it was the Second Vatican Council claim that all persons of good will whether they are "separated brethren" (Protestants, Eastern Orthodox or other Christians), or Jews, Muslims, or even pagans, agnostics, or (God forbid!) atheists, all can be saved. It was that Vatican II teaching that really shocked Catholic traditionalists. Adhering to a formula that dates back to Pope Pelagius in 585, conservatives continue to staunchly believe that "Outside the Church there is no salvation" – this despite the kind of explanations I received as a youngster from the good sisters who taught us about "Baptism of desire". This meant that people of good will, if they really knew God, understood God's will, and followed Christ's commands, would duly line up for Baptism and thus get themselves saved, even without actually joining the Catholic Church, because God would surely not hold them responsible for not knowing any better.

Admittedly, such a liberal reinterpretation of that old belief has its own problems. For example, did Hitler, who was baptized a Catholic, really think he was following God's will or doing good when he engineered the extermination of six million Jews? – or did Joseph Stalin, a former student for the priesthood in the Georgian Orthodox Church, really think that the starvation of millions of Ukrainians who revolted against forced collectivization or the slow murder of millions that were sent to the gulags of Siberia, really believe he was doing something good?

But aside from that difficulty, the main tactic used by dissenting conservative Catholics is to deny that anything taught by the Second Vatican Council is really official Church doctrine. Yet if an ecumenical council is not considered authoritative enough to make chnages in Church teachings, then what is?

Heresy in the Church

From the above point of view, I will venture to say that the Church has always been somewhat complicit in heresy, picking and choosing from its vast biblical and other traditional heritage what it sees to be most valuable and deserves promotion and leaving aside what no longer is applicable or even eliminating what is detrimental. It has done this for a long time, even setting aside the use of certain psalm verses – or in one case, a whole psalm (Ps. 109) as being too vindictive to be squared with Christian attitudes. Nor did the Church insist entirely, even to begin with, on Christ's prohibition of divorce and remarriage, perhaps realizing, without actually saying it, that Jesus' seeming promise that his predictions would be fulfilled within the lifetime of at least some of his listeners was, to be honest about it, somewhat premature.

Such discrepancies bring up, at least to my mind, what seems to me to be the greatest and most prevalent heresy among Christians. It is an error, or really heresy in the technical sense, because it is contrary to the defined doctrine drawn up at the Council of Chalcedon in 451. It reads, to quote verbatim, that not only was Jesus "consubstantial with the Father in his divinity" but also "consubstantial with us in our humanity." In other words, the Church teaches that Jesus was as much truly a human being as his being truly divine. But somehow it was decided not to add that statement to the Nicene Creed, so that despite the official doctrine drawn up at Chalcedon, most ordinary Christians — except perhaps some liberal Protestants whose error is in the opposite direction — are, in fact, much like the Coptic Christians I had met in Egypt, "monophysites", a technical term meaning that they see Christ as being of *one* or a single nature, that nature being divine, but taking a human shape or form. This term first turned up after the council at Chalcedon had ended and the Egyptian or "Coptic" Church and its close relatives in Abyssinia (Eritrea and Ethiopia) and a few local churches farther east refused to accept the

Chalceldonian formula, which was derived from a famous letter sent to the Council by Pope Leo I (Leo the Great).

The reason for this squabble, which probably was as much political as theological, is really quite simple. It is because the balance between the divine and the human that was attempted in 451 has proved almost psychologically impossible to maintain. Think of it as standing in the middle of a see-saw or teeter-totter and trying to keep both ends evenly off the ground. Inevitably, as soon as we think of Jesus as God incarnate, the weight of his divinity carries the day. But in doing so, the whole idea of the Incarnation is put in jeopardy, and with it, at least to some degree, our redemption or salvation as well. For as some of the early Church theologians boldly put it "What was not assumed was not redeemed." If Jesus only suffered in his body, but not in his soul, his cry on the cross ("My God, my God, why have you forsaken me?") remains incomprehensible, and the worst of human suffering, that of the mind, remains unredeemed.

This monophysitism shows up in Catholic and other traditional Christian thinking in many ways. My first venture into probing this issue was in writing a review of Martin Scorcese's sensational 1988 film adaptation of Nikos Konzantzakis' disturbing (to pious believers anyway) 1953 novel, *The Last Temptation of Christ*, a book which almost earned the author an excommunication from the Greek Orthodox Church. In Konzantzakis' book, Jesus is strongly tempted by Mary Magdalene – this presumably being before she was converted. Nevertheless, Jesus goes ahead with his mission of preaching love and peace, and when he finds himself being crucified is tempted again, this time to come down from the cross, move in with Martha and Mary, or even marry the by now converted Magdalene and thereafter, live a normal life. I spoke of the scandal that most believers would probably take from the book or film as being an unconscious sign of the monophysite heresy. What readers of that review made of it I'm not sure. But I presume it raised a few eyebrows.

My second venture into this same issue of taking Jesus' humanity seriously was in a book I wrote in the late 1990s as a

Chapter 9

sequel to my 1990 book, *Faith Security & Risk*. I based this new book on the premise that if Jesus really had a human nature similar to ourselves, then he too must have gone through the various stages and struggles of faith. So I gave it the title *The Faith of Jesus: The Jesus of History and the Stages of Faith* and sent the manuscript on to Paulist Press, which had also published the previous book and which had done fairly well. But their board sat on it for about a year or so until they apparently decided it was too risky for them to publish. Although the head of the press, who was a scripture scholar and seemed intrigued by my approach to the subject, there also seems to have been pressures coming from Rome's Congregation for the Doctrine of the Faith which at that time, near the end of Pope John Paul II's pontificate, had forced certain Catholic publishing houses to recall some books they'd already published. Apparently this caused Paulist Press, which is among the most visible Catholic publishing firms in the USA, to not risk the same thing happening to them.

So I set the project aside for several years, then revised the manuscript and sent it to a press that is independent of ecclesiastical oversight or censorship. It was published in 2006 with an additional final chapter that I titled "Faith in Christ: A Christological Postscript". In it I summed up the present predicament – what theologians have called the "Chalcedonian Problem" or maybe we should say "the Christological Conundrum". I suggested that we abandon the old formulas based on ancient and questionable philosophical notions such as the Platonist concept of the naturally immortal soul, a concept which the earliest Christian apologist and philosopher, Saint Justin Martyr, thought was clearly mistaken. Justin seems to have believed that it is only through God's power that we can escape from our mortal condition. If so, then I suggested that perhaps we need to make a fresh start in understanding the humanity, as well as the divinity, of Jesus. It should be based on a more dynamic model of human nature drawn from evolutionary science, one that suggests that Jesus had been sent to us by God as a prototype and through God's special predestinating grace, as a fully achieved exemplar of what we are *all* called to be, that is, (in the words of 2 Peter 1:4) "participants in the divine nature."

My third and probably last attempt to use this approach has been in the final chapter of my 2015 book *Einstein and the Image of God: A Response to Contemporary Atheism.* There I even turned to quoting Saint Augustine's treatise on "The Predestination of the Saints" and his words about Christ being "the Saint above all other saints" to try to get this same point across. However, in the course of writing that same book, I also came to a rather disconcerting conclusion – that most Christians really don't want a Christ who shares our human nature entirely with all our frailties and messiness. They really don't want a Jesus who is too human.

The key to understanding this insight was Einstein's own admission that while he could only envision God as "a superior reasoning power" or "an infinitely superior spirit that reveals itself in the little that we can comprehend in the knowable world," he could not believe in what he called "a personal God... a God who concerns himself with the fate and doings of mankind." Einstein seems to have also had his own personal reasons besides his dislike of the seemingly capricious God of the Old Testament. The failure of his first marriage and his shortcomings as a husband and father may have had something to do with it. Yet he nevertheless conceded, albeit reluctantly, that most people require a personal God and that "I wonder whether one can ever successfully render to the majority of mankind a more sublime means in order to satisfy its metaphysical needs." In other words, although Einstein stoutly maintained the superiority of what he called his "cosmic religion", he nevertheless understood most people's need for a God who answers prayers and perhaps even threatens us if we don't live up to God's expectations.

In any case, I have concluded that if God is really the superior reasoning power that Einstein believed, that God, despite what Einstein thought, is in some sense really a person: if not, why would the Big Bang have taken place 13.8 billion years ago instead of say, 30, 50, or 100 billion years ago? It seems that someone or something had to make a decision. If so, then it makes sense to believe that this same God is concerned enough about our own welfare to have sent us an image of himself in Jesus, an image who struggled to the very end to accomplish his heavenly Father's will, despite sharing all the weaknesses of our human nature. A God who is a "prime or unmoved mover" (Aristotle's concept of God), "an infinitely superior intelligence" (Einstein's concept of God) or simply "the force" (the God of "Star Wars") is not enough. Most people require an image of God who is deeply involved in our struggles, even to the point, as the evolutionary philosopher Alfred North Whitehead put it, a God who deeply "cares" about us and reveals himself as "our fellow sufferer."

But, as I was finishing that last book, I realized that enough is enough, and this same God must be, in the end, an uncontested winner. This is why the humble, persecuted, and murdered Jesus of history will never be enough for the devout and committed Christian. In the end, even despite the persistent danger of a lop-sided monophysite view, the divine and risen Christ of Faith will always come out the victor.

Where I Stand Now

As for myself, whether I am a heretic or not, I'll have to leave that to the reader to judge. It's not that I haven't honestly struggled with these questions. In fact, back in 2006, I began to write my own commentary on the creeds (both the short "Apostles' Creed" as well as the longer Nicene Creed) just to see whether I could honestly conform to what was expected from me as a representative of the Catholic Church. Despite the brevity of what I wrote (a total of only 106 pages including an index) the process was a rather long one, especially when the local bishop, who had first encouraged me to write it, after a long delay became alarmed by my interpretations and I ended up sending it to my own diocese downstate instead. There my efforts met more success in securing the official Church *imprimatur* that had been requested by Paulist Press after slightly altering my remarks on the nature and origin of the human soul (a matter which although, strictly speaking, is more a question of philosophical viewpoint, is still seen as essential for a traditional

Catholic understanding of the faith). However, by the time this whole process was completed, Paulist Press insisted on printing it with a cover that pictured the older translation of the Nicene Creed which started with "We believe..." instead of the newer "I believe..." version mandated by the Vatican – a switch that almost immediately outdated my efforts after the book went to press in the autumn of 2010. So it seems that even my four years long effort to prove to myself that I am sufficiently orthodox to be included within that traditional "We" were undermined almost from the start. Some day, if I live long enough, I hope to republish that little book the way it was written to begin with. Meanwhile, my orthodoxy remains in a state of suspense.

So at one point some years back I discussed my dilemma with a close priest-friend, who suggested that maybe (and here I quote his exact words) I might have "to fake it to make it." By that I presume he simply meant being a good actor – which I'm not. And this of course brought back to my mind the old family friend's prediction back when I was still in college — that I'd find myself someday teaching one thing for the sake of the people but no longer believe it myself — and my resolution back then that I'd never allow myself to compromise or destroy my own sense of integrity. It is for that reason that after much prayer, especially after the changes in the wording of the liturgy that took place in November of 2011 made my difficulties all the more obvious, that I eventually, some months later, composed a letter in which I resigned, not from the priesthood or the Catholic Church, but from all active ministry, this on the grounds that I am, at least technically speaking, a heretic (or more specificially, a "modalist" who leans toward Nestorianism). I then sent copies of the letter to both my bishop down in Lansing and to the local bishop in the area where I live, and several years later to his successor. I assured them of my continued prayers for the Church and my intention to keep writing with the goal of reaching out to those who have left the Church and attempting to reconcile them to God and Christianity.

If one wants to know what I meant in that letter by my "modalism", I would explain it this way. Christianity has for long

Chapter 9

time, in regard to the triune nature of God, used the word "person" or the term "three persons" this regard. However, I now believe (as did the 20th century's greatest Catholic theologian, Karl Rahner) that because the word "person" has drastically changed its meaning over the centuries (it originally meant an actor's mask or a person's face) that to continue to use that word in this trinitarian context is a serious mistake, making it sound as if Christians are "tritheists" or believers in three Gods. Instead, I believe that it is wiser if we (as I did in my little 2010 book about the creeds) to speak of the one God in terms of the three functions of creating, redeeming, and sanctifying – although now I would prefer to use the term "saving" (primarily from death) rather than "redeeming" us from Adam and Eve's sin.

And as for my reference to Nestorius or Nestorianism, since it is not clear as to what exactly Nestorius held, other than he wanted to emphasize a distinction between the divine and the human in Jesus, I'm using the adjective "Nestorian" in the broad sense of a general disavowal of monophysitism. That monophysitism is still alive and well among Christians today I think was more or less confirmed by the results of some three-way talks a few years ago between Catholic, Eastern Orthodox, and Coptic Church theologians. The result was a consensus that their supposed disagreements were mostly semantic. But if that is the case, then it would seem that either the monophysites (or as they would prefer to say *"miaphysites"* meaning a mixed or combined nature) are orthodox or else all of us are heretics! Not only that, I tend to agree with those scholars who believe that monophysitism, or at least the confusion caused by the debates over the identity of Jesus which became widespread in the Middle East, and the overall incoherence of the official doctrine that resulted, seems to have paved the way, as a reaction, for the rise of the much more simple beliefs of Islam.

If so, all this again confirms my doubts that the Church, whether taken collectively (the *"sensus fidelium"*), or in an Ecumenical Council, or even in terms of solemn papal pronouncements on matters of faith or morals, is in fact infallible. Instead, much like theologian Hans Küng, I believe that God's Holy

Spirit will help us evenually to discern the truth more fully and make corrections accordingly. In the meanwhile, we would be wise to take a hint from the mystics and the greatest theologians who confessed that in the end they knew very little for sure. In other words, we need a healthy dose of humility or of practicing what the Eastern theologians called *"apophaticism"* (meaning "beyond what can be said") or, again, what the great 15th century churchman Cardinal Nicholas of Cusa termed "learned ignorance".

As I see it today, looking back on all this it, it seems to me that we, as part of a collective "we", too often will tend to hold or at least tolerate viewpoints or opinions for the sake of the common good that we, as responsible individuals, might never agree to on our own. It seems that I, much like Rousseau's "Savoyard Vicar" (whom I once wrote about in a short essay first published back in 2006) tolerated pious myths – in the sense of "sacred stories" expressing existential, but not historical, truth – for the sake of the common good, even while privately thinking otherwise. So I asked my readers what they thought: was the vicar a hero (for suppressing his own opinions) or a hypocrite? When one of my readers, a devout Catholic, wrote me expressing her own opinion (that it was a case of the latter) I could only see myself as being the same. And as I see it now, while such collective "group-think" can generate great power, even for the good, it can also cause great harm – just think of the medieval crusades, or today's Islamic jihads.

So now, as I write this, I ask myself: should we repress our own opinions as independent persons for the sake of the greater whole, thinking only in terms of the common "we", especially realizing that as solitary persons we will probably never completely understand all that the human mind has discovered or understood on the collective level?

Yet, when it comes to particular instances of this, I still wonder. Cardinal Newman once admitted (I think it was back when he was struggling with his own decision over whether or not to leave the Anglican Church to become a Roman Catholic) that if all the bishops in the Christian world (estimated to have numbered about eighteen hundred at the time) had showed up at Nicea in 325AD, compared to the three hundred and eighteen bishops who are said to have actually attended the council, would not Arianism have prevailed and would have been considered to be "orthodoxy"? And if so, was the Nicene Creed with its declaration of Christ being *homoousios* or "consubstantial" (of the same nature as) God the Father really the result of a divine intervention? Or was this result due to pressure from Emperor Constantine who, although he had not yet declared himself to be a Christian, conspicuously sat among those bishops and was determined to see Christianity united in its doctrine, lest his newly reunited empire fall apart?

This example is of great importance to me because even if I don't agree with Arius' attempt to solve the so-called and still on-going "Christological Conundrum" (who or what Jesus really was) by means of using Platonist philosophical categories, I still have great sympathy for him and what he was attempting to do – which was trying to see Jesus Christ as divine without equating him with God the Almighty.

So what should one do when one finds oneself in such a position? Just pretend that you agree with the official line ("Fake it to make it," as my friend said) or separate oneself from the majority lest one cause trouble? And if it is the latter, shouldn't I then at least keep the reason for my separation a secret for the benefit of the rest? And if so, then shouldn't I refrain from even publishing these thoughts?

But then I think that if everyone remained silent, acquiescing to the majority (or presumed majority) opinion, would or could there be any advance in understanding at all? I doubt it. Instead, look at Copernicus or Galileo – or for that matter, Jesus. Hence the Evangelical question: "What Would Jesus Do?" And if so, what must I do? If I were to really imitate Jesus – who, to say the least, was highly critical of the religious establishment of his own time – I could end up, at least figuratively speaking, being "crucified". But more likely, I shall end up being ignored or more or less consigned to oblivion.

It is this latter likelihood that brings back to mind memories of much more accomplished theologian, Fr. Piet Schoonenberg, a Dutch Jesuit whose book, *The Christ: A God for Man*, had been published in English back in 1970. With my busy teaching schedule back then, it had taken me a couple of years to getting around to reading it, but when I finally did, I was much impressed with his idea that God's "Wisdom", as personified in the later Old Testament books, and again personified as God's "Word" in the prologue of the Gospel according to John, only became a *person*, in the contemporary meaning of that word, in the humanity of Jesus Christ. In other words, up to that point in time, to speak of a "second person" in God (seen as a trinity of persons) was more or less just a figure of speech. But with the arrival of Jesus, it became an actuality.

The summer after I had finished reading that book, I learned that Schoonenburg was in Michigan, spending some time at Saint John's Seminary after having taught a summer course at Siena Heights College in Adrian. So one day I drove over to Saint John's to meet him and ask him more about this novel approach, which to my mind made a great deal of sense, by both giving us a more plausible understanding of the dual nature of Christ (both divine and human) as well as a more dynamic understanding of God as a trinity. So I asked him what the reaction to his book had been among other theologians, particularly in his homeland and Europe. His answer was not encouraging. Apparently his idea was considered to be too far out of the mainstream of traditional thinking, even though in another article, he attempted to defend his view (and his own reputation) in terms of the long established history of "Spirit Christology" wherein the action of the Holy Spirit gradually "divinizes" a human being into becoming an image or replica of God.

However, it may be that Schoonenberg, who is believed to have collaborated with another avant-garde Dutchman, the Dominican theologian Edward Schillebeeckx, in writing the popular but controversial 1966 "Dutch Catechism", was already under a cloud of official suspicion. It seems that little more was heard of Schoonenberg, at least on this side of the ocean, even though he lived to the ripe old age of eighty-eight, only dying in 1999. His younger co-author in that catechism, Fr. Schillebeeckx, continued to attract criticism even longer, dying at age ninety-five in 2010. So maybe I should ask if being a contrarian adds to longevity?

So as I come close to concluding this account of my life up until now, it seems that whether it be simply the result of a series of odd personality quirks and the flip-flops of fate on the one hand, or the guiding hand of God on the other, that I have ended up living in a state of life where I have been given both the freedom as well as perhaps the obligation to try to contribute to the progress of Christian thinking, even if that means teetering on the edge of what most churchmen might consider to be heresy. If so, I see it as a price that I must pay to be of any use to the Church of the future. Other than that, my goal as a hermit, is trying to live, as closely as possible, in conscious union with God.

Yet even that goal, it seems, plunges me deeper into what probably appears to be a "heresy" by some, at least when expressed paradoxically in what has become one of my favorite expressions or ways of putting it. It is that (strictly speaking) "God doesn't *exist*: instead, God simply *is*."

So why do I put it that way? It's because I feel that it is the best or most effective way of jolting people, including myself, into a realization of what God really is, as Saint Augustine put it in his definition of God, *ipse esse* or "Being itself". Existence, on the other hand – again strictly speaking – implies a state of being that takes its being *from* or which depends *on* (*ex* in Latin) something else. Thus, apart from God's being, nothing else could possibly exist!

So how did I – or more importantly Augustine – come to this realization? I suspect that it came from his study of the pagan philosopher Plotinus, whom Augustine credited with leading him to his eventual conversion to Christianity. Although, at least from my limited familiarity with his vast amount of writings, it seems that Augustine seldom, if ever, quoted Plotinus directly, I did find, in my attempts to read Plotinus, a puzzling sentence which, after I tried my best to untangle Plotinus's Greek and his translator's dense prose, I think sums it all up. It is, and here I'll italicize as well as underline several key words for emphasis: *"God is not only everywhere; God is the everywhere within which everything else in that everywhere exists."*

However, I do not believe anyone has to go back to Plotinus or even Augustine to grasp or defend what I have to say on this matter: it is plain to see even in the New Testament, in the Acts of the Apostles where Saint Luke relates that the Apostle Paul, in speaking to the Greeks who had gathered to hear him in Athens, even appealed to one of their own ancient poets to describe the "Unknown God". That quote (and again I'll italicize it for emphasis) reads as follows: *"In him we live, and move, and have our being."* Need anything more eloquent than that be said?

I know that many of those who might read this will think that this sounds like "pantheism" – that God is everything or, inversely, that everything that exists is God. I also realize that the famous 14th century Dominican preacher Johann Eckhart ("Meister Eckhart") was hauled up before the Inquisition and accused of being a pantheist for saying something rather similar; that everything or everyone is divine, because everything that exists shares in God's being. Eckhart managed to defend himself by quoting Augustine, but also upset his interrogators by implying that maybe they were too stupid to understand. But at least he was not burned at the stake! But admittedly, this picture of God is a far cry from most of the depictions of God that we find in the Bible, especially in what Christians call the Old Testament, and even more from what even Christians too often think of and rather too flippantly refer to as "the man upstairs".

Instead, the view that I have only gradually come to adopt (too bad I didn't follow that philosophy professor's advice years before) is what the "Process Theologians" or those who follow the thought of the evolutionary philosopher Alfred North Whitehead call *panentheism.* It is the belief (emphasized by that additional *en* – the Greek for "in") that everything is in God and that God is in everything and that, again in Whitehead's own words, God is a God "who cares" and who, in that caring, is "our fellow sufferer." But again, if that really is the case – to take this theme beyond what

Whitehead dared to do – then should we be surprised or scandalized by the fact that Jesus, whom Paul calls the "Son of God" and whom the later scriptures call "the image of the invisible God" (Col 1:17) and the "exact replica of the divine nature" (Heb 1:6) or God's "Word" (Jn 1:1) had to die on the cross and yet had to overcome death by rising from it?

In adopting this emphasis on the presence of God in everything everywhere, I believe that not only can we avoid such alienating ideas of God as some mysterious being far off in a distant heaven, but even throw new light on such deep or puzzling doctrines as the Trinity and the divinity of Christ. If God were to be seen as contained within and supporting the existence of the universe that He created, would it be any wonder that someone like Jesus could be filled with God's spirit in such a way as to be the embodiment or the incarnation of God's wisdom or "Word" or that he might have access to God's power in ways that (despite the skepticism of modern biblical scholars) defy our pre-conceived beliefs? In an age when even nuclear physics has succeeded in unlocking only a tiny fraction of the energy contained within matter, how can we presume to limit how and when God's power might reveal itself (or in the case of what traditional Christians have called "sacraments") in new and surprizing ways?

However, in adopting these rather radical ideas, I have, as already mentioned above, found myself more critical of some of the traditional ideas that have long-served as explanations for the death and resurrection of Christ, particularly those couched in terms of "atonement" and "expiation". Such ideas, associated with bloody sacrifice, were repeatedly criticized by many of the Old Testament prophets. So why do we Christians keep using them? The answer, I think, lies in our own psychological needs. If we feel we have wronged someone, our own conscience bothers us unless we feel we have done something to try to "make up for it". Thus, in explaining why Jesus died on the cross, the early Christian theologian Origen wrote "God emulates man with magnificent generosity." In other words, Christ was acting out the priestly role of expressing not God's but our own needs. Nevertheless, such explanations, which are found in abundance in the New Testament epistles are, as I see them, much the same as the various third level traditions or explanations found in the Gospels: they are varying viewpoints adopted by the different writers to try to illustrate a particular point or even to try to explain what sometimes or even often seems to be otherwise inexplicable. And the fact that they once accomplished this purpose attests to their authors' genius and divine inspiration. But that does not mean that they continue to do so with equal effectiveness.

So instead of continuing to repeat, over and over again, a theory of redemption based on bronze-age concepts of a vengeful God and bloody sacrifices offered in expiation for sins, I think we need a much broader concept of "At-one-ment" with the God who is, as Whitehead said, "our fellow sufferer" in the evolutionary process which, as Teilhard once said "resembles nothing so much as the Way of the Cross." In fact, Whitehead's concept of God's "consequent nature" (as the result of God's presence in the course of evolution) is not all that different from Teilhard's understanding of the *"Pleroma"* of the later Pauline epistles. It is, not just a fulfillment or completion of the universe, but it is, as Teilhard once confided to a friend, "in some sense, a completion of God" – echoing Saint Paul who wrote about the God who, when everything, including death, "has been subjected" (to Christ) "becomes all in all" (1 Cor 15:28).

I have not adopted these rather esoteric and, no doubt to some, strange ideas in order to dazzle people or much less, upset them. I have, instead, felt compelled to adopt them because they really are, or at least it seems to me, the only way that Christianity can make sense not just now, in the world, or even more, in a universe that is infinitely larger than our ancestors could have possibly imagined. In fact, even Teilhard was hard pressed to figure out a way to incorporate the Christian teaching about the Incarnation of God in the person of Christ into his conviction, based on Edmund Hubble's dicoveries of thousands of galaxies, each consisting of millions of stars, and which (if the latest findings, which multiply these estimates by many thousands, even billions, more are accurate) probably include who knows how many inhabited or "thinking planets". A singular "inoculation of the Universe" as Teilhard once put it? Or would it require, as I'm tempted to surmise, multiple incarnations? Either way, I'm tempted to say that just as Teilhard's understanding of evolutionary biology undermined the foundations of traditional Christian anthropology (the understanding of humanity as having "fallen" from a primordial state of innocence) that Teilhard's attempts to expand the redemptive significance of the Incarnation to the whole universe have become increasingly overwhelmed by contemporary cosmology. Thus my late atttaction to Whitehead, the son of a Anglican clergyman, for whom it seems to have been enough that Jesus was "The brief Galilean vision of humility [that] flickered throughout the ages, uncertainly."

Yet if God is everywhere, and everything exists in God, why look elsewhere for God? As I once wrote in a reply to someone who asked me how to become a saint (not that I am one), the key is to see God in everything and everyone. But that is only the first step. The next step – and I should have added by far the more difficult one – is acting accordingly. In other words, instead of arguing over the identity of Jesus (whether he should be seen as divinely human or humanly divine?) or trying to see how the Incarnation could affect the whole universe, perhaps we need most of all to concentrate on "the Imitation of Christ", that is, living like Jesus.

By that last measure, I must admit that I still have a long way to go. But I haven't given up on that goal, and even aspire to live long enough to get somewhere near achieving it. Meanwhile, I can only pray that the reader will have benefited in some way from reading this long story even if, in some ways, I could be considered a heretic. But if so, then I hope my relentless seeking for new understandings of ancient beliefs in the light of today's science will be seen as a particularly stubborn form of faithfulness.

Some Afterthoughts on the Afterlife

After nearly thirty-five years of living in solitude and wrestling while in prayer or engaged in writing about the ultimate issues, it is unlikely that I will ever be able to say this book will be finally finished. It is more likely that it will undergo periodic updates until the day I die.

Facing the inevitable end of one's life is never an easy thing. Yet for anyone attempting to philosophize or to be a theologian, especially as one who lives a contemplative life, to avoid this subject (death) would be a dereliction of duty. And as this story of my life has indicated, the specter of death, "The Grim Reaper", has made its way into my life and thinking on numerous occasions, even during my boyhood, especially with the sudden loss of one of my buddies even triggering my decision to enter the professional religious life or priesthood as soon as I could make up my mind which of the two it would be. And then there were other traumatic events in which sudden or even premature deaths, like the assassination of President Kennedy, prompted me to write reflections, or on that occasion, quote Teilhard de Chardin's anguished words at the sudden loss of a colleague and his desperate profession of faith in the survival of the human spirit. And again, after my personal confrontation with death and brief taste of what lies beyond for those who have faith, there was (and what still is) my own stubborn belief and conviction that the hope and promise of eternal life is at the very heart of Christianity. If it isn't, then in my opinion, as the southern Catholic novelist Flannery O'Connor once said about Catholic belief in the Eucharist, "If it's just a symbol, then to hell with it!"

Yet, as I explained in the last chapter, symbols, if they are valid at all, are a way of expressing a deeper reality. For example, following the reasoning expressed by the Apostle Paul in his First Epistle to the Corinthians (Chapter 15), Pope Benedict has argued that the resurrection of Christ represents a kind of "evolutionary leap" or promise of our own resurrection in what Paul called "a spiritual body". Yet, for this helpful clarification, Benedict has been denounced by some Catholic traditionalists as a heretic.

Eventually, in response to questions posed to me as a priest, even as far back as the late 1970s, I finally got around to writing and publishing (in 2012) my own short book on the subject of death and the afterlife, which I titled *Forever: Evolution and the Quest for Life beyond Life,* in which I not only drew heavily on Teilhard's reasoning, but also, rather boldly, I think, attempted to re-present Pascal's famous "wager", this time rethought in terms of an evolutionary view of human nature. My conclusion was, and still is, that either we evolve, with God's help, into a higher and more permanent level of life or else evolution itself will eventually come to a dead end.

Yet, when it comes to the question of facing our own death, one keeps postponing it, as if by doing so one might stave off the inevitable. For me, in particular, having had at least one grandparent (my mother's father) who lived well into his mid-nineties, this postponement is particularly tempting. Yet I couldn't avoid the uncomfortable fact that once I had passed my seventy-fifth birthday, I had already lived three years longer than my father did, and one year longer than my mother. Accordingly, based on that background and with modern medicine, I could probably count on about five to ten more years at most here on earth until I ended up under it. But then, as I first wrote this, I found myself on the verge of turning eighty-five.

Nor has reaching that age been without its setbacks. Back in December of 2004, I began a course of radiation treatments for cancer of the prostate. It was something that I would have liked to think my vows as a celibate would have spared me. But of course such thinking would be naïve – like believing that not eating might save one from ulcers. Nor was I in any immediate danger of death. In fact, the specialists said I could probably survive another ten years even without any treatment. Nevertheless it came as a grim reminder of my mortality. Then, five years later, it finally became apparent that, like both of my parents, I probably could use a cardiac pacemaker due to an abnormally slow heart-rate — something that I was long aware of, especially after a Palestinian doctor had become quite alarmed when I visited the "French Hospital" in Bethlehem to get help in overcoming a sinus infection back in the spring of 1981.

The radiation treatments, which continued on into 2005, also occasioned a change in scene that brought about another sobering reminder. In order to be closer for my daily trips to the hospital, in February I moved into a summer home belonging to my cousin (the one who I used to consider to be my nemesis back when I was a kid) just outside Petoskey, Michigan — a scant fifty miles away from my cabin, but only five miles from the hospital where I could receive daily radiation treatments for five weeks to wipe out any remaining vestiges of the cancer. As a trendy high-scale resort area, it was a world of difference from my normal backwoods existence. It also afforded me quick access to several ski-resorts that offered free lift-tickets to old fools my age and of which I took liberal advantage despite my declining strength as the treatments progressed. But on the other hand, there I was also confronted with the constant reminder, just from being there, that my cousin, although still at home in Florida, was herself slowly dying from a cancer that once had seemed cured but had returned.

This period also comprised my longest stay outside of my hermitage in over twenty years, and I was there for over two months' time that both covered the period of treatment and its aftermath, when trying to move back into my cabin would have been unwise. Plus, due to the accumulated snow blocking the half-mile or so into my place from the nearest regularly-plowed road, the return with my books, computer, and other stuff would have been nearly impossible without having to hire someone with a bulldozer to get me back in.

It was also a period which, tempered by the awareness of our frailty as human beings, that I thought a lot, not so much about the traditional "Four Last Things" (Death, Judgment, Heaven, and Hell) but more about how the incredible complexity – and I use that description quite seriously – of Christian beliefs might be condensed to some general facts or principles, perhaps something like the "Four Noble Truths" of Buddhism. And what they boiled down to was what I would see as three inescapable or at least uncomfortable realities and a Christian corollary. As I detailed them in a three-page

Some Afterthoughts

"Afterward" to a collection of my short essays that was first published in 2008, but will state in four sentences below, they are:

First, that physically nothing in this world, and perhaps not even the whole universe, will last forever;

Second, that psychologically speaking, few if any of us are comfortable with that physical reality;

Third, that in terms of spirituality, most religions or philosophies seek a way to escape or transcend those first two realities; and...

Fourth, that Christianity confronts all the above by inviting us to squarely face, accept, and pass through these realities in the pattern set by Jesus.

Of course, there are probably some who might object to any one of these assertions, particularly the last. Nevertheless, it was not a Christian but the cultural anthropologist Ernest Becker, although Jewish by birth and an agnostic, who claimed, in his Pulitzer Prize winning 1973 book *The Denial of Death*, that *only* Christianity had succeeded in facing these truths. Becker was strongly criticized for his opinion. Nevertheless, basing my own opinion on the psycho-dynamics championed by Viktor Frankl, I believe that Becker was correct. However, as of now, as I update this summary, I would also add that while I believe that while Buddhism, especially in its original or primitive form, embraced that "cloud of unknowing" that the medieval mystic spoke of, that it is most of all passing through what the theologian Jürgen Moltmann called the "godforsakenness" that Jesus experienced on the cross that the Christian can confidently hope that his stubborn faithfulness will be rewarded with eternal life.

If this is so, then what are the implications of all this for our, or I should say, speaking for myself, our own lives? After writing, back in the autumn of 2014, a critique of Dr. Ezekiel Emanuel's *Atlantic* magazine article titled "Why I Hope To Die at 75" (an opponent of euthanasia, he nevertheless believes life is, in terms of the general average, all downhill after our seventy-fifth year) I wrote a letter to my general practitioner telling him why I hope he can keep me going until I'm ninety or perhaps even beyond.

One reason I gave for this wish is the length of time it takes me to write a book (this one has taken me about 15 years, and like I have already said, it may not be finished yet!). And, as a result of attending and participating in a series of biannual meetings over the past two decades of a society dedicated to the search for ultimate reality and meaning, I have already declared my intention and even secured an ISBN listing for a book titled *Time and Meaning*, but which I have yet even to begin. But then I begin to worry that if I manage to live long enough to finish such a book, or even longer, will I be able to manage to do so on my own?

That last question raises still another. If God really is to be found in everything, then must not God be encountered in our diminishment and death as well? We have to learn to accept the limitations of life in this world as part of God's creative activity, the *Creative Evolution*, the random play of nature without which free creatures such as ourselves would never have come to be. As I see it, in this world, without chance there can be no choice. And if, again, as Teilhard put it, "...the human epic resembles nothing so much as a way of the Cross", I pray for the strength to carry mine when the time comes.

And then what? The early Christian treatise known as "The Epistle of Barnabas" speaks of the "hope of life" as being "the beginning and end of faith." If so, then it seems that without the promise of eternal life there is no point in being a believer. This no doubt seems selfish to some, and perhaps it is – that is, until you go back to square one, so to speak, the first of the four points I made earlier, that as far as science (and here I mean genuine or "hard science" as apart from flights of speculative fancy) is able to take us, eventually the universe, or at least *"our* universe" should there be others, even if it lasts forever, will, according the reckoning of current cosmology, end up cold and lifeless. And even if there were to be another universe after this one, how would that involve us or give any meaning to our own lives? So while my argument in favor of there being an "afterlife" may seem to be, on the surface, rather

Some Afterthoughts

egocentric, it is, in the end, cosmological as well as theological in nature. For if unless there is the possibility that at least some individuals survive beyond death (a kind of "survival of the fittest" argument) then evolution, at least on this planet, will have reached a dead end. And while I can imagine a God who might have created an evolutionary process that ends in a final dissolution (a celestial fireworks show for his own entertainment), I don't think I could possibly worship such a God, much less consider him to be a God who is "Love".

As to how such a transition from this life to another might occur, I must admit, to begin with, that I do not believe, as did Plato and his followers, that we begin life having an immortal soul. Instead, I believe that the energy that is expressed in our physical life and psychological or mental activity (much like Teilhard de Chardin's belief that the *weltstoff* that makes up the universe is an amalgam of matter and spirit) can be transformed, with God's help, into a non-material or spiritual existence when we die, but that this transformation is conditional, that is, determined by the way we have lived this life. I also believe, in accordance with the teaching of the Second Vatican Council, that this transformation is open or available not just for Christians or believers in God, but also to all (even atheists or agnostics) who have sought for what is genuinely good.

So while, instead of asking such tough and perhaps still unanswerable questions, it would've been nice to have spent the final chapter of these memoirs recounting all the wonderful experiences I have enjoyed during my thirty-some years of life in Michigan's north woods living as I do, among the deer, elk, bears, eagles and ravens, and now it seems "coywolves" (a recently discovered interbreeding of eastern coyotes with northern timber wolves), I did not come up here for that purpose. And I suppose that, had I been determined to live the eremitical life in the ancient pattern adopted by my Ukrainian hermit friend in Ontario (no electricity, no indoor plumbing, no vehicle for transportation, etc.) my life deep in the "Northwoods" would have turned to be much less complicated by the affairs of the

Some Afterthoughts

world – although the last time I visited him I saw that even he had acquired a car and that someone had set up a solar-electric panel outside his cabin, which presumably gives him some contact with the outside world. Apparently some friends had become concerned for his safety in his advancing old-age.

Nevertheless, despite my preoccupation with the major issues and hard questions listed in the pervious chapter indicate, I still came up here to achieve one major goal, which is to find God. In fact, it is this quest alone, I think, that can justify how I can, both as a priest (a vocation which by definition must be dedicated to serving others) and as a theologian (whose vocation must to be, again, by definition, to explore and expound on the nature of God) be excused for what I have done in leaving behind the work of a pastor in his parish, a preacher in his pulpit, or a lecturer in his classroom. Otherwise, what I have done is only so much self-deception.

So, you may well ask, "Have I achieved that goal?" And my answer must be, if I am to be honest, "Not yet!" But still, I remember hearing that there is a Zen Buddhist tradition that holds that the last decade of life, whether it be in the seventies, eighties, or even nineties, is apt to be the one in which a person finally achieves enlightenment. So, now I can only pray that I'm finally getting close.

This is why I began the introduction to this book with a quotation from the unknown author of *The Cloud of Unknowing*. Yet it could have just as well been from the writings of Saint John of the Cross, with his warnings about the necessity of passing through both the "Dark Night" of the senses as well as of the soul before we can reach full union with God.

Such advice, of course, does not sit well with rationalists, who even if they admit that the whole idea of God is beyond them, nevertheless refuse to believe that there is anything that transcends the capacities of our own intellects. That is a curious belief indeed, especially considering that it has so far taken about four and a half billion years of evolution on this planet before anything emerged that became self-aware enough to make such a claim. Instead, I think that we should seriously remember the observation of Teilhard who was continually under suspicion of heresy because of his scientific views on human evolution, yet who was equally convinced that "mysticism is the highest form of research."

Keeping all this in mind, then, I turn again to a prayer recommended to me by a holy priest who was my spiritual director for a number of years before he went to his reward. It goes:

> Serene Light – shining in the ground of my being: draw me to
> yourself; draw me past the snares of the senses, out of the mazes
> of the mind: free me from symbols, from words, that I may
> discover the Signified, the Word unspoken in the darkness that
> veils the ground of my being....

When my friend, and truly he was a friend for many years, handed me this prayer, he told me that it was "from an Eastern liturgy", but whether he meant from an Eastern Rite Christian liturgy, a Sufi ceremony, or even a Buddhist or Hindu ritual, I still do not know. But does it really make any difference? Do we not all take our origin from the same "ground of being" whom we've become accustomed to call God, *Allah*, *Brahman*, or perhaps simply, "the Ultimate"?

All this brings me back to a conclusion that I reached many years ago. It is that when all is said and done, that the strength or attraction of the Christian faith ultimately lies in its ability to give people hope in the face of the sufferings and vicissitudes of life in this world. But I also realize that in this function it may not be all that different than other religions, even Buddhism, although Buddhism seems to concentrate more on overcoming suffering here and now in this life rather than promising any eternal reward. However, when all is said and done, I find it remarkable that the reverent agnosticism of Buddhism (often mistakenly called "atheism" by uncomprehending Westerners) is not that much different than the "Cloud of Unknowing" of Christian mysticism.

Some Afterthoughts

Thus, for both the Buddhist and the Christian, advance into the ultimate is an advance into the unknown.

Yet, when it comes to dying, for the Buddhist, death offers the hope of *Nirvana* – the cessation or literally, the "blowing out" – of those desires that shackle us to the ceaseless cycle of reincarnations and with them, the miseries of life. On the other hand, for the Christian, death offers the promise of fulfillment of all those desires that only eternal life can fulfill. So which is it? Or are they not ultimately the same? And should they both be wrong, will either know it, with no self remaining, even to know they are dead? And if that should turn out to be the case, can we say that life, at least for us even now, has any lasting or ultimate meaning?

(As updated on November 15, 2017)

Appendix

How and What I Believe: a Profession of Faith

It has been said that *faith* is not so much a noun or thing as it is a verb or action, or it is primarily a longing of the heart, or a matter of fidelity. This is in contrast to belief, or more exactly, the *beliefs* or the mental ideas or constructs that express that faith. But that being said, it must be realized that these ideas exist within a mindset or philosophical framework that is largely defined by our worldview or perspective on the world in which we find ourselves to be living. In today's world, that perspective is predominantly evolutionary in its outlook. Accordingly, my core beliefs, both as a Christian as well as a believer in evolutionary science, could be summarized as follows:

I believe in that mysterious or hidden force or being that has created the universe and which believers have traditionally called "God" and within which everything else lives and moves and has its existence.

I believe in Jesus of Nazareth, as the Christ, and as the exemplar, the "Word" or the "image of God", the prototype of what humans might become, and who both died and overcame death to reveal God's love for us and who is indeed our "fellow-sufferer".

I believe that God's Holy Spirit is available to all who seek God or whatever is truly good and who both guides and inspires the Church, as well as corrects it when necessary.

I believe in God's promise of eternal life, not just for Christ's followers, but for all who strive to rise above their material existence and cares, — so that once death has been finally overcome, God will become "all in all", the God in whom the universe will reach its final fulfillment.

Richard W. Kropf
December 3, 2016

Index

Index

Carmel, Mt., 177

Carmelite Order, 44, 198

Carthusian Order, 49, 57, 58, 76, 97, 100

Castellot, John, Rev., 40

Catholic: Church, 4, 15-16, 93-94; schools, 11; theological mandate, 108

celibacy, celibates, 52, 62, 86, 99, 106-07, 131, 198

Central Michigan University, 141

Centre Cultural (Chantilly, France), 134-35

Chalcedon, Council of, 228

Chicago, 5-7; University of, 5-6, 117

Creeds, book on, 232-33

Christ: of faith, 232; as image of God, 238; imitation of, 240; as Word of God, 238

Christ in the Desert Monastery (Abiquiu, NM), 109

Christian Anthropology, 145

Christian Family Movement, 70, 84

Christeros, 64

Christology, 145, 230-31

Cincinnati (Ohio), 19

Civil War (US), 11, 12

Cloud of Unknowing, The, viii-x, 170, 247

Coleman, Thomas, Fr., 86

Coughlin, Charles, Fr., 35, 59

Copper Country (Michigan) 2-4, 8, 12, 26

Copperweld Steel Corporation, 8-10, 12, 13

Copts, Coptic Church, 180-82, 228

Conan, Paul. S.J., 144

Confirmation, 16; age of, 91

Congregational Church, 2

Connecticut, 15-18

contemplative life, orders, 49

consciousness, vii

cosmology & theology, 212-13

Constantine, Emperor, 226, 235

consubstantuality, 228, 229

Csaky, Anton, Rev. Dr., 75-76, 84, 98, 106

C.T.S.A. (Catholic Theological Society of America), 185, 204

Cuernavaca (Mexico), 46-47, 101

Curran, Cyril, MD, 92-93, 97, 107

Cursillo movement, 91

Cusa, Nicholas of, 234

-D-

D'Armagnac, Christian, S.J., 134-35

Davis, Charles, 107-08

deaconate, 61

Dead Sea, 167

death (experiences of, reflections on), 13 , 26, 30-31, 60-61, 243

Deely, John, Ph.D., 125

Denali National Park, 159

Denmark, 136

depression, the great, 1, 12

Desharnais: Gabriel, 53- 58, 60; Gaston, 58-59

Detroit: 46, ethnic mix of, 36; poverty in, 48

DeVeuster, Damian, Fr., 55

divine nature, human participation in, 230

Doctrine of the Faith, Congregation for the, 230

dogma, dogmas, 227

Doherty, Catherine, 126-27

Dollar Bay (Michigan), 2-4, 158

Index

Dominic, St., 82
Dominican Sisters, 6-7
Dostoyevsky, Feodor, 108
Douglas (Ontario), 187, 205-08
Dunnigan, Raphael, Fr., 69, 90

-E-
Eckhart, Johann, 239
Einstein, Albert, 120, 224, 225-26, 231-32
Eisleben, Saxony (Germany), 2
Egypt, viii, 179-84, 214
Emmanuel, Ezekiel, MD, 246
energy, nuclear, 240
England, 59
Ephesus, Council of, 183
Erie, Lake, 13
Europe: first trip, 53-60; second trip 132-36
Evans, Ed & Nick, 34, 42
Evil and Evolution (book):145, 163, 176, 217-18
evolution, 224, 225, 243-44, 247, 249
expiation, 218

-F-.
faith; and belief: crisis of, 95-96; difference between, 203, 221; leap of, 210; stages of, 203, 220, 229
Farm Point (Quebec). 131-32, 136
father (see Kropf, Richard B.)
Fedele, Stephen, DO, 93
Fedewa, Matthew, Fr., 75, 90
Fenn, Lyman, Fr, S.S., 40, 50-51, 115
Fermi, Enrico, 5
Foley, Francis W. (grandfather), 3, 243; Aileen (mother), viii, 2-5,

28-29, 31, 102, 108, 147, 244; Gretchen (cousin), 30, 151-52; Frank (cousin), 13, 148; James (uncle), 60-61, 91; John (uncle), 23 Nora (cousin), 9, 71-72, 91; Robert (cousin), 158; Thomas (cousin), 136
Fondation Teilhard de Chardin, 132, 133
Ford, Henry, 36; automobiles, 36; tractors, 41-42
Fowler, James W., 203, 220
Franciscan Sisters, 7
France, 53, 57-58, 59
Francoeur, Robert, 65
Frankl, Viktor, 202-03, 220, 246
fundamentalism, 220, 221

-G-
Galilee, 170, 174-75, 177
Gaylord, Diocese of, 201-02; weekend ministry in, 200-02;
Geitzen, Robert, 26, 30-31
Gerazim, Mt., 171
Germany, 2, 53,
Gethsemane Abbey, 33, 74
girls (see women)
God: as "Being", 236-37; completion of, 241; "existence" of, 236-37; immensity of, 213; as love, 213, 225, 247; as person, personal, 231-32; proof of, 112-13; suffering of, 232; will of, 83, 96-97, 98, 106 Word of, 240
golf, golfing, 41

Index

Index

of, 215, 225
John XXIII, Pope, 223
John-Paul II, Pope, x, 202, 230
Johnston, William, S.J., 170, 192
Joshua, Book of, 225
Junior Dates, 25-26
Justin Martyr, St., 230

-K-
Kant, Immanuel, 121
Kavanaugh: James, 93-94;
    Robert, 85
Kennedy, John F., 25, 79, 243
Kenai Peninsula (Alaska), 160
Kerrin, Charles, Fr., 40
kerygma, 219
King, Ed, 77
King, Martin Luther, 25
Kinget, Marian, Ph.D., 80
Konzanakis, Nikos, 229
Korean War, 32-33
Kropf: Richard B. (father) 1, 18, 31,
    35, 51, 87-88, 98, 147-49, 244;
    Georgia (aunt), 15, 101, 118;
    Rudolph R. (grandfather) 2,
    196; Wilhelmina (aunt
    "Billie"), 15,101
Kubsz, Charles J., Er.Cam., 103-06,
    162
Küng, Hans, Fr., 192, 234

-L-
L'Arche (Trosly-Breuil, France),
    135
LaGrange (Illinois), 7-8, 13
Lansing (Michigan): Community
    College, 139, 141;
    Diocese of, 33, 50, 63, 102, 139
Lantern Hill Camp, 13-14, 23
Latin (language), 25, 36, 40

Lebanon, 178-79
LeBlond, S.J., 134
Legion of Mary, 66-67
Leitrim, County (Ireland), 3
Leo I, The Great, Pope, 228
London, 59, 132, 136
Louvain, University of, 30, 55, 136
Luke, St., Evangelist, 219, 239
Luther, Lutheran, 2, 169, 199
Luxor, 180-81

-M-
Madison, Wisconsin, 1-2
Madonna College, 143
Madonna House Apostolate, 125-
    28, 138-39, 188; Associates,
    205; Yukon mission, 153
marriage and remarriage, gospel
    teachings on, 228
Marcarius, St. (monastery of), 181-
    182
Magdalene, Mary, 229
Malewitz, William, Fr., 72, 106
Mar Sabas, Monastery of, 170
Marcenkowski, Jerome, 196
Maria Pilar, 54, 58-59
Maritain, Jacques, 125
Martin, Francis, Fr., 128
Masons, 2
materialism, 216
matter & spirit, 248
Mayotte, Msgr., 68
McGoey, John H., 83
McKeon, William, Fr., 249
McNamara, William, 110-11, 113
Mehm, Walter, Msgr., 85
Meier, John P., 219-20
Melancthon, Philip, 2
Melkite (Greek Rite) Catholics, 168
Mercy College of Detroit, 141-42,

Index

Index

Pearl Harbor, 10

penance, 188

Pentwater River (Michigan), 94-96,103

Phoenix (Arizona), 110, 113

Pigeon River Country State Forest (Michigan), 196

Pius IX, Pope, 227

Pius XII, Pope, 19,

Pleroma, the, 241

Plotinus, 238

Psychology, psychological:
conditions, 21,144;
hospitals, 70- 73, 89, 92-93
studies in, 40-41;
test results, 32, 38;

Polish (language), 36

Popocatpetl, Mt., 45

poustinias, 127, 147-48, 188, 197

poverty, vow of, 138-39, 209-10

Povish, Kenneth, Bishop, 200, 202

predestination, 22

prayer, 188

priests, priesthood: reflections on, 47- 51

"Process Theology", 238

promotion, self-, self-centered, vii

Purcell High School, 20-21

-Q-

Quebec & Quebec separatism (the October Crisis), 137

-R-

racial tensions, 84, 100

Rahner, Karl, S.J., 233

Reimarus, Hermann, 218

Renaud, Jean, 196

Residence Dechatelets, 119, 121, 131

Roebling Corporation, 3

Roosevelt, Franklin Delano, 1, 15

R.O.T.C. (Reserve Officers Training Corps), 32

Rome, 56, 163

Royal Oak (Michigan), 35

Rousseau, Jean Jacques, 235

Russia, Russians, 2, 126,156, 160

-S-

sacraments, 238, 243

St. Benedict's Monastery (Snowmass, Colorado), 109

St. Joseph Parish, Battle Creek (Michigan), 70-75

St. Michael Parish, Grand Ledge (Michigan), 75-88

St. Mary's College, Orchard Lake, Michigan), 148

St. Monica Parish, Kalamazoo (Michigan), 88-99

San Angel (Mexico), 44

San Antonio (Texas), 42-43

San Miguel de Allende, 46

Sartre, Jean-Paul, 121

Satan, 217

Schoonenberg, Piet, S.J., 237

Schweitzer, Albert, 218-19

schism, schismatics, 215

school: public & parochial, 11; junior high, 14-15, high, 19-21, 23, 31

Schweitzer, Albert, 219

scientific method, 216

Scorcese, Martin, 229

Scotland, 136

Scouts: Cub, 9, 16-17; Boy, 13, 17

scrupulosity, 9-10, 20-21, 22, 31

sea voyages, 53-54, 60

Index

Index

Other Books by the Author

Teilhard, Scripture and Revelation: A Study of Teilhard de Chardin's Reinterpretation of Pauline Themes, published by Fairleigh Dickinson University/Associated University Presses (1980).

Evil & Evolution: A Theodicy, originally published by Fairleigh Dickinson University/AUP (1984): 2nd revised edition published by Wipf & Stock Publishers (2004)

Faith: Security & Risk: The Dynamics of Spiritual Growth, published by Paulist Press in 1990 (republished by Wipf & Stock, 2003).

The Faith of Jesus: The Jesus of History and the Stages of Faith, published by Wipf and Stock Publishers in 2006.

(with Joseph P. Provenzano) *Logical Faith: Introducing a Scientific View of Spirituality and Religion,* published by iUniverse, Inc. (2007, 2009).

Views from a Hermitage: Reflections on Religion in Today's World, published by Lexington Books, Rowman & Littlefield Publishing Group, in 2008; 2nd edition, Stellamar Publications, 2013.

Breaking Open the Creeds: What Can They Mean for Christians Today?, published by Paulist Press in 2010.

Forever: Evolution and the Quest for Life beyond Life, published by Stellamar Publications, 2012.

Einstein and the Image of God: A Response to Contemporary Atheism, published by Stellamar Publications, 2015.

Made in the USA
Coppell, TX
09 June 2021

57162629R00154